Editors

Melody Bridges studied English and Drama at Cambridge University and has written, acted and directed for theatre before working in TV where she developed, wrote, produced and directed two television series. In addition to contributing to *Celluloid Ceiling*, she writes a weekly page for a newspaper, and is Artistic Director of Worthing's WOW Festival. In 2014, she was a Finalist as Influential Woman of the Year at the NatWest Venus Awards. She has recently given a TEDx talk about inspiring change. www.melodybridges.com

Cheryl Robson is a producer/director of several short independent films, most recently *Rock 'n' Roll Island* which was nominated for Best Short Film at Raindance, London 2015. She worked at the BBC for several years and then taught filmmaking at the University of Westminster, before setting up a theatre company. She also created a publishing company where she has published over 150 international writers. As a writer, she has won the Croydon Warehouse International Playwriting Competition and as an editor, she recently worked with Gabrielle Kelly on *Celluloid Ceiling: women film directors breaking through*, the first global overview of women film directors. She also received a Gourmand Special Jury Prize for Peace with author Robin Soans, for *The Arab-Israeli Cookbook*. www.cherylrobson.net

First published in the U.K. in 2016 by Supernova Books

67 Grove Avenue, Twickenham, TW1 4HX
www.supernovabooks.co.uk
www.aurorametro.com

Cover design © Greg Jorss 2016 www.upsidecreative.com.au
Front cover image Margery Ordway *Photoplay* 1916
Back cover image Lillian Gish directing *Remodelling her Husband*
Inside cover image Mary Pickford with camera ca. 1920

We have made every effort to ascertain image rights. If you have any information relating to image rights contact editor@aurorametro.com

Typesetting by Head & Heart Publishing Services

ISBNs:
978-0-9566329-9-9 (print version)
978-0-9932207-0-8 (ebook version)

SILENT WOMEN
PIONEERS OF CINEMA

EDITED BY

MELODY BRIDGES
AND
CHERYL ROBSON

SUPERNOVA BOOKS

CONTENTS

FOREWORD   9
Bryony Dixon, Curator of silent film, BFI National Archive

INTRODUCTION   13
Melody Bridges and Cheryl Robson

1. GIRL FROM GOD'S COUNTRY: The History   19
of Women in Film and Other War Stories
Karen Day

2. EARLY AFRICAN-AMERICAN FEMALE   35
FILMMAKERS
Aimee Dixon Anthony

3. THE SILENT PRODUCER: 69
Women Filmmakers Who Creatively Controlled the
Silent Era of Cinema
Pieter Aquilia

4. WOMEN WERE WRITING: 95
Beyond Melodrama and Hot House Romances
Patricia Di Risio

5. DOING IT ALL: Women's On- and Off-screen   109
Contributions to European Silent Film
Julie K. Allen

6. FEMALE LEGENDS OF THE SILVER SCREEN   131
Melody Bridges

7. DIRECTORS FROM THE DAWN OF HOLLYWOOD   146
Francesca Stephens

IMAGES   163

8. INTERVIEW WITH DIRECTOR DOROTHY ARZNER   179
Kevin Brownlow

9. WOMEN FILM EDITORS FROM SILENT TO SOUND   201
Tania Field

10. WHO WAS THE FIRST FEMALE CINEMATOGRAPHER IN THE WORLD?   228
Ellen Cheshire

11. WHEN THE WOMAN SHOOTS: 241
Ladies Behind the Silent Horror Film Camera
K. Charlie Oughton

12. CRITICS, REFORMERS AND EDUCATORS: 255
Film Culture as a Feminine Sphere
Shelley Stamp

13. U.S. WOMEN DIRECTORS: The Road Ahead   280
Maria Giese

INDEX   305

FOREWORD

Bryony Dixon

Curator of silent film, BFI National Archive

With the significant hurdle of a best director Oscar going to a woman *finally* being cleared, it has become increasingly shocking that the number of women at the top of the film industry is still so low. As we cast around for reasons why this may be so, it is well worth looking back at film history to see what women were doing in the film business, in the way that the other arts have been re-evaluating their respective areas since the 1970s. Linda Nochlin's ground-breaking article 'Why Have There Been No Great Women Artists?' published in 1971 should be required reading for anyone asking the question: 'Why Have There Been No Great Women Film Directors?' Her well-argued findings can easily be applied to the film industry. One of the first jobs she tackles is to look a bit harder at art history to see if it is entirely true that there are no great women artists. She discovers a huge number of women artists – Artemisia Gentileschi is probably the only name worthy of the name 'great' that people may have heard of now, but there are plenty of others. You could apply the same criteria to music or sculpture and similarly reveal artists of the calibre of Clara Schuman or Barbara Hepworth. We are undergoing this research in the field of film now, a few decades late – but film history is young. We start with those extraordinary and rare creatures – women film directors from the early days – Alice Guy-Blaché, Lois Weber, Dorothy Arzner, Ida Lupino and so on.

This is good. This gives us an instant answer when asked 'the question'. But it's not enough. We have to look further and deeper into what women were doing in the film industry in the past. We have to understand the conditions for producing film works to see if there were systemic reasons why women have not produced great film works in the past. And indeed there were. Nochlin also recommends that we examine the myth-making mechanisms which perpetuate the (male) individual as 'genius' – we can swap her Picassos and Goyas for our Hitchcocks and Kubricks. Constant repetition of the pantheon in books, TV programmes, references and now particularly online journalism's '10 best' and 'bluff your way' culture perpetuate this reductive state of affairs. She concludes that:

> ...art is not a free, autonomous activity of a super-endowed individual, influenced by previous artists and more vaguely and superficially by 'social forces' but rather that the total situation of art making, both in terms of the development of the art maker and in the nature and quality of the work of art itself, occur in a social situation, are integral elements of this social structure and are mediated and determined by specific and definable social institutions, be they art academies, systems of patronage, mythologies of the divine creator, artist as he-man or social outcast.

When you take barriers such as those social institutions and academies, or their film industry equivalents, out of the equation as in literature for example, you find that women can compete on more equal terms with men. Literature is an exception, it seems. There are lots of famous women novelists and poets that everyone can name. But this is because to write you only need paper, a pen and time (I'm not implying that creative writing is easy). There is no male-controlled institution to prevent you. This couldn't be further from the case with filmmaking. There are so many barriers to entry in the world of film, it's a miracle anything gets made.

Once you know that the reason women have historically been prevented from doing certain jobs by institutions and social mores you can get down to examples. If it was so impossible systemically for a woman to direct a film how did those few remarkable individuals manage it? Discussing artists, Nochlin notes that nearly all the women artists, to whom we can apply the word 'great', were the daughters of artists. Is this true of filmmakers? There are certainly a lot of partnerships in the lives of women directors perhaps implying they were well-supported – Lois Weber and Phillips Smalley, Alice Guy and Herbert Blaché and our very own Ethyle Batley with her husband Ernest. Ethyle who? I hear you cry. You can be forgiven for not having heard of her but she directed at least sixty-five films in Britain between 1912 and 1916. She was an actress turned director for the British and Colonial Film Company working on the cusp of the commercialisation of the film business, another example of a woman director working in the early film industry just before the institutional barriers went up that prevented later women from following her lead.

But having established and investigated our list of remarkable individuals we must avoid the trap of imitating the male-centric concept of 'greatness'. Film is a fundamentally collaborative medium that has become astonishingly complex and is getting more so over time. Today's director is quite a different animal from his/her predecessors. So although the first job is to be able to name the few women directors that there *are,* we should be looking at the industry as a whole. The creative impetus for a film work may, in any event, not be from the director. If we get over our need to compare what we conceive of as the creative pinnacle, the *auteur* director, then the history of women in film becomes much more interesting. The creative talent in any film may be the vision of various people, often the writer. To take another British example the films of Manning Haynes (director) and Lydia Hayward (screenwriter) made in the 1920s are a good example – all perfectly well directed – but the primary creative talent was with the writers W. W. Jacobs, the author of the original stories, and Lydia Hayward who transformed his literary works into cinematic gold. And there are many, many others of this kind. Alma Reville, later Mrs Hitchcock, is the obvious example in British cinema – a filmmaker in her own right, who reached assistant director level before she married 'Hitch', was still working on *The First Born* (1928) (rather appropriately) when pregnant and thereafter worked in all kinds of capacities, with and without her husband and in credited and uncredited roles. She was, in her quiet way, one of the most important people in the film business from the 1920s to Hitchcock's retirement. Of course in the mythology of 'genius' this places her as 'the great woman behind the great man' – true, up to a point, but the real story is so much more interesting. If we want to know where the women were in film we also need to look under the level of director. And it is well worth the look because here are fascinating lives and careers. Within these pages you'll find a whole range of inspiring women making films in all kinds of ways.

And what of the future? Does it help future women filmmakers to know about these stories of women working against the prejudices of their age? I think so. Many of the institutional barriers to women working in film are long gone, social attitudes take a bit longer but may be as good as they are going to get. So to any aspiring filmmakers – take heart and inspiration from the past and go out and win that second Oscar. Now is the time.

INTRODUCTION

Melody Bridges and Cheryl Robson

This book explores the incredible contribution of women at the dawn of cinema when, surprisingly, more women were employed across the board in the film industry than they are now. It also looks at how women helped to shape the content, style of acting and development of the movie business in their roles as actors, writers, editors, cinematographers, directors and producers. In addition, we describe how women engaged with and influenced the development of cinema in their roles as audience, critics, fans, reviewers, journalists and the arbiters of morality in films. And finally, we ask when the current discrimination and male domination of the industry will give way to allow more women access to the top jobs.

Silent Women: Pioneers of Cinema is not just a book about women working in film during the silent film era. The term 'silent' also refers to the silencing and eradication of the tremendous contribution that women have made to the development of the motion picture industry. Why have women such as Alice Guy-Blaché, the creator of narrative cinema, been written out of film history? Why have so many women working behind the scenes in film been rendered 'invisible' and 'silent' for so long?

SILENT WOMEN

When looking back at the era of silent cinema, names such as Charlie Chaplin, Harold Lloyd, Buster Keaton, Rudolph Valentino and Douglas Fairbanks loom large. Female stars such as Mary Pickford, who started as a child star in the U.S., became the 'nation's sweetheart' and co-founded United Artists, are rarely mentioned. It's claimed that Pickford was the most powerful woman who has ever worked in Hollywood but few would know this today. In recognition of her significant contribution to motion pictures, she was awarded an honorary Oscar in 1976.

Other stars such as Louise Brooks, Theda Bara and Clara Bow are celebrated for their erotic intensity or mesmerising performances, but remain largely forgotten as their careers suffered when sound was introduced. From that era, only Swedish actress, Greta Garbo has become a cinema legend. Her famous line: 'I want to be alone,' from the star-studded movie *Grand Hotel* (1932) immortalised her in cinema history. She made around a dozen silent films before successfully crossing over into talkies in 1930 and became the most popular actress in the U.S. with her films consistently breaking box office records. She continued until the war changed the public's taste in movies and her last film *Two-Faced Woman* (1941), directed by George Cukor, was badly received by the critics. Garbo was nominated three times for the Academy Award for Best Actress, finally receiving an honorary award in 1954. Director George Cukor said of her in an interview:

> She had a talent that few actresses or actors possess. In close-ups she gave the impression, the illusion of great movement. She would move her head just a little bit and the whole screen would come alive, like a strong breeze that made itself felt. (*George Cukor: Interviews*, Robert Emmet Long, 2001, University of Mississippi Press).

As researchers have recently discovered, women were a significant part of the commercial success of cinema both in their appreciation of the new art form as the majority of ticket-buyers and as consumers of cinema-related products such as hair care and make-up. Their likes and dislikes not only influenced which films were made and which stars were cast but also the kind of costumes, make-up and hair styles which the actors wore.

Nell Shipman achieved fame and success initially as an actress in silent movies but wanting greater control over her work, she decided to write, direct, edit and produce her films as well. Seeking to escape the studio system, she moved to Idaho and set up her own production company near Priest Lake, making her one of the first truly independent filmmakers operating entirely outside the studio system. Karen Day, writer and filmmaker, tells us in her chapter about the making of her documentary film *Girl From God's Country*, which explores this incredible, multi-talented filmmaker. She goes on to uncover other pioneering women filmmakers such as Marion Wong, a talented Chinese-American who acted in, produced and directed her own films too.

U.S. academic Aimee Dixon Anthony, an expert in early African-American filmmakers, explores the work of black women filmmakers such as Maria P. Williams, Eslanda Goode Robeson and Zora Neale Hurston, who struggled to work within a white, male-dominated film industry.

Writer and Professor Pieter Aquilia explores female producers and the complexity of the 'director/producer' conundrum in the U.S., U.K. and Australia and asks why the power shifted from men to women as cinema developed in the years before World War II.

Patricia Di Risio looks at the art of scriptwriting and the vivid characters created by early writers such as Frances Marion and Gene Gauntier. Were they aware they were 'breaking boundaries' with their strong feisty characters and thrilling girl adventures?

Julie K. Allen looks at women behind and in front of the camera in early European silent film giving us a wider scope and understanding of the many women working with and for Pathé, Gaumont and Nordisk.

Writer and filmmaker Melody Bridges explores the influence of the screen legends of silent cinema and asks when female representation on-screen will achieve gender balance.

Francesca Stephens examines the lions of early cinema roaring their stories: female directors Arzner, Weber and Guy-Blaché. She argues that we should, we *must* recognise their significant contribution to the industry.

Kevin Brownlow, a well-known expert in cinema of the silent period, used his 2010 Oscar acceptance speech to underline the necessity of preserving precious film. In this book, he shares a (hitherto unpublished) interview with legendary female director, Dorothy Arzner. It was one of the last interviews with her which he recorded and which has been transcribed and published for the first time. You can read for yourself his notes from their conversation, and see a photo taken on the day it was recorded by Kevin's former collaborator, photographer David Gill.

Writer and filmmaker Tania Field explores the contribution of female film editors to the process of filmmaking in the U.S., U.K. and Europe and shows how their collaboration with leading directors often went unacknowledged within the industry.

Writer and academic Ellen Cheshire looks at the history of cinematography and asks: were camera operators always male? Has she discovered who the first female cinematographer really was?

Writer and academic, Dr K. Charlie Oughton, looks at the horror genre in early films, from the earliest version of *Phantom of the Opera* to the importance of Alma Reville to the *oeuvre* of Alfred Hitchcock.

Writer and Professor Shelley Stamp, an expert on early film culture, explains the influence of female reviewers, fans and audiences on the ways in which cinema developed. She also discusses the early use of film for educational and moral purposes.

Screenwriter and feature film director, Maria Giese challenges some of the prejudice and discrimination against

INTRODUCTION

women and minorities taking place in the U.S. entertainment industry today. In our final chapter her call to arms asks us: if not now, then when will change come?

This book is an explicit challenge to cultural commentators and film historians – to shout as loud as they can about the incredible contributions of women in film. Chapter upon chapter names and celebrates fantastically talented women whose work has gone unrecognised and unappreciated for too long. The Women Film Pioneers Project at Columbia University must be credited with undertaking and compiling much of the research to date. Their website provides a wealth of information for those who wish to learn more or contribute to the project: https://wfpp.cdrs.columbia.edu/.

In our recent global overview of women film directors, *Celluloid Ceiling: women film directors breaking through* (eds. Gabrielle Kelly and Cheryl Robson), we provided many examples of women all over the world finding it easier to produce and direct films when a film industry was in its infancy. As film industries mature and become more profitable, men seem to dominate, taking on the main production and decision-making roles, while women are excluded.

We see this process in action across the various geographies and crafts which are explored in this book. What is now undeniable is that from the earliest days of cinema, women involved in the suffrage movement, Zora Neale Hurston, Alice Guy-Blaché, Lois Weber and many more were involved in making films of all kinds, whether documentary or narrative, educational or commercial, offering a female perspective on the world. Remarkably, they were able to achieve success as filmmakers in greater numbers than we see in the so-called liberal age of today. During the 1930s, economic downturn, technological change and a less forgiving moral climate created a more difficult environment for women to work in. The categorisation of jobs together with increasing control by male-led trade unions limited the mobility of workers to move up the career ladder. Despite this, a few women did remain at the forefront of both technical innovation and artistic expression as well as pushing the boundaries of what was considered acceptable on-screen. In 1923, an article in *The Business Woman* detailed a range of around thirty different jobs that women carried out in the motion picture industry from actress to secretary, costume designer to script girl, film editor to laboratory worker, set designer to casting director, department manager to director, publicity to producer.[1]

There were real pioneers like Nell Shipman who broke away from the studio system, becoming one of the first independent filmmakers and there were those who were able to successfully navigate the system, subverting it from within, such as Mary Pickford and Dorothy Arzner.

Well-known female directors such as Jane Campion and Kathryn Bigelow may be seen as today's 'pioneers' but they are standing on the shoulders of generations of women filmmakers, whose contributions to both the art and the business of filmmaking, have gone before. This book goes some way to providing recognition, beyond the realms of academia, to the notable achievements of a small number of the real pioneers working in the nascent years of the motion picture industry. But there is much more to discover about this fascinating period of cinematic history and more work to be done.

We hope this book acts as inspiration for future creators of content, whatever their gender, to express themselves visually in new media, overcoming the many challenges which remain. We invite them to be as dauntless as the women filmmakers in this book, to unleash their unique perspectives on the world and let their talents shine brightly.

---

1 .Gebhart, Myrtle. 'Business Women in Film Studios', *The Business Woman*. December, 1923, 67–68.

1. GIRL FROM GOD'S COUNTRY: The History of Women in Film and Other War Stories

Karen Day

Nell Shipman (1892–1970)

Shipman once wrote 'Applause and recognition are the handmaidens of creativity.' The truth and irony of this pioneering filmmaker's insight are apparent in the fact that her legacy of writing, producing and starring in seventy silent films remained buried for nearly a century. In 1984, Shipman's obscurity nearly dissolved when Professor Tom Trusky, at Boise State University, stumbled on mention of this unknown filmmaker in a 1933 Idaho publication. The professor began a seven-year, transatlantic search to rediscover and restore Shipman's lost body of work, including the complete re-mastering and digitization of her 'obtainable' films from 1912 forward.

Boise State University also published the first volume of Shipman's dusty autobiography, *The Silent Screen and My Talking Heart*. Written a year before her death in 1970, the autobiography had been carefully preserved by Shipman's son, Barry, in the hope that his mother might someday earn recognition. Trusky, however, suffered a fatal heart attack in 2009 and with his passing, the filmmaker's name faded once again. In credit to his own legacy, the professor did succeed in amassing a comprehensive library of Shipman's personal papers, her writing and eight of her films.

SILENT WOMEN

I'd been producing and directing independent documentaries for twenty years when I saw a head shot of Nell Shipman displayed at the Idaho Historical Museum. The black and white photo was a studio-manufactured image, mandatorily glamorous, but unusual in that its 'star' lacked the typical pouted lips and corkscrew curls of the silent era. More wholesome than stilted beauty or sultry vamp, Shipman offered an adventurous image, completed by a luxurious, lynx fur hood and the title, 'The Girl from God's Country: Idaho's First Filmmaker'.

Two thoughts continued to haunt me for weeks after I'd seen the photo. First, I wanted one of those coats despite its scandalous political incorrectness. More importantly, I wondered how had I lived in Idaho for fifteen years and been making movies for twenty, yet never heard of Shipman? I spent the next two years of my life searching for the answer. Eventually, the truth revealed was so unjust and purposefully entombed, I felt compelled to produce and direct a feature-length documentary on the *Girl From God's Country*.

In the beginning, I envisioned the film as the shocking, untold story of one bold and forgotten female film pioneer. By the end of post-production, I was shocked by the naïveté of my original vision.

Before proceeding further, professional integrity demands a disclaimer: I am not a film historian nor academic. As a journalist and documentary filmmaker, credibility demands fact checking, but the human story fuels my focus. My words and films concentrate on 'giving voice to those who don't have the opportunity to speak for themselves.' Working in warzones, I've specialized in places that will never see a Club Med – South Sudan, Kandahar, and Baghdad. I go there in pursuit of stories that would not be heard if I didn't go. In other words, my work has been a matter of life and death for many and not surprisingly, a few times, the life at stake was my own. The final results are worth the risk when counted in lives saved and wrongs righted. The people my work has served always prove humbling in their courage and grace. Hence, I've avoided assignments about Hollywood celebrities, no matter how altruistic their cause. In my initial ignorance of all silent filmography beyond Charlie Chaplin, I dismissed Nell Shipman as a superficial object of attention.

What possible pertinence could a turn-of-the-century woman offer twenty-first century female filmmakers like myself? This was the Oscar-era of *Zero Dark Thirty* and action-adventure Pixar heroines! Silent films were the dark ages of cinema, overacted with batting eyelashes and flailing sheiks. If you'd seen one Rudolph Valentino film, you'd suffered too many, was my belief. I wasn't alone in my pop cultural vindications. Today, tweets and blockbusters rule as our makers of meaning. Ask anyone younger than seventy years old about actresses in silent films. Even the screen queens, Lillian Gish and Mary Pickford, in my recollections, smear into black and white blurs between simplistic intertitles. Therefore, I confess it was curiosity and coat envy, rather than scholarship or artistic appreciation that finally sparked my research into Nell Shipman.

Wild at Heart

Nearly a century apart, Shipman and I both chose to relocate from California and make films in the state that still boasts the most wilderness in the lower forty-eight. This commonality indicated she was a kindred spirit, a fellow cultivator of worthwhile risk. Idaho has as much landmass as Texas, but remains obscure, surrounded by five more-famous western states and Canada. The population was 436,000 when Shipman moved here in 1922, equating roughly to thirty-three square miles per person. (Current residents can only claim eight square miles.) Already a successful silent film writer, producer and movie star, Shipman boarded trains then tugboats to travel 1,280 miles from Glendale to the Priest Lake, fifteen miles south of the Canadian border. Her life was an orchestrated spectacle even in the wilderness. She brought along her ten-year-old son, her married lover-director, a future Academy Award-winning cinematographer and a zoo of seventy abused, animal actors, including bobcats, bears, elk, eagles, deer and sixteen sled dogs.

The more I read, the more brightly Shipman's boldness shone. Her daring was like a dimmer switch, turning up the light on early female independence. Seeking space enough to create herself and her films *on-location*, not on veneered sets, this firebrand rejected interference from 'suits' like Sam Goldfish (soon to be Goldwyn) who offered her a seven-year studio contract with a guarantee of stardom in velvet handcuffs. Shipman writes in her autobiography:

> 'Cheekily, I turned down the offer... Probably as silly a move as any neophyte ever made. But I did not like the way they dressed their contract players. This was the period of curly blondes with Cupid-bow's mouths... This long-legged, lanky outdoors gal, who usually loped across the Silver Screen in fur parkas and mukluks, simply gagged at such costuming.'

Independent, audacious, lover of animals *and* fur coats, determined to make films *in dangerous locations* – here was a filmmaker and a female I could relate to, albeit a century later! Imagine, she rebuffed Goldwyn to start her own production company the same year the U.S. Postal Service destroyed 500 copies of James Joyce's new novel, *Ulysses*.

I suddenly wished I could take this woman to lunch. Surely, we'd drink martinis and share dessert and disdain for the latest Mad Max movie. This revelation, coupled with the fact that today, Idaho still boasts only three female filmmakers and two million cattle, spurred me to walk into the Special Archives library at Boise State University and ask to see 'The Nell Shipman Papers'.

My purse and phone went into a locker. I was handed a pair of white gloves and guided into a transparent room, all walls being windows into the library. Students looked up from their laptops and texting. Stripped of technology, I stared at my feet, feeling strangely exposed.

A young woman with blue hair and cat glasses wheeled in

three file carts with forty-four boxes labeled meticulously with cross-referenced file folders. 'Good luck,' she said. 'You may use those pencils and paper to take notes.'

Pencils and paper? What fresh hell is this? I sat down and opened 'Box One.' The first folder was labeled 'Birth Certificate'.

She was still-born, according to record, on 25th October 1892, on Victoria Island B.C. Her mother, a victim of Victorian repression and British upbringing, refused to cry in public and ran with the dead babe in arms to the blustery cliffs overlooking the straits. There, in gale-force winds, Helen Barham-Foster fluttered her blue eyes and was reborn. 'A creature as foreign to her parents as *Siwash,*' Shipman later wrote. 'A being made of fire and water and gutter-muck, a half-wild, ornery, often vulgar, and brave-beyond-reason child who would forego convention, dodge proper education, refuse to be a lady and instead, become an actress at the age of thirteen.'

Vaudeville Years

Apparently, circus acts and shamelessly-black-faced musicals welcomed child labor at the turn of the 20th century. 'You're pretty, and tall for your age... but what idiot told you you were an actress?' Shipman relates her failings with wry and sardonic wit in her autobiography. 'A shabby little tramp in a backwoods troupe in a one-night stand company as there ever was... But, at last I am a professional actress!' she wrote home from a pool-table stage in Wallace, Idaho.

Touring with stock theater companies from her childhood home in Seattle to New York and as far as Alaska, the eighth grader learned fast what it meant 'to sit on my theater trunk so the local sheriff could not attach it for the troupe's unpaid hotel bills, to go hungry, cold and study one part while rehearsing another and playing a third'.

Shipman's descriptions of her pubescent years on filthy pillows made me wince as a mother. As a filmmaker, however, I understand artistic passion as both a gift and affliction. The applause and hardships were life's boot camp, building a maverick girl before women could even vote. Sexism and feminism had not been named nor cursed yet, but resilience, determination, independence and the ability to fry mascara in a tin cup over a smoky kerosene lamp became Shipman's armory for life as an untamable artist and liberated woman forty years before Betty Friedan published *The Feminine Mystique*.

By her eighteenth birthday, Shipman had mastered the road, living off two dollars a week and stirring crowds in plays like *Queen of the Highway*, where she performed a horse-rearing stunt and manure-dodging death in two performances daily. These talents, plus her intact virginity, spiked the interest of a 'posh', thrice-married, Broadway promoter.

'Men like Ernie Shipman made the 90s gay,' she wrote. 'He was one of the great cocksmen of his time, not immoral, but amoral, not lascivious, but lusty.' This amiable rake and slippery gentleman gave Shipman a beloved son, Barry, then shoved her off the stage and into 'moving pictures', while touring with another leading lady.

In 1912, every town had a Vaudeville 'house' and those theaters where Shipman reared her horse were quickly converting to cinemas. Around the world, film companies were springing up as fast as the cameras could be cranked. So raw was the industry that Kalem, Selig and Biograph, the 'biggies' printed their company names on the lower left hand corner of every frame to stop hijacking. Ernie Shipman smelled money and advised his young wife how to earn it, writing melodramatic scenarios for Vitagraph at $25.00 a reel.

Before Hollywood

By 1915, Ernie Shipman's exceptional spending ability and promotional perspicacity had propelled his wife into writing two-reelers for the new Universal. He even sold her first novel, *Under the Crescent* for a startling, thousand-dollar advance. The money evaporated quickly. Ernie Shipman went to jail for unpaid bills pre-dating the marriage. Nell Shipman pawned the first of many family heirlooms lost to debt, bail and broken dreams. Ironically, it was while writing scripts that Nell Shipman was elbowed into directing, when a director on a Universal set in Tahoe ran away with the leading lady.

'You wrote this mishmash,' shouted the lead actor, 'you can direct it.' Shipman picked up the megaphone and from then on, only put it down when she applied Stein's thick-greased make-up to play the part of the female lead. Even two-year-old Barry earned his first of a thousand film parts.

Hollywood didn't exist yet. Burbank, Pasadena and Glendale (where the Shipman family and two pet bears, resided within a population of 3,000) were individual production towns. Nell Shipman's persistence of vision and empty bank account, coupled with the boom time of silent film, catapulted her career when she wrote the script and starred in *the first multi-reel feature shot on-location.* Vitagraph provided a staggering $90,000 budget to produce *God's Country and the Woman,* adapted from the popular outdoor novel by James Oliver Curwood. Logline: Queen of Dog Sleds Conquers Canadian Tundra.

Temperatures regularly slid to thirty below, according to Joseph Walker, the future Oscar-winning cinematographer on the set. He later published an autobiography about his work with Hollywood's most beautiful women. In *The Light on Her Face,* he describes Nell Shipman in near angelic terms and that film location as a polar hell. Cameras had to remain outside or their lenses would shatter if brought inside the cabins at night. The lead male actor died of pneumonia and was replaced half way through shooting while the director, Bert Van Tuyle, suffered crippling frostbite on one foot that would eventually drive him delusional with pain. Nell, on the other hand, emerged from the harsh landscape a true movie star – with Van Tuyle, her clandestine paramour.

Witness here the birth of the first action-adventure-heroine in a box-office blockbuster. Stunt queens, like Helen Holmes in the *Perils of Pauline* were at their zenith in 1915. These cliff-hangers were packaged as 'serialized' entertainment, but *God's Country and The Woman* was a feature-length film. Box-office receipts soared and investors garnered 300%, while Nell's pay lagged until last. More valuable, however, her public persona blossomed as the heroine who paddled canoes and drove dogsleds. Fans loved the *Girl From God's Country*. This marketing moniker would prove as true as it was successful.

This Curwood epic and its sequel, confirmed Shipman's uncommon bond with wild animal actors. Bears, cougars, elk, skunks and vicious dogs – she considered all four-legged creatures to be as worthy of respect as any actor, insisting they be treated as humanely by refusing to allow guns, whips or chains on her sets. Even the most dangerous animals returned the favor.

At this point in my research, I felt like I'd struck documentary gold! How utterly *cool* was this woman? And better yet, she'd mysteriously disappeared! I dug deeper into the archives and my production budget.

The box-office success inspired Ernie, Nell and author Curwood to abandon Vitagraph and create an independent production company to make, *Back to God's Country*. This rebellion provoked a contentious relationship with the studio establishment for a price Nell alone would pay the rest of her life.

Freedom is Never Free

Shipman's rejection of tyranny, particularly against the patriarchal construct, made me cheer. She embodied the archetypal dilemma of all women, then and now, the choice between security and freedom, of the predictable turn and the unknown road – or as the author, Karen Von Blixen described it, 'the lion hunt and bathing the baby.' As twenty-first-century women and mothers, we owe these female provocateurs of change, women like Susan B. Anthony, Charlotte Perkins Gilman and Nell Shipman, a debt. Our freedom is no less free, but we have the advantage of looking back on their sacrifices and bonfires. We know the price of freedom demands a loss of innocence and a fight. As a director and woman, I suddenly began to understand this story was much bigger than Nell Shipman and this film, more than a documentary. It had become a personal journey and homage to all these anarchic sisters I'd never met.

In 1919, Nell Shipman was female liberation in the flesh, literally. *Back to God's Country* premiered with Nell flashing the first nude scene in film history. (Lois Weber's film, *Hypocrites*, is a spectacular runner-up and Hedy Lamarr's 1933 nude scene in *Ecstacy* still generates far more press). 'Don't book this movie unless you want to prove the NUDE IS NOT RUDE!' dared a 1920 advertisement for this Curwood-Shipman Production. Five years later, Nell performed a second nude debut in her own film, *The Grubstake*. This grainy, black and white swimming scene would rate PG 13 today, but a woman's naked shoulders still shocked in 1924. The footage, shot on location at an icy, high-mountain stream, typifies Nell performing her own stunts no matter the risk.

By the time *The Grubstake* premiered, Shipman had escaped the partnership with her philandering husband and author Curwood, took up with her married director, Van Tuyle, acquired her own zoo of seventy rescued wild animals, and moved them all, including ten-year-old Barry, to the Idaho wilderness to produce her own films. Never again would a man control her destiny, income or scripts. Writing, producing, starring in and selling some twenty-five films, (mostly extant) Nell nearly died swimming white-water rapids, driving sled dogs in sub-zero temperatures, and *always*, rescuing the male lead. Her storylines of courageous women overcoming physical challenges and befriended by wild animals in the wilderness refuted the cinematic Cinderella formulas of the large studios taking shape in California in 1925. Looking back in Hollywood's history tomes, production giants like Universal, Paramount and Metro-Goldwyn were considered renegade 'start-ups' at the time, created by packs of male visionaries like Carl Laemmle, Adolph Zukor and Samuel Goldwyn. Meanwhile, far away and forgotten at her Lionhead Lodge on

Priest Lake, Nell went on writing what she knew and every film was a reflection of who she was – an unrelenting, unrepentant talent and self-reliant film pioneer.

The Beginning of the End

Making movies has always been an expensive business, which explains why fledgling studios began courting Wall Street. Shipman, on the other hand, was no different than myself or other independent filmmakers today – hopeful vampires in constant pursuit of financing angels. No doubt, the Queen of Dog Sleds would have been the Queen of Crowdfunding had her birthdate been a hundred years later.

Free from constraints, Shipman created her best work from 1918–1924. Unfortunately, neither her talent nor middle school education extended to accounting. Investors balked when her personal epic, *The Girl From God's Country* ran over-budget at $10,000 a day. So she followed her muse to Idaho, making movies on traded fame, local labor and borrowed credit. As the film industry transformed into an entertainment monopoly that swallowed production, distribution and theaters, she cleaned fish to feed her zoo and kept writing and staring in *The Grub Stake* and *Tales Of The Northwind*. Independent distribution died in the new studio paradigm and none of her films made money. By 1924, the animals were reduced to half-rations and Nell, to eating the animals that finally fell in twelve-foot snow drifts.

Living her individualistic dream, this *truly*-starving artist suffered murderous locals, sub-zero winters, several near-death experiences, bankruptcy and ultimately, the loss of her lover, her film company and her beloved zoo. Her rugged individualism also placed Shipman on an unspoken 'studio black list' for future collaboration in Hollywood. Despite life-long disappointments, Nell continued to write articles, pitch scripts and adopt homeless animals until her death in 1970. She completed her autobiography in one year, at the age of seventy-seven. The book is as full of brave passions and great heart as the writing women herself, transmuting her adventures in silent film and the Idaho wilderness into an Artemis-like legend. Even her descriptions of the indignities of old age and poverty are laced with humor and resilience.

'Another call from the Motion Picture Relief Fund,' wrote Nell. 'This time, they're asking for a condensed biography of my life and work. Appears I am non-existent.'

Holding their final letter of denial of benefits in my own hands, I wondered how Nell must have felt in 1969, reading the words, 'We can find no record of your name in any film credit.'

How morally unjust! How tragically romantic! How radically modern! Forget The Hunger Games*! Surely, Nell Shipman must be singular in her early proto-feminist heroism, animal activism, self-propelled stunts and bare booty!*

Here is where I must defer to my favorite quote in my own documentary as it resounds as one of the most surprising and horrific moments in my directing career – '*How wrong you are!*'

Female Ghosts

We should all say 'Thank You' to Dr Jane Gaines, Director of the Women Film Pioneers Project at Columbia University. The professor enthusiastically shared this declaration about half way through our interview. Since 1993, this ivy-league powerhouse has dedicated her career to reassembling the invisible history of thousands – no, really, *thousands* – of women in all facets of the silent-film hierarchy.

'When we started, we knew about a few women: Alice Guy-Blaché, Germaine Dulac, Lois Weber… by the time we were ready to publish, we had so much material, the paper was three feet off the floor!'

As early as 1907, women in France, China, Japan, Russia, India, Poland, Brazil, Germany Italy, U.K., Mexico, America and more, were cranking cameras, writing scripts, directing short films, splicing reel and schlepping their films, many just like Nell Shipman, up and down Fourteenth Street in New

York City. The Women Film Pioneers Project at Columbia University, my documentary and this book serve as testimonials to the legacies of these forgotten film professionals. Hopefully, many more studies will follow.

Every writer, filmmaker and perfectly awful talk show host knows the best stories begin with a question. So, how is it I could have been making movies for twenty years and never heard of Nell Shipman *and her huge posse of female film pioneers?* What happened to their films? More perplexing, why did all these she-mavericks disappear around 1925?

Following these doomed trailblazers took me down a rabbit hole inhabited with flickering, female ghosts. In silence, Helen Gibson made crazy leaps onto fast-moving trains, Mary Pickford signed the contract to form United Artists as a full partner with Fairbanks and D. W. Griffith and Chaplin, while Alice Guy-Blaché directed more than 1,000 short films! I liken the experience to waking up in the Jurassic period of Hollywood, the lost era when women were giants in the global silent film industry.

More stunning were the works of minority directors that surfaced. Assets were sparse, but profound. The family trust of Zora Neale Hurston generously donated the only surviving footage of a film shot by the Pulitzer-Prize-winning author. The clips are jaggedly spliced, like black and white stanzas folded into an unfinished poem about the African-American experience, vivid and true. Watching the footage in my documentary, few realize the hypnotic singer is also the famed writer.

Then along came Marion Wong. Truthfully, if I hadn't already fallen in love with Nell Shipman, I would have refocused my entire documentary on this founder of the Mandarin Film Company in Oakland, California in 1914.

Chinese–American history is unique in that the Chinese Exclusion Act prohibited Asian integration into white culture from 1882 until the end of World War II. Especially on stage and screen, the 'Yellow-face' was stereotyped as inferior. Anna May Wong, the most popular Chinese-American actress of the 'silents' described herself as 'the woman who died a thousand times but has never been kissed', since interracial touching was forbidden by law. Amazing that in this crucible of discrimination, Marion Wong managed to smelt art from the suffering of many. Her feature-length film, *The Curse of Quon Gwon: When the Far East Mingles with the West,* was the first to authentically document the Chinese-American experience.

I met Marion's grand-nephew, Greg Mark, at Sacramento State University, where he is Director of Asian-American Studies. His story hypnotized me as much as the film.

> 'I was introduced to the film by my grandmother, Violet Wong, in June of 1968. She took me into the basement of our family home in Berkeley, and there, in a corner, she showed me an old canister with three reels of 35mm film… *The Curse of Quon Gwon* had been preserved through three generations and they were handing it on to me.'

Watching this film, I felt like I was witnessing dust being blown off lost pages of American history. It's a love story, but a foreign story, in our own country – the exotic foot-binding shoes, dangling headdresses and Chinese villages amidst the *empty* Berkeley hills – every set is so richly detailed and every intertitle so nuanced with the unfamiliar, I could not look away from title screen to final scene.

Violet Wong, Marion's sister and Greg Mark's grandmother, is the flawless female lead in a newlywed couple's struggle to integrate Chinese tradition into their new life in a 'closed' American society. Surprisingly sophisticated, the plot revolves around reverse discrimination toward the lovers by the unaccepting, Chinese purists instead of the obvious white perpetrators.

'How did this twenty-year-old woman get this idea?' asks Greg Mark in my film. 'She wrote the script, directed the film, played the villainess, and she was the producer – she raised the money! Plus, three generations of women in my family were involved in film. The baby is played by my mother!'

Marion Wong, the Mandarin Production Company and *The Curse of Quon Gwon* faded into historical anonymity around the same time Nell Shipman and all women-owned silent film companies disappeared. Why that happened, how that happened can be attributed to economic and cultural changes in the evolution of American society. Male-dominated ownership of production, distribution and theaters, the infusion of power and money from male-dominated Wall Street into the male-dominated film studios, the male-dominated perception that women wanted – *or needed* – to be dominated at home and in the workplace; in other words, Hollywood had entered the Stone Age. More difficult to understand is why the same cave rules continue to reign over women in film today.

Then and Now

I found the answer in *Thelma and Louise,* or more precisely, Geena Davis, aka Thelma. (FYI: I can confirm she is devastatingly tall, beautiful and preternaturally intelligent and I would hate her if I didn't respect her so much.) The Oscar-winning actress and her Institute on Gender in Media have amassed the most comprehensive body of research on gender-bias in entertainment. It turns out there's no evil conspiracy in Hollywood against women today. Sure, men under thirty-five in baseball caps are still making most of the decisions on which male star to greenlight in the next male-directed blockbuster. Albeit, no women cinematographer has ever been nominated for an Oscar. And yes, only four women directors have ever been nominated for an Academy Award. But the good news is that Katherine Bigelow won! And Geena, and Meryl Streep and Patricia Arquette and legions of mouthy women in every aspect of the film industry are working to inform, rather than alienate the public and the powers in baseball caps.

The time has come, let us all chant, to give women equal

screen time, power and pay in media. Why? Because women are half the world's population and more than half of movie audiences and we say it's time, for ourselves, and our daughters. After all, a little girl can only be what she can see and no matter our gender, we *all* want our daughters to see themselves in presidents and astronauts and in baseball caps.

That's why Nell Shipman and her contemporaries matter today. There are generations of young girls (and boys), especially minorities, who believe they can't succeed, who believe no one sees or hears them because they don't see themselves reflected on-screen or off.

Ironically, it's a generation of *Silent Women* that can now inspire us to project our voices in film, art, literature, business, education and politics. Nell Shipman, Zora Neale Hurston, Marion Wong: these astounding pioneers had no one to look to for guidance. They blazed their own trail and in so doing, dare us all to follow them into a future with parity for all.

Author Biography: Karen Day

As a photographer, filmmaker, journalist and author, Karen makes a habit of ignoring the punitive warnings of military dictators, Christian and Islamic fundamentalists, political pundits and her four children. Consequently, her resumé includes house-arrest in Myanmar, lunch with Dr Anthrax in Baghdad, fashion reprimands from a warlord in Kandahar and happy hour with the Dalai Lama in Manhattan. Her professional pen and camera focus on the human element in every story, whether the subject is war-torn refugees or Hollywood celebrities. A member of the Society Of Professional Journalists and Reporters Without Borders, Day has reported from Afghanistan, Cuba, Iraq, Myanmar, Rwanda, Uganda and South Sudan for national publications, including *Newsweek 'O', Elle, Motherjones.Com, Body And Soul, Marie Claire* and *The Los Angeles Times*. Her news features have aired on NBC Nightly News with Tom Brokaw, CNN, and the BBC. Day is co-producer and host of the Emmy award-winning television series on Plum TV, *Women With A Cause* and has written, directed and produced eleven documentaries, including *Between The Earth And Sky* (2012) and *From The Ground Up* (2014) with Harvard. In 2010, Day published *Seal: The Unspoken Sacrifice*, about working with the

Navy's Special Operations Forces. She recently presented a TED Talk about the Afghan Women's Justice Project, the organization she founded to support women and children imprisoned in Afghanistan for moral crimes. *Girl From God's Country* is Day's favorite film to date – but she always says that about her current project.

Director's Statement

Girl From God's Country: The History of Women in Film and Other War Stories is my way of saying Thank You to courageous female film pioneers, like Nell Shipman. I realize I could never be making documentaries to empower women and girls around the globe if these women in film hadn't come first. Their work deserves to be rediscovered and appreciated and in so doing, the public can better understand how history is repeating itself as women in film continue to experience gender disparities in today's media industry.

www.karenday.net

2. EARLY AFRICAN-AMERICAN FEMALE FILMMAKERS

Aimee Dixon Anthony

In recent years, film scholars have focused much attention on the earliest histories of African-American men in the film industry. Aside from the acknowledgment of William Foster of Chicago in 1910 and the Lincoln Motion Picture Company, founded in Los Angeles, California in 1916 (Sampson 1–2) as the first African-American makers of film, a great deal of writing has been devoted to Oscar Micheaux, considered 'the most prolific and important African-American independent filmmaker in the first half of the twentieth century' (Bowser and Spence xvii). While the significance of Micheaux to the history of film cannot be underestimated, there is still a great void left in the scholarship of early African-American cinema, namely, the study of women of African-American descent. Outside of three articles – one by Gloria Gibson, an article by Kristal Brent Zook of *LA Weekly,* and a more recent article by Elizabeth Binggeli – little has been published. From my research on this topic, it is suggested, between these sources and an unpublished thesis by Yvonne Weldon titled 'Sisters of Cinema', that there were approximately eight African-American women who were a part of the film industry in the silent era, ranging in their respective roles in the industry from women who produced films, like Eloyce King Patrick Gist and Alice B. Russell, to women who directed films like Tressie Souders and Maria P. Williams to women who managed their husbands' careers like Eslanda Goode Robeson. The degree to which these women were actually filmmakers, is a question that Gibson raises in her investigation:

> Since references are few and footage scant, queries sometimes arise such as: Can these women be 'filmmakers'? or: How important are film fragments? These are serious questions with dire consequences for film studies scholarship, especially as they pertain to filmmakers of color.' (Gibson 195)

While the era of the Harlem Renaissance was focused primarily on literature, poetry and the fine arts, there was a desire by some of its members to penetrate Hollywood. Kristal Brent Zook discusses the difficulty of being a well-known African-American writer (male or female) with a desire to be included in the Hollywood system but never able to make it 'in':

> It must have been a lonely existence — to be black, creative and intoxicated by the power of one's own quiet imagination. How many days were wasted with worry about how to make ends meet? [Langston] Hughes had files full of story ideas right up to his death in 1967. And yet even he, who may have been the first black writer in this country to actually make a living from his work, was locked out of Hollywood. *(LA Weekly,* 26th October 2000)

And, as the industry began to grow even white women in the film business lost their power:

> Could she have a husband and also run a film company? Gaines wondered. It was a question that, like the films themselves, had a brief shelf life. In 1916, no one knew the outcome of the drama. But by 1925, the film industry had been thoroughly masculinized, and she was sent home, said Gaines. *(Harvard Gazette,* 6th November 2003)

However, at this same point when white women's role in film history was diminishing, the kernels of African-American women in film began to sprout. Zora Neale Hurston was not only the first African-American female to make films but also the first anthropologist with a focus on African-American culture to ever make ethnographic films (Gibson 206). It may be true that Hurston was the first African-American woman to record ethnographic films, but it can be argued that she was *not* the first to make films.

While many of the early African-American female film-makers were middle-class, none of them, simply by the complexion of their skin, would have the freedom to create in the same way as their white counterparts. Thomas Cripps speaks to this dilemma for African-Americans in Hollywood in the early days of cinema:

> …The only film role for African-Americans was to serve powerful whites and to act as models for screen characters. The resulting dependent class of blacks was never able to deal with the studios as equals. Blacks found they could not compete in this world. (Cripps 90–91)

Yet, while the numbers for African-American films produced in the early years of cinema is far less than those of white filmmakers, African-American filmmaking tended to be on a smaller scale and was often carried out by both men and women. In the U.S., alternative production practices such as the New York avant-garde, black film companies and studios based in Chicago have been excavated. Small in scale though these may be, they point to a cinematic potential that the dominant paradigm denies or suppresses. (Andrew 182)

With an interest in the relevance of a 'less dominant' film group, this chapter's purpose is to respectfully uncover and debate the possibilities of a history for African-American women of color that places these women in earlier parts of cinematic history where they, undoubtedly, played a role. Just as the African slaves, the majority of whose names are unknown, helped to elevate the country from an untapped source of wealth and richness, it is in these types of stories and histories of all people that we can see a fuller picture of how the American film industry developed.

Searching for the Traces

It appears that it was not until the twenty-first century that anything was written about an African-American female filmmaker from the silent era. What you would have found prior to 2000, is that African-American filmmaking seemed to begin in the late twentieth century with filmmaker Julie Dash. As important as Dash is to the history of film, she produced her very first film in the 1970s (Welbon 65). It seemed implausible that over the course of almost eighty years, since the beginnings of film, that no African-American woman had created a moving picture.

The filmmakers included in this chapter are women with a variety of roles in film and the film industry, from directors to writers to theater owners. In this search, sometimes clues appeared in the banal details through which other sources materialized. In other instances, information was uncovered from histories of other filmmakers where scholarship only briefly indicated a role for an African-American woman in the filmmaking process. Through a case study, Gloria Gibson examined the films of Zora Neale Hurston and Eloyce King Patrick Gist and reflected upon their work as 'firsts' in this area of film history.

Another writing on African-American women in early film stands out because of its specificity and focus on one aspect of this period of history. Again, a study of anthropologist and novelist Hurston, this essay explores her attempts, like others in the Harlem Renaissance, to break into film unsuccessfully (Binggeli 1). Similar to her foray into film through anthropology, her interest in the adaptation of her novels into movies was a means to an end, at least as is implied by most of the writings on Hurston as filmmaker. Binggeli emphasizes the importance of pushing research beyond the usual path:

> While it is commonplace that Hollywood narrative production in the studio era was conservative, particularly in regard to race, Hollywood narrative consumption was

> strikingly ecumenical. This consumption has not been
> adequately interrogated because scholars examining
> literature-to-film adaptations generally approach archival
> material from the film backwards — that is, from
> produced adaptation back through screenplay versions,
> production notes, and early readings of the source text.
> Such an approach utilizes only a tiny fraction of extant
> archival material. (Binggeli 2)

I would argue that even beyond the realms of the studio and
film system, archives need to be 'dusted off' to find more
information about these women, their film products and their
film ventures. With the majority of the women in independent
productions, there is little information on their work outside
of the black press. The newspapers that were run by and for
African-Americans at a time when the country was segregated
proved an important component in the success of many
African-American films and filmmakers:

> By responding to white racism and promoting self-
> determination, the black press had begun to play a role
> in African-American film history. Between 1918 and
> 1929, African-American newspapers exerted a positive
> influence by applauding the efforts of companies that
> produced films appealing to black audiences. They helped
> expand the market for black productions by providing
> reviews, advertisements, behind-the-scenes gossip, and
> discussion of these films. (Regester 37)

Much of what is written about early African-American women
in film is found from the black press. With more and more
investigation of these archives, it is my firm belief that more and
more African-American women involved in the film industry
of the early years will surface. Yvonne Welbon's dissertation
speaks to this need to search more deeply in the papers of
the African-American press. Her writing on African-American
women in film suggests that there were approximately eight
women who directed films since the beginning of film in 1896
until 1989 (Welbon 3); however, in my own limited research,

there were still other women who could qualify as filmmakers, not just behind the camera as directors but also as significant players in the process of making films and making sure that films were seen by an audience.

Extant Films

There are a small number of extant films that were, if not all, in part, the work of African-American women. The current best source for many of these films is to be found in the Library of Congress in Washington, D.C. There is an archive of several reels in 16mm of Zora Neale Hurston's footage of ethnographic films during her time in the South. The titles of the films appear to relate mainly to their subject. The first of Zora Neale Hurston's films called *Children's Games* suggests that the footage comes from Alabama. The footage lasts approximately ten minutes. The other films in the library are titled under the Margaret Mead Film Collection. There are eight film clips in the group, also on 16mm. Like the former film footage, the images include frames of children playing; shots of an elderly man, Kossola, supposedly one of the last slaves in America at the time; a younger man doing various activities, including posing for the camera; moving shots of the countryside where workers chop wood and approach a steam engine; African-Americans in a stadium setting where a man plays a saxophone and the women dance for the camera in white dresses; footage of a woman's baptism; and various other short takes of locations or people gathering. Additionally, there is film footage housed in the Library of Congress within the Margaret Mead/South Pacific Ethnographic Archives Collection where Hurston was involved as the 'onsite project director' (Balkansky) with anthropologist Jane Belo in another ethnographic field study of church rituals and spiritual experiences of church-goers in Beaufort, South Carolina.

Eloyce King Patrick Gist worked with her husband James Gist to write, direct and produce films which had a strong, moral dimension. They showed their films mainly in churches with the aim of providing religious and moral education. The extant footage consists of three reels, more specifically of the films *Hellbound Train* (1930) which preaches temperance and *Verdict Not Guilty* (1933) which explored the justice system. While originally shot on 16mm, the format offered to viewers in the Library of Congress is VHS. The footage, with a hand-held feel, tells stories of everyday African-Americans in situations where they must use their moral compass to do the right thing, but it is the title cards, such as, 'Little Girls shouldn't be Impudent to Mothers', and 'Thou Shalt Not Steal', that offer the viewer a didactic message of the right path to choose in these religious films. In addition, they are different from Hurston's countryside locations as the stories are set in the streets of a northern city or town and several scenes shot outdoors show snow. The people appear more sophisticated in their carriage and their dress. Other footage of Gist's films are period pieces in abstract settings, again telling the demise of falling prey to the devil.

Another film in Howard University's Moorland Springarn Research Center, also in Washington, D.C. is the ethnographic footage of Eslanda Goode Robeson's trip to Africa in 1936. But her son, Paul Robeson, Jr. has control over the viewing of the film and due to its poor condition, restricts access. Presumably shot on Cine camera, Eslanda Goode Robeson refers to this machine in her writings *African Journey* (1945).

The only other known film to exist, with an African-American woman contributing as 'filmmaker' in the earliest years of cinema, is the Hollywood film *Hallelujah* (1929). Also housed in the Library of Congress, the feature, produced by Metro-Goldwyn-Mayer, is significant primarily because it is considered the first all-black cast film produced by a major studio. It is also the first sound film of director King Vidor who capitalized on this new technology with the use of musical numbers throughout the film. Listed low in the credits of cast members are the Dixie Jubilee Singers. The choir director of the Dixie Jubilee Singers was Eva Jessye. She not only directed the gospel-based choir but also claims to be the composer of the music in the film:

> Although in all publicity the matter of singing in the picture was stressed, and although it played an outstanding part in the picture … I was receiving no credit whatever for my part in composing much of the music, arranging the spirituals, as director of the now famous Dixie Jubilee Singers, or my service in directing all synchronized singing, timing and vocal sequences, etc., for which ability I had been engaged by contract. King Vidor evaded the issue, and Wanda Tuchok informed me that since it was not stated in the contract that credit was to be given for the music, I could not hope to successfully demand recognition. (Jessye 592)

On the Internet Movie Database website, *Hallelujah* does now list Eva Jessye as the musical director but she was 'uncredited' on the film itself.

Non-Extant Films

Either no-longer extant or still to be found, there are several films by African-American women that were produced in the early years of cinema. The earliest project that involves a woman behind-the-camera is *Shadowed by the Devil*. However, accounts differ regarding the name of the filmmakers as well as the year of the production. Henry Sampson cites the film several times in *Blacks in Black & White* but while one reference credits the film's story to Mrs. M. M. Webb (Sampson 92), an earlier mention of the film cites her husband, and the main producer of the film as Miles M. Wells (Sampson 71). And while every mention of *Shadowed by the Devil* suggests a release date of 1916 (Sampson 8, 71, 92), *The Chicago Defender* refers to the film doing 'big business' in 1915 in their section 'Among the Movies' *(Chicago Defender*, 20th November 1915).

Madame E. Touissant Welcome (sister of famed African-American photographer James Van Der Zee) produced in partnership with her husband the documentary film *Doing their Bit* (1918) on 'Black soldiers in action in World War I', (Sampson 277) for Touissant Motion Picture Exchange based in New York City (Welbon 42). Welbon suggests that E. Touissant Welcome directed one of the films included in the twelve-part documentary which would make her the first African-American woman to direct a film. (Welbon 42–43)

Other African-American women credited with a major role in the production of a film in early cinema include Tressie Souders for *A Woman's Error* (1922) which is often referred to as the first feature film made and given distribution by an African-American woman director. Others include Dora L. Mitchell who is credited with being an actress and writer on *Right of Birth* (1921) and writer and social activist Maria P. Williams who produced, directed and acted in *The Flames of Wrath* (1923).

Maria P. Williams is credited with producing, writing and acting in her own films, however she is not officially credited as a 'director'. For this reason, Tressie Souders is sometimes considered as the first female director of African-American descent. But the role of director and producer was sometimes interchangeable and they were not distinguished in the way that they are nowadays.

Research reveals that women supported the film industry in a variety of roles from directors to writers to movie theatre owners and even projectionists. The beginnings of film history incorporate such men as Marcus Loew and Carl Laemmle who both started in the film industry through their work in exhibitions. Equally, African-American women participated in the film industry in many ways such as Sadie Dorsey, who was a member of the Maryland Board of Censors in 1924. (Welbon 50). Of the women who owned movie theaters, one of them also produced a film. In 1929, A. Leila Walker, daughter of famed entrepreneur, C. J. Walker, produced a promotional film 'with a narrative structure' (Welbon 45) about their hair care business that was shown around the country. A year prior, they had opened the Walker Theatre on the company's campus in

Indianapolis, Indiana. Whether the film is still in existence is unknown at present.

Zora Neale Hurston and Eslanda Goode Robeson

In this chapter I focus on two women: Zora Neale Hurston and Eslanda Goode Robeson. These two women offer a unique vantage point into early African-American film. While Zora Neale Hurston and Eslanda Goode Robeson represent, at first glance, two very different involvements in the film industry, they were both associated with the intellectuals of the Harlem Renaissance and mixed in the same circles of writers, artists and poets. In an era when almost no blacks went to college, an educated group of African-American intellectuals was making significant contributions to American literature, music, and the arts. They were also redefining race relations in a still virulently racist American society.

A seminal anthology *The New Negro: An Interpretation,* published in 1925 at the height of the Harlem Renaissance, reflected the vision of such luminaries of this group. Alain Locke, professor at Howard University cites in the introduction of the book which he edited:

> This volume aims to document the New Negro culturally and socially, to register the transformations of the inner and outer life of the Negro in America that have so significantly taken place in the last few years. (Locke ix)

The book (which includes a play by Zora Neale Hurston called *Spunk*) reflects the society of which both Hurston and Robeson were an integral part. Hurston, considered a member of the Harlem Renaissance through her work as a writer, later in her life lost favor with the core members of this group, in particular Langston Hughes, over a professional dispute. Eslanda Robeson gained entrance into this group primarily through her husband's stature as a performing artist, but also to some degree, because of her own accomplishments as a graduate of Columbia and her comfort level amongst the intellectual society and the black elite.

Both Zora Neale Hurston and Eslanda Goode Robeson were born in the South near the turn of the century. Zora Neale Hurston was born on 7th January 1891 in Notasulga, Alabama and later moved to Eatonville, Florida when she was still a very young child. As Hurston describes in her autobiography, *Dust Tracks on the Road* (1942), Eatonville was a special place for the South in that period of time in America:

> I was born in a Negro town. I do not mean by that the black back-side of an average town. Eatonville, Florida, is, and was at the time of my birth, a pure Negro town – charter, mayor, council, town marshal and all. It was not the first Negro community in America, but it was the first to be incorporated, the first attempt at organized self-government on the part of Negroes in America. (Hurston, 'Folklore' 561)

In Eatonville, Hurston's father was both minister and mayor. He encouraged all children of the township, including his own nine, to get an education. Hurston, upon her mother's death and her father's remarriage, left a comfortable yet modest home to make a life of her own at the young age of fourteen. Eventually she ended up in Baltimore where she received her first secondary degree at Morgan Academy, later to become a student of Morgan State College. (Turner 90)

Eslanda Goode Robeson, born on 15th December 1896 in Washington, D.C., a more cosmopolitan town of the South than Eatonville, and yet, while not an all-black city, was a city with one of the nation's largest populations of African-Americans in the early twentieth century (Taylor) as well as many with education and affluence. Her family, as is noted in several of the African-American newspapers of the day, came from a distinguished lineage:

> Mrs. Robeson was Miss Eslanda Goode before her marriage. Her father, who has been dead for many years was very prominent in the social life of Washington, D.C. in the 1890s… On her maternal side, Mrs. Robeson is the

granddaughter of the late Francis Cardozo, Sr., a graduate of Cambridge University, England. He was later during reconstruction times State Treasurer for the State of South Carolina. (*Afro-American* Baltimore, 12th November 1927)

Both women, Hurston and Robeson, went on to receive not only undergraduate degrees but Hurston earned a doctorate from Columbia University while Robeson pursued a PhD at Hartford Seminary. These accomplishments for women, African-American women in particular, were extremely rare and unprecedented. Zora Neale Hurston was the first African-American woman to graduate from Barnard College in 1928. Robeson was initially conferred a Bachelor of Science degree across the street at Columbia University in 1923 (Robeson Letter to Erik Barnouw). In addition, while there are differing accounts of Eslanda Robeson's professional position, she became the head histological chemist of Surgical Pathology at New York-Presbyterian Hospital or a bacteriological analyst at Bellevue Hospital. In either case, she was the first black and the first black woman to hold such a position. ('Eslanda Goode Robeson'; *Afro-American* Baltimore, 12th November 1927). So, not only were these women setting precedents unheard of for their time but they were doing it almost simultaneously. Interestingly enough, both women, eventually, pursued degrees in anthropology. Both Hurston's bachelor's and doctorate were in the field of Anthropology and Robeson went on to study Anthropology too, inspired by her interest in Africa. With her husband and others Robeson helped establish the Council on African Affairs, which advocated African solidarity and campaigned against apartheid in South Africa.

Because of her ethnographic filmmaking of Southern African-Americans, Zora Neale Hurston has been credited by some film scholars as the very first African-American woman to make films (Gibson 206). Through the encouragement and urgings of her renowned professor, Franz Boas, Hurston, with the support of Guggenheim and Rosenwald fellowships, as well as backing from white patrons, was able to travel through the South to document various aspects of African-American folklore and society.

Eslanda Robeson's exposure to the film industry came through her relationship with her husband, Paul Robeson, as his manager and wife. She was even afforded an opportunity to act in a film because of her constant interaction with filmmakers. But a part of her desire to explore film as her own medium arose due to her own ambition and determination to make a mark on the world. Also, through Robeson's studies in anthropology, her only existing footage as a filmmaker documents her trip to Africa.

In the early twentieth century, the history of people of African descent was minimal. Both Hurston and Robeson have suggested in their writings their desire to explore and document the realities of their own histories so that future generations could have a documented history to look upon regarding people of African ancestry. But more immediately, both of them desired to find out more about their own roots to understand their place in history. According to Robeson:

> In America one heard little or nothing about Africa. I hadn't realized that consciously, until we [the Robeson family] went to live in England... I began to read everything about Africa I could lay my hands on ... the reading and the questions landed me right in the middle of anthropology (a subject I had only vaguely known existed)... At last I began to find out something about my "old country", my background, my people, and thus about myself. (Robeson, *African Journey* 9–11)

It was concern regarding the loss of African-Americans' Southern histories and customs that encouraged Hurston to make the trip. Along with the mentorship of Franz Boas, she took the adventure to document the folklore of the Southeast. In the opening sentence of her book, *Mules and Men* (1935) which documents her first journey as an anthropologist, she states succinctly how she felt about this opportunity: 'I was glad when somebody told me, "You may go and collect Negro folk-lore".' (Hurston, 'Folklore' 9)

Despite many commonalities between the two women, they were very different. Hurston's life was her own. That is to say, her career pursuits were to satisfy her own needs as an artist. Eslanda Robeson's life choices were based on her husband's career. In an article from the *New York Amsterdam News*, the subtitle for one portion of the news story is called 'Gave up Her Career':

> And now more about Eslanda Goode Robeson, manager-wife. 'Years ago I gave up my professional career, that of being a chemist, to become my husband's manager. To this job I have [sought] a scientific approach and [it] has been genuine fun, as in chemistry, watching reaction and results,' she says. (*New York Amsterdam News,* 6th August 1938)

Like many women of her era, Robeson directed her energies towards her husband's goals and used her talents to further his career.

Outside of the more immediate differences between the two women, Hurston and Robeson's personalities couldn't be more different. Hurston has been described as wild, care-free and independent in spirit while Robeson has been considered ambitious, disciplined, focused and strong-willed. These women did know each other as well. In fact, there is an extant letter by Zora Neale Hurston to Eslanda Goode Robeson, replying to another letter from Robeson:

> Dear Eslanda,
> Your letter was altogether satisfactory. I had not written you because I feared that I might be seeming to lay an obligation upon you – to be trading on sentiment… So I just sat back and waited until I heard from you. I know that if ever anyone bought the movie rights to the book and if ever anyone wrote a satisfactory scenario and if it suited you all, I mean if you liked it, Paul will act in it anyway so I feel fine. (Kaplan 299)

While no film project came to fruition, and this letter represents the interests of both parties in the actor Paul Robeson, it is quite interesting that the negotiations and business exchanges that are taking place around this prominent African-American male are between two African-American women. These two women who lived in Harlem in the beginning of the twentieth century were well-acquainted with each other but chose very different paths despite their many commonalities..

Zora Neale Hurston: Dramatic Ethnographer

Most of what is written about Zora Neale Hurston is, understandably, about her work as a writer of novels and anthropology. Fairly prolific in both of these areas of literature as a professional writer, it was her experiences in the dramatic arts that was her longest career pursuit. Her first foray into theatre was, in fact, her first job. At a young age, Hurston was hired as a wardrobe girl in a Gilbert & Sullivan repertory company (Hemenway 17). The exposure to this world more than likely ignited her interest and lifelong pursuit of the theatre and drama:

> …she had eighteen months as lady's maid to an actress in a Gilbert & Sullivan troupe, and that association did as much for her as more standardized education in opening up a vista of books and music to be absorbed. (*New York Times*, 29th November 1942)

Hurston, herself, suggests how her work in theatre affected her ability to become a playwright: 'I have learned a lot about the mechanics of the stage, which will do me good in playwriting.' (Kaplan 227)

Considering the overall body of Hurston's work as a writer, it is true that she is known for her literature in both fiction and non-fiction, but her consistent drive was to do works that showed a dramatic inclination. Theater was not only comfortable to her with her background in that arena, but it was also accessible in a way that film was not. She was encouraged to pursue theater through her experience of success in writing such plays as *Color Struck* (1925) that drew her into the rich artistic and influential world of the Harlem Renaissance, as well as her plays *Spunk* (1925) and *Sweat* (1926) which caught the eye of established author and screenwriter,

Fannie Hurst who would later become a mentor in her writing career. Opportunities to work in drama as an instructor came through a variety of different institutions and organizations. She had been offered roles teaching theatre and starting drama departments at several schools throughout the country from Bethune-Cookman College in Daytona Beach, Florida to Fisk in Nashville, Tennessee (Kaplan 165). Perhaps the most interesting of these work experiences was through the government run Works Progress Administration.

> Given her training in folklore, Hurston was an obvious choice for the Federal Theater Project, newly organized in 1935 through the Works Progress Administration. She was hired as a drama coach at $28.36 a week and worked with such professionals as Orson Welles and John Houseman. (Kaplan 171)

Not only did these theatrical experiences play a significant role in her development as an artist, but they were the cornerstone in her approach towards her work. While she became more established through literature, drama was the core of her work and, to her, the core of the African-American voice:

> Yet, despite her convictions about the power of theatre as the source for the African-American expression, it was literature that defined her to the public and to many of her patrons, specifically Charlotte Osgood Mason, or as she affectionately calls her 'godmother'. (Hemenway 108)

The fight to push towards a more dramatic form of creativity was thwarted by Hurston's obedient behavior (at least with regard to her white patrons, a point of contention for her Harlem Renaissance peers, specifically Langston Hughes) and her need to make ends meet financially. It was a daunting profession for a woman of color to pursue without the support of a wealthy person to back her and Mason was not in favor:

> Hurston's theatrical ambitions were difficult to realize. Mason was determined that Hurston not 'waste' her

material on the commercial stage. Funding was difficult
to come by. (Kaplan 173)

Determined, Hurston did continue to pursue theatre, but she
started to focus more on what was low-hanging fruit for her
creative and anthropological pursuits. Her natural curiosity
into the folklore and nature of African-Americans of the
South as well as religious behaviors of people of African
descent directed her career, at least earlier in her development,
towards ethnography.

Ethnographic films

When, on her first voyage as an anthropologist, Zora Neale
Hurston recorded footage of games, customs and characters
of the South, her trip was a precedent in ethnological study.
Under the tutelage of the most prominent anthropologist of
her time, Dr Franz Boas, Hurston was encouraged to travel
towards her own roots to the South to penetrate communities
of African-Americans and record any and all information she
could acquire from the people. Being an African-American
woman, a first for anthropological study of African-
Americans, Hurston utilized her knowledge and comfort with
the people, even making Eatonville a base of operations (*New
Republic*, 11th December 1935), so that she could ascertain as
much information as possible. Written, shortly after her book
based on her findings, *Mules and Men,* that Hurston 'prowled
about the countryside, living in turpentine camps, railroad
camps, a phosphate mining village. Everywhere she went, she
cajoled people into telling her all sorts of tales, "big old lies",
a townsman called them.' (*New Republic*, 11th December 1935)

It was this expedition that led to the film footage now
housed in the Library of Congress. And it was this trip for
Hurston that Hemenway called '…a combination of luck,
pluck, and accident, Zora Neale Hurston had the opportunity
to become the authority on Afro-American folklore'. Hurston
describes to Dr Franz Boas in a letter marked as 21st April
1929, the collection of material she gathered:

> I am through collecting and I am sitting down to write
> up. I have more than 95,000 words of story material,
> a collection of children's games, conjure material, and
> religious material with a great number of photographs.
> (qtd. in Kaplan 137)

Hurston was also afforded a second opportunity to study the African-Americans in the South through support of her patron, Charlotte Osgood Mason. Mason had supplied Hurston with '\$200 per month for a year, and promised to provide a motion picture camera and an automobile to facilitate the collecting' (Hemenway 109). A portion of Hurston's footage, which I had the opportunity to view in the Library of Congress, comes from that expedition as is suggested by what was written on the canister: 'Believe this is Charlotte Mason's notes,' which read: 'loc. maybe: Alabama.' In my viewing of this reel, Hurston's approach to shooting the footage indicates an understanding of her subject's actions and its importance. Of course her motivation, and directive from Mason, was to 'collect all information possible, both written and oral, concerning the music, poetry, folklore, literature, hoodoo, conjure, manifestations of art and kindred subjects relating to and existing among the North American negroes.' (Hemenway 109)

But despite the scientific motivation behind the project there is a sense that the 'director' is present. It is not footage that is voyeuristic in nature but, on the contrary, the action seems, almost staged. This leads to the question that Gibson poses: 'How did Hurston intend to use the footage?' Further she makes the salient point that '...more research needs to be conducted' (Gibson 209). However, Hemenway indicates that Mason was concerned that Hurston would use the footage for commercial purposes. Not only did Mason, apparently, dictate Hurston's direction in her usage of ethnographic footage but, perhaps, also directed her potential for narrative filmmaking. In my estimation, the rebellious nature of Hurston slips into the films and there is that underlying desire to create stories and drama, as was Hurston's natural inclination. While her anthropological writing is highly regarded, it is of a dramatic nature in itself: music, folklore, and stories all are told in *Mules and Men* through a colorful griot's voice. A taste of her writing from *Mules and Men* demonstrates this dramatic and visual approach to her work;

> I thought about the tales I had heard as a child. How even the Bible was made over to suit our vivid imagination. How the devil always outsmarted God and how that ever-noble hero Jack or John, not John Henry, who occupies the same place in Negro folklore that Casey Jones does in white lore and if anything, is more recent. *(Folklore* II)

There is no indication that Hurston had any crew with her to shoot the film. The intriguing and interesting simplicity of the camera work and the gaze of many of her subjects suggests a one-woman team. Additionally, there was a real desire from Hurston, and more importantly her advisor, Boas, that this investigation be about 'manner rather than matter, style rather than substance' (Hemenway 91). In order to achieve those pure and natural results, Hurston could be hampered by a 'crew.' Her abilities to freely roam the familiar towns of Florida, from Jacksonville to Palatka, Sanford and her hometown of Eatonville (Hemenway 84) almost demanded her freedom and need to be independent in her task of collecting folklore.

Hurston's other footage, also in the Library of Congress, consisted of eight reels of film clips that total twenty-three minutes long. Marked as a part of the 'Margaret Mead Film Collection', they were possibly the footage obtained from her earliest explorations of the South. Despite the anthropological drive to create these films, there is a signature style to Hurston's footage. It is a style that suggests a narrative: each take of film shows action and space. The subjects of the films move about the frame purposefully, and it is suggested, through title cards (they are difficult to read but seem to suggest names of the people presented in the films) that Hurston did direct the actions of her subjects more than not. The focus of their gaze towards the camera implies the presence of a 'director.'

Back down South to the West Indies and beyond

Hurston's trips to the South did not end her pursuit of anthropological information. If anything it sparked a continued curiosity about folklore and traditions of people of color throughout the globe. Hurston was now officially an anthropologist who pursued exploration beyond the familiar territory of her home state of Florida. One of her next trips for collecting materials is related in her book *Tell The Horse* (1938) which follows her journeys through Jamaica and Haiti. But Hurston also traveled to the Bahamas on more than one occasion to pursue a developed interest in the connection between African-American and Afro-Caribbean culture (Hemenway 127). In a letter to Langston Hughes in the winter of 1929–30, she relays to him information about film footage secured during her travels: 'Hope you see the Nassau dances I sent G. ("Godmother" or Charlotte Goode Mason). Three reels if they don't cut them at the laboratory. The drum is in New York now.' (Kaplan 157). A trip to Beaufort, South Carolina demonstrated a more advanced approach to securing the film when she traveled with a 'crew' to document the religious practices of the African-American church. This 'crew' came through her partnership with fellow anthropologist, Jane Belo. She, and the three men of the crew (Norman Chaflin, Lou Brandt and Bob Lawrence) wrote to Belo an enthusiastic letter of their experiences thus far:

> …we've been shooting, shooting, and shooting – We've been begging and wheedling – and bluffing to get current – But we've got records… Not that all we planned worked out. We don't have any synchronization because our motor lay down on us before we started, so we were hand cranking all the four hundred foot rolls and using the spring on the one hundred foots… We really did shoot some wonderful reactions I hope that they prove satisfactory for study purposes. (Kaplan 459)

The footage depicts prayers, songs, sermons, trances and general religious services at the Commandment Keeper Church on Saturday 18th May and Sunday 19th May 1940. Another suggestion that there was more ethnographic materials on film is offered through a letter in 1944 to Jane Belo. In it Hurston asks her:

> Have you a motion picture camera now? We will need it badly. I have a line on some truly sensational material. Come and bring all the equipment that you can rake and scrape. You know that I know what I am talking about. All I need is time and equipment… (Kaplan 507–8)

Hurston was talking about a possible trip to Honduras through a recent connection with an 'adventurer' named Reginald Frederick Irvine who owned a ship that could take her to Latin America. She eventually made a solo journey which led to her novel *Seraph on the Suwanee* (1948).

Hurston circles Hollywood

While the bug to be involved in making films for Hollywood could have been spawned by her relationships with peers from the Harlem Renaissance, it is just as likely that Hurston's own interests in drama and narrative encouraged her pursuit of writing for film. But probably a more significant influence on her curiosity was that she also was surrounded by women, from the white community, who were writers and also had success in Hollywood. Women like Fannie Hurst and Marjorie Kinnan Rawlings had transitioned their novels into films, specifically with the motion pictures *Imitation of Life* (1934–1959) and *The Yearling* (1946).

Ironically, her brief tenure as a story consultant in Los Angeles at the Paramount Studios proved less than interesting to Hurston who spoke of her work in a letter written from Paramount Pictures on 30th December 1941 as '…not the end of things for me. It is a means' (Kaplan 463). Hurston was not entirely naïve to the prejudices of Hollywood and relayed her determination to her friend Van Vechten late in November 1942:

> Having been on the writing staff at Paramount for several months, I have a tiny wedge in Hollywood, and I

> have hopes of breaking that old silly rule about Negroes
> not writing about white people. In fact, I have a sort of
> commitment from a producer at RKO that he will help
> me to do it. I am working on that story now. (Kaplan 467)

That story turned out to be *Seraph on the Suwanee,* a novel published in 1948 that focused on a story of poor white Southerners, not African-Americans. Hurston paid out of her own pocket to send copies of the novel to Berg-Allenberg, a Hollywood agency associated with a 'motion picture offer' (Binggeli 10). Later, it was Anna Silva of the Warner Brothers, New York office that began the approval process. Along with a twenty-two page summary of *Seraph* was also a recommendation for 'executive attention' (Binggeli 13): 'Make no mistake about it, *Seraph on the Suwanee* is no first-rate novel...' Despite these reservations, however, she does recommend Hurston's novel for studio purchase. Silva concludes with the assertion that this story 'of a domestic nature' would be 'dear to the heart of women' and 'should not be expensive to film.' (Binggeli 14)

However, the story did not make it into celluloid. Hurston's attempt was unsuccessful yet this was not a deterrent. Soon after she began another project, a story of epic proportions called *The Life* of *Herod the Great,* that was 'filled with dramatic potential that was perfect for Hollywood'. Hurston pushed the project with many of her friends and patrons in the hopes of stirring up interest and support for the book and film idea. But, according to Kaplan, her more promising project coincided with her initial failure of the Herod story. Entitled *The Golden Bench* of *God,* it was her interest in the life of Madame C. J. Walker and Annie Pope Malone. Walker and Malone's fame rested upon their success in the hair care industry which made both of them millionaires. Kaplan writes: 'She [Hurston] discussed her book about them in more than fifteen known letters written in the early 1950s, and she returned to the novel over and over, developing it variously as a novelette, a play, and a movie script' (603). There is no manuscript available of *The Golden Bench* of *God.* Nor did a film or a book come out of the concept.

Other works by Hurston also passed through the offices of Hollywood studios and agents' desks. Among such attempts by Hurston to gain screenplay credit are *Moses, Man* of *the Mountain* (1939) her autobiographical *Dust Tracks on a Road* (1942) as well as a galley form of *Their Eyes were Watching God* in July 1937, two months before it was published. But Hurston still made it to the list of firsts in film with her ground-breaking ethnographic studies of African-Americans of the South. While we can speculate what her vision as a director or producer of film might have looked like, it is through her writing as a novelist and anthropologist where it is evident her gift was in the richness of her visual representation of folklore, people and stories that come to life through her profound command of the language both of dialect and description of life. Had she been a man or a woman of means, perhaps we would be writing not only about her literature but about her body of work in film.

Eslanda Goode Robeson: The Woman behind the Man

When Paul Robeson presented Gerry Neale with a proposal of marriage, she turned him down delicately and offered this advice to her dejected suitor:

> …She looked him straight in the eye and gently told him that she could not live life in his shadow. Her firm, almost motherly advice was that he should marry Eslanda, who was both willing and emotionally equipped to put his career and needs ahead of her own personal ambitions. (Robeson, Jr. 51)

While this information was acquired from a biographical book on his father's life as an artist, Paul Robeson, Jr. takes an historical approach to his dissemination of information on his father, as well as his mother. However, what he provides that other authors have not, is a more holistic perspective of the life of Paul Robeson. It affords the reader a closer peek into the evolution of an artist which includes a chapter and anecdotes throughout the book, about his mother's role in the shaping of his father as an artist. This particular quotation demonstrates the significant presence of Eslanda in Paul Robeson Sr.'s life. Based upon the information gathered about Eslanda's role in Paul's life as 'manager-wife' *(New York Amsterdam News*, 6th August 1938), she was very conscious of the power she parlayed. Although Eslanda's personality was strikingly different from Paul's, what they shared in common was compelling – they were both scholars, and both harbored strong ambitions. Paul became aware that Eslanda had decided to put off going to medical school until the following year so that she could devote more time to their relationship. He knew she was risking more for him than he for her, but he was wary of her powerful will. (Robeson, Jr. 48)

Perhaps, it was Eslanda's 'powerful will' that helped her to work in a very male-centric business environment. In an essay by June Mathis called 'The Feminine Mind in Picture Making' (1925), she discusses the lack of women in the film industry in the early years and how that absence was noticeable:

> There were only a few women at that time who were working in the industry, I mean, working side by side, or rather as silent aides to the directors and production heads. Somehow, these men prospered and succeeded in quite a remarkable way, outstripping most of the others; and it was half-heartedly acknowledged throughout the industry that a woman could do something to aid in the great development of the motion picture business. (Lant 663)

There is no indication from the writing of Eslanda Robeson or the comments made by those who knew her that she was deterred by what were, more than likely, major obstacles in front of her in her role as Paul Robeson's manager. Even during World War II, Eslanda held fast her duty to her husband and his career and the significant role she could play in their success. Much like her role as manager, Eslanda took pleasure in driving her husband to his appointments, much to Paul's delight as he did not care to drive. Her fortitude and commitment was truly tested during the filming of *The Proud Valley* (1940):

War came in the middle of filming. On September 1, 1939, Hitler invaded Poland, and Britain and France declared war on Germany… The filming at Ealing stopped for a couple of days. However, it soon resumed and Eslanda drove Paul for the thirty-minute trip back and forth to the studio. This exercise became quite a problem when Paul had to work late, since the blackout rules often forced Eslanda to drive home in almost pitch darkness. Somehow, she always managed. (Robeson, Jr. 330–331)

Eslanda's vision for Paul's life was far-reaching. She did not limit her view of his success to the more traditional field of law which would have been the expected path for the Columbia law school student. Even Paul was hesitant when after, having reluctantly performed with a group of African-American students in a drama called *Simon the Cyrenian,* he was approached to appear in a professional production of *Taboo* as its lead:

Paul was again inclined to refuse the part, preferring to concentrate on law school, but Eslanda … kept at him. After much discussion, and having determined he could continue his law studies simultaneously, Paul agreed to take on the role. (Duberman 43)

Upon meeting Eslanda, the artist Antonio Salemme, who had wanted Paul to model for a sculpture, described her 'twice as businesslike … hard-boiled, absolutely adamant and independent. Drove a hard bargain and didn't make friends.' (Duberman 68). And Eslanda's goals for Paul did not end at theater (and law and singing). She had set her sights on the big screen. In a letter to Carl Van Vechten, Eslanda shared her secret wish to act in films. She confided to Van Vechten that she had:

…quite settled one thing in my mind definitely – as soon as I get home I'm going to make a try to get into the movies – isn't that funny? Of course, I shall keep Paul's mark first always. I suppose I'll never get over that! We talked about that particular weakness or was it strength, on my part one night, remember? Well, anyway, I've always longed to act in the movies.

And in response to her letter, Carl replied: 'I'm awfully excited about your movie ambitions. I don't see why you shouldn't realize them.' (Duberman 91)

Perhaps that is the underlying motivation for Eslanda's devotion to her husband Paul. While she had the drive and determination to make his career a success, it was, in fact, through Paul that she could realize her own artistic interests and dreams. Eslanda's significance in Paul's career was apparent to others, at least others who agreed with her point of view. Rebecca West, writer and a friend of the Robesons commented: 'But if she hadn't pushed, Paul wouldn't have got anywhere so quickly.' (Duberman 94). Paul agreed that Eslanda was largely to credit with his abilities to broaden his talents into such areas as film. Writing to Eslanda from Europe about his newfound conviction that he must broaden his career, Paul concluded that this was 'just what you have believed all along but what you have been sensible enough to let me find out myself'.

While she was not completely naïve around her own film desires mixed with management of her husband's career, she did, occasionally show her lack of film business knowledge at the onset of her role as manager. While Paul did not fully integrate himself into the film world in the 1920s, he did make his debut in Oscar Micheaux's *Body and Soul* where he played both parts of twin brothers. Acting as his manager and showing her lack of knowledge of the film business, Eslanda contracted her husband to receive a modest $100 per week for the three weeks work on *Body and Soul*. True, Paul was to receive 3% of the gross above $40,000 (Musser 91). But despite her naïveté, on set, Paul saw Eslanda as an asset to him. While filming *Body and Soul*, Paul wrote Eslanda a note to indicate how much he loved her and how much he valued her guidance:

> You see everything so clearly, and I understand you so quickly. I shall never worry about any future play. You, better than anyone, understand any false *move* or accent or tone. You're marvelous. I only hope to be as useful to you when you begin [an independent career]. (Robeson, Jr. 82)

As time progressed, Eslanda honed her managerial skills and knew to push for information in advance of the project. The next opportunity for Paul to work on a film project was quite different than their last experience with Micheaux. The silent film, *Borderline* (1930), was an experimental feature about inter-racial relations by a member of the Pool Group 15 and editor of the film journal *Close Up* (1927–33), Kenneth Macpherson. It also involved the poet H. D. (Hilda Doolittle), as one of the lead actors. Eslanda proved a more sophisticated manager when approached by Macpherson. He talked over an early draft with Eslanda and promised to incorporate her suggestions, yet, when she asked to see the final version prior to their arrival in Switzerland, Macpherson sent word that he 'did not think it advisable to send the scenario as it is not like stage acting, not sustained.' (Duberman 130) He did promise to discuss all the shots with her upon arrival.

In part, Eslanda's involvement in the production was a means to protect Paul from a performance or film experience he would regret, like his first entrée into film on *Body and Soul* which, according to an essay by Charles Musser, became a 'taboo' subject for both Eslanda and Paul and an experience that '…he and his wife avoided mentioning in writings and interviews' (82).

Despite Macpherson not following up with his promise to share his writing with the manager-wife prior to their performances in *Borderline* (both Eslanda and Paul appeared in the film), the experience for the couple was memorable and a release from the weight of working as an African-American in American films. It was not an opportunity for profit as much as it was a chance to do something new. It was also a chance for Eslanda to make her screen debut. No one was paid and the total cost of making the film was $2,000. In her diary, Eslanda treated the experience as being something of a lark for them and apparently they had 'great fun,' in part because they liked everyone connected with the filming. When they were shooting the interiors, Eslanda wrote in her diary: 'Kenneth and H. D. used to make us shriek with laughter with their naïve ideas of

Negroes so that Paul and I often completely ruined our make-up with tears of laughter, had to make up all over again… We never once felt we were colored with them.' When Eslanda expressed her hesitation about her ability to act, the director reassured her. (Duberman 130–131)

As time progressed, Eslanda's skills as manager became more sophisticated and developed. Not only were Eslanda and Paul concerned with the profits they received from the projects in which Paul was involved but also the control Paul had in approving the script, songs and edits of the films became a more significant part of negotiations. Too many times, starting with his experiences on *Body and Soul* to the negative portrayal of African-Americans in *Sanders of the River* (1935), did Paul feel that the power he carried, as a representative for the African-American race, was spoiled by the end product of the films for which he played a part. Eslanda was quite alert to this and 'in her role as his manager at the outset of his career, was well aware of how her husband created a new representative of the black man.' (Stewart 63–64)

Eslanda's toughness and know-how was revealed in the deal-making around the Hollywood production of *Showboat* (1936). Her preliminary negotiations with Universal Pictures for *Showboat* resulted in agreement on a huge salary, all expenses paid for both Paul and herself, approval of the location (Paul was still refusing to go south of the Mason-Dixon Line), and the promise that he would have no lower than fourth place in the billing. The only provision left unresolved was Paul's demand that he have the right to approve not only the script but his actual takes. (Robeson, Jr. 226–227) Eslanda became more and more shrewd with production companies and studios and she protected her husband's image and interests more effectively as time went by.

Eslanda Robeson managed to negotiate roles for Paul in three films that were to be made by major film companies and completed before their departure for Moscow in October 1949. This time she made sure that Paul was contractually entitled to script approval (including shooting scripts) for all three movies throughout the filming process, as well as approval of the takes of his songs (Robeson, Jr. 237). Yet Eslanda did not see her role in Paul's life purely as manager. In fact, Eslanda considered herself quite important in the assessment in his work as an actor and performer: 'I am the most critical audience my husband has,' Mrs. Robeson replied when asked if she goes to his play and concert rehearsals, or visits the lot when the movies are being made. (*Newspaper interview*, 6th August 1938)

Over time, Paul's promiscuity pushed Eslanda away from her devotion solely to her husband's interests. During the period when they separated as man and wife, she did explore her own desires as an artist yet she maintained her duties to his professional pursuits too. Eslanda tried not to question, or dwell upon Paul's comings and goings, and continued to take care of his career. For his part, Paul tried to preserve the dignity of their social life by maintaining their unrelenting schedule of activities as a charming couple. With regard to business matters, the status quo continued. Eslanda carried on her full-time job as manager-agent-treasurer-accountant, complete with power of attorney. (Robeson, Jr. 100)

Of the many interests that Eslanda hoped to pursue were performance, production and the writing of plays and films. One such project that she often referred to in her writing was both a film and play. The former was called *Black Progress* which she hoped to adapt to a film scenario and the other was a play called *Uncle Tom's Cabin* (154). From that experience, Eslanda felt empowered and wrote to her friends:

> The role of Tom could be played wonderfully by Paul, but he isn't NECESSARY to the play at all... I mean to PROVE that I made Paul what he is, by doing the same for myself that I did for him. I mean little Eslanda to speak up. And loud, too. (157)

In a letter to Professor Barnouw of Columbia University, Eslanda wrote to inquire about participating in a class he offered on radio writing. In the letter she even informed him of her background:

> I am a B.Sc. in Chemistry, 1923, from Columbia, but have been working with my husband for the last 10 years in theatre, music, films and radio. I want very much to learn something about the technique of radio writing. I work very hard at anything I undertake, and am no dilettante. (Robeson Letter to Barnouw)

Soon thereafter, Eslanda sent Barnouw two postcards. Each postcard front was an illustrated image of Los Angeles broadcasting studios for films. The two-postcard correspondence was to inform Barnouw that she:

> ...came out here to transact some film business for my husband... Enjoyed very much the little technical bits, and especially the great informality of the whole proceedings... We live in the deep country now, in Connecticut, but in a really country part. But for this, you would have seen me again in your classes. (Robeson Postcards to Barnouw)

Again and again, Eslanda attempted to insinuate herself into the film industry in a more significant, acknowledged, and creative role outside of her bit parts in the films *Borderline* (1930) and *Big Fella* (1937).

Eslanda's opportunity to become a filmmaker would finally be explored in a similar means to Zora Neale Hurston – through ethnographic studies.

In May 1936, Eslanda and her son, Paul Jr., traveled by way of ship to Africa to pursue a dream of Eslanda's – to study and learn about the place where African-Americans originated – the motherland. They started their journey in South Africa and made their way north through the continent via Mozambique, Congo, Uganda as well as visiting Kenya and Egypt. Throughout her book, *African Journey* (1945), Eslanda makes references to taking photographs and having a Cine camera. Upon their arrival in the Congo, they were required to meet with a customs official who asked Eslanda to fill out forms regarding her equipment:

> I had to fill out three forms each for Pauli [Paul Jr.] and me, and one for the Cine camera. He clamped a seal on the camera. He did not ask whether I had another camera with me, and I didn't say. (Robeson 138)

Until the footage can be examined, scholars will have to wait to find out whether Robeson's film offers more than a simple record of her travels. However, the journey did lead Robeson to become passionately involved with the struggle for independence by African nations, for which she was honored by East Germany with the German Peace Medal and the Clara Zetkin Medal.

Conclusion

In my research, not only have I discovered gray areas due to the variety of roles women have undertaken during the early days of cinema, but also a great deal of possibility for more research to be completed. My approach was simply to include African-American women who did something in the film industry that has made a mark on film. I would venture to say if this same group of women lived in the twenty-first century where technology affords even a child from the remotest areas of the planet an ability to make films, many of these women would have become filmmakers of a more significant nature.

It is with great pride that I viewed the scant footage of Hurston and Gist at the Library of Congress. The images of African-Americans on film and video that represented an earlier era was thrilling to explore as a person of African-American heritage myself. To know that women of African-American descent participated in the early film industry in roles from writers to directors to projectionists excites me as an historian too.

A deeper investigation into the roles of the women mentioned in this chapter is necessary. In addition, there are strong possibilities for more extant films to be found; for example, the footage of Eslanda Goode Robeson's trip to Africa. With these potential discoveries and deeper research into this subject, the many important contributions of African-American female filmmakers to the history of early cinema will finally be revealed and ultimately, receive the recognition they deserve.

This is an extract from a dissertation submitted to the Film Division of the School of the Arts of Columbia University in 2010.

Author Biography: Aimee Dixon Anthony

Award-winning film director, Aimee is a graduate of the Rhode Island School of Design, Maryland Inst College of Art, and Columbia University. Born into a home of politicians she started her career in fashion eventually to become a filmmaker. *Vivian*, a surrealistic women-centric comedy, marked Aimee's award-winning first venture into writing and directing. A member of the Costume Designers' Guild as a costumer, Aimee has worked with such talents as Julie Dash, Debbie Allen, Geoffrey Lewis, Maz Jobrani, Taraji P. Henson and Oscar-nominated costume designer, Ruth Carter.

A contributor to the Women Pioneers Film project, Aimee is a doctoral student at George Mason University in Cultural Studies.

References

Balkansky, Arlene. 'Zora Neale Hurston and the Beaufort, South Carolina Church Footage: The Recovery of Sound and Film'
Orphans III: Listening to Orphan Films Symposium. http://www.sc.edu/filmsymposium/archive/orphans2002/program.html

Binggeli, Elizabeth. 'The Unadapted: Warner Bros. Reads Zora Neale Hurston', *Cinema Journal*. 48.3, 2009, 1–15.

Bordwell, David, Janet Staiger and Kristin Thompson.*Classical Hollywood Cinema: Film Style and Mode of Production to 1960*. New York, Columbia University Press, 1985.

Bowser, Pearl and Louise Spence. *Writing Himself into History: Oscar Micheaux, His Silent Films, and His Audiences*. New Brunswick and London, Rutgers University Press, 2000.

Carson, Warren. 'Hurston as Dramatist: The Florida Connection', *Zora in Florida*. Steve Glassman and Kathryn Lee Seidel. Vols. Orlando, University of Central Florida Press, 1991.

Cripps, Thomas. *Slow Fade to Black: the Negro in American Film, 1900–1942*. Oxford University Press, 1993.

EARLY AFRICAN-AMERICAN FEMALE FILMMAKERS

Duberman, Martin B. *Paul Robeson*. New York, Knopf, 1988.

Gaines, Jane. 'First Fictions', *Signs: Journal of Women in Culture and Society*. 30. 2004, L: 1293–31 7.

Gibson, Gloria. 'Cinematic Foremothers: Zora Neale Hurston and Eloyce King Patrick Gist'

Bowser, Pearl, Jane Gaines and Charles Musser, Eds. *Oscar Micheaux* and *His Circle*. Vols. Bloomington and Indianapolis, Indiana University Press, 2001.

Hemenway, Robert E. *Zora Neale Hurston: A Literary Biography*. Urbana, University of Illinois Press, 1977.

Hughes, Langston and Zora Neale Hurston. 'Mule Bone: A Comedy of Negro Life' 1930.

Hurston, Zora Neale. *Dust Tracks on a Road*. NY, Harper Perennial, 1996.

---. 'Color Struck: A Play', *Fire!!* 1. November 1926.

---. *Folklore, Memoirs and Other Writings*. New York, Literary Classics of the United States, 1995.

---. *Moses, Man of the Mountain*. Illinois Books, Ed. Urbana, University of Illinois Press, 1984.

---. *Mules and Men*. New York, Perennial Library, 1990.

---. *Seraph on the Suwanee*. New York, C. Scribner's Sons, 1948.

---. 'Spunk', *The New Negro: An Interpretation*. Alain LeRoy Locke and Winold Reiss, Eds. New York, A. and C. Boni, 1925.

---. *Sweat. Fire!!* (Nov. 1926), 40–45.

---. *Tell My Horse*. Philadelphia, P. Lippencott Co., 1938.

Jessye, Eva. 'The Truth about Hallelujah'. 1930.

Kaplan, Carla. *Zora Neale Hurston: A Life in Letters*. New York, Random House, Inc., 2002.

Zora Neale Hurston: Critical Perspectives Past and Present. Henry Louis Gates, Jr, Ed. Harper Collins, 1999.

Musser, Charles. 'Troubled Relations: Robeson, O'Neill, and Micheaux'

Potier, Beth. 'Radcliffe Fellow explores early female film pioneers', *Harvard University Gazette*. Cambridge, 6th November 2003.

Regester, Charlene. 'The African-American Press and Race Movies, 1909–1929'

Reid, Mark A. *Redefining Black Film*. Berkeley and Los Angeles: University of California Press, 1993.

Robeson, Eslanda Goode. *African Journey*. London, Victor Gollancz Ltd, 1945.

Paul Robeson, Negro. New York and London: Harper, 1930. Print.

Robeson, Jr. Paul. *The Undiscovered Paul Robeson: An Artist's Journey; 1898–1939*. New York: Wiley, 2001.

Postcards to Erik Barnow. Western Publishing & Novelty Co. MS. Columbia University Rare and Book Manuscript Library.

Sampson, Henry. *Blacks in Black and White: A Source Book on Black Films*. 2nd ed. Metuchen, NJ. Scarecrow press, 1995.

Stamp, Shelley. 'Presenting the Smalleys, "collaborators in authorship and direction"', *Film History*. 18. 2. 2006, 119–128.

Steedman, Carolyn. *Dust: The Archive and Cultural History*. New Brunswick, Rutgers University Press, 2001.

Taylor, Quintard. 'Five Centuries of African American History in the West'. ProQuest LLC, 2005.

Turner, Darwin T. 'The Negro Novelist and the South', *Southern Humanities Review*. 1 1967, pp. 21–29.

Welbon, Yvonne. 'Sisters in Cinema'. Chicago, Northwestern University, 2001.

White, Patricia.'Feminism and Film,' *Film Studies: Critical Approaches.* John Hill and Pamela Church Gibson, Eds. New York, Oxford University Press, 2000.

Wiegman, Robyn. 'Race, Ethnicity and Film', *Film Studies: Critical Approaches.* John Hill and Pamela Church Gibson, Eds. New York, Oxford University Press, 2000.

Zook, Kristal Brent. 'From Harlem to Hollywood: The Renaissance that wasn't', laweekly.com. 26th October 2000.

Filmography

Baptism. Dir. Zora Neale Hurston. 1929. Film.

Big Fella. Dir. Elder Wills. British Lion Studios, 1937. DVD.

Borderline. Dir. Kenneth Macpherson. Pool Films, 1930. DVD.

Children's Games. Dir. Zora Neale Hurston. 1928. Film.

Daughters of *the Dust.* Dir. Julie Dash. KINO Features, 1991.

Diary of *an African Nun.* Dir. Julie Dash. 1977

3. THE SILENT PRODUCER: Women Filmmakers Who Creatively Controlled the Silent Era of Cinema

Pieter Aquilia

The existence of the female producer is as old as the film business itself, although controversy over terminology has often left women un-credited for their creative contributions in the silent film era. From the 1880s to 1929, many female pioneers in the industry labelled as actresses, scenario writers and directors have not been acknowledged for roles that today are associated with producing. Perhaps, the most clear-cut example of a woman producer was French *directrice*, Alice Guy-Blaché who made her first film in 1886, supervised over 150 films as Head of Production at Gaumont Chronophone, before setting up her own film production company in New York in 1910 (McMahan 2002). But generally in Hollywood, career paths were not as clearly defined. The idiosyncrasy of the female producer is illustrated in the U.S. studio system of 1890–1929, which used the terms 'director' and 'producer' synonymously to describe the filmmaker of a silent reel (Cooper 2010, 40). Likewise, a 'producer' or a 'producing director' often headed production units within a larger company; many of these were women.

To complicate matters further, after the turn of the century, the term 'actor-producer' came into vogue, leading to many star-name companies, such as Olga Petrova, Leah Baird, Marion Leonard, Hel Gardner, Ethel Grandin, Gene Gauntier and Florence Lawrence. Women often ran these independent production companies, wanting more control over the films in which they starred (Mahar 2006, 155). The movie star Mary Pickford successfully secured a picture deal that allowed her a greater share of the profits as well as increased creative control. By 1916, Pickford's salary equalled many of her male counterparts, including Charlie Chaplin. Soon after, she established her own film production unit, 'insuring that she had a voice in selecting her own projects, assigning directors, casting roles, and designing publicity' (Stamp 9). In 1918, signing with First National, Pickford was guaranteed complete creative control from script to final cut. However, despite her successful jurisdiction over her own films she was never awarded a 'producer' credit. This chapter attempts to delve deeper into the anomaly of the female producer in the silent era, tracing the highs and lows of women trying to take greater ownership of their films. While history shows women struggled to be defined as producers, the female characters, storylines and themes, which they supported, commonly herald their legacy.

The Role of Producer in the Silent Era

Alejandro Padro (2010) explains that early film producers 'as the greatly forgotten ones' and 'unsung heroes' of cinema (Prigge cited in Pardo 2010), were shadowed by the creative roles of actress, director and cinematographer. Helen De Winter laments that to many cinema historians the term 'producer ... seems nebulous and evasive' (2006, 1). Since the beginning of cinema, the responsibilities of the producer have precariously swung between the diverse skills of financing, technical knowledge and creative input, with the emergence of the Hollywood system tipping 'the balance toward technical knowledge or, less frequently, towards its creative capacity' (Pardo 2010, 2). Indeed, Irving G. Thalberg defined moviemaking as 'a creative business ... in the sense that it must bring in money at box office, but it is an art in that it involves, on its devotees, the inexorable demands of creative expression' (quoted in Thomas 1969, 252). David O. Selznick, perhaps the most renowned of the studio producers 'considered himself an excellent judge of talent and commercial story properties, a capable writer and film editor, and a demanding production executive' (Selznick 1937; 1988, 473–474):

> The producer today, in order to be able to produce properly, must be able not merely to criticize, but be able to answer the old question what or why. He must be able, if necessary, to sit down and write the scene, and if he is criticizing a director, he must be able not merely to say 'I don't like it', but tell him how he would direct it himself. He must be able to go into the cutting room, and if he doesn't like the cutting of the sequence, which is more often true than not, he must be able to recut the sequence (ibid. 475).

For women producers operating in the golden age of silent cinema, this important merger of technical, creative and economic skills was often conflated into inadequate terminology such as *actrice, directrice* or translated into a studio nomenclature. Film directors were often called 'producers.' Job titles such as producers, production executives, studio managers or heads of production were given to persons who managed smaller studios within a larger film entity (Cooper 2010, 40). Gaines and Vastal (2011) believe this practice 'credited women who were involved in production companies as "producers" as a means of adding a facet to a career, understanding, however, that there is more variance under the term "producer" than under "director."' As Stamp suggests in her seminal work on women in silent film:

> …when searching for models of female authorship in early Hollywood, it is important to look beyond the title "director" or "screenwriter," for many women assumed positions of creative control in other capacities. Many female stars, for instance, formed independent production companies in the late 1910s, seeking to

have more input over the projects in which they were involved. (2012, 9)

In terms of fulfilling the technical knowledge required by the producer, Wright Wexman (2013) notes the difficulty in 'ascertaining the precise contributions' of women filmmakers in the silent era due to the complication of ambiguously worded phrases like 'adaptation by…', 'story by…', 'titles by…', 'continuity by…', 'dialogue by…', 'editorial supervision by…', and so forth. This chapter notes that the job portfolio of women producers often included casting, location management, script writing and editing. Women's contribution to the financial control of the silent film industry is full of contradictions and speculation. Cooper (2010) and Mahar (2006) believe that in many husband-and-wife film companies, the men controlled the money and business, while Gaines and Vatsal (2013) suggest men were often the ones who were financially irresponsible in these familial businesses citing Harry Solerer, Florence Lawrence's partner in the Victor Company and Herbert Blaché, Alice Guy-Blaché's husband and partner in Solax Company. However, researchers believe women such as Mary Pickford 'demonstrated remarkable business acumen':

> Charlie Chaplin, for instance, recollects Mary Pickford at the meeting to form United Artists in 1919: 'She knew all the nomenclature: the amortizations and the deferred stocks, etc. She understood all the articles of incorporation, the legal discrepancy on Page 7, Paragraph A, Article 27, and coolly referred to the overlap and contradiction in Paragraph D, Article 24.' (Chaplain cited in Gaines and Vatsal 2013)

The diffuse literature in this field suffers from significant inconsistencies and seeming deficits of information. In the last twenty years, researchers in the United States have carefully documented the successes of the female filmmaker in the silent era (Stamp 2012; Mahar 2006; Slide 1996; Gaines and Vastal, 2013), but often filmographies are hampered by a lack of documentation or understanding of crew roles. British research has followed slowly behind, consolidating the legacy of women producers, albeit often without clear demarcation between actor, director and producer (Gledhill 2007; Newey 2000; WSBC 2015). Australia has been more vigilant in its celebration of its early female directors, but many female producers fall into the shadows (Dooley 1997; Toulmin 1988; Chapman 2002; Shirley 2015). And many other nations that boasted active film industries in the silent era are yet to consolidate the fragmented primary narratives and forgotten interviews that reveal the important contribution that their women made to the business of film. While female filmmakers proliferated in the major film industries of Europe from the 1890s to 1914, there is little published material that acknowledges Alice Guy-Blaché's career in France as the first prolific female film producer in history or analyzes Italy's Elvira Notari as the creative genius behind the first films to give voice to continental feminism. In response to this lack in literature, this chapter attempts to gather the often sporadic discourses of women who managed the creative, technical and often financial aspects of film in the years since 1890 to 1929, an era which marks significant milestones of early feminism, by highlighting women producers' most remarkable achievements.

Alice Guy-Blaché

In 1895, twenty-two-year-old Alice Guy was a secretary to photographer Leon Gaumont in Paris when she attended a demonstration by film engineers Auguste and Louis Lumière of the first moving image projector. Guy quickly realized the potential of the new medium and was one of the first filmmakers to create dramatic content for the moving reel. Until then, film had been used to record places and people, usually real time documentation of actual events. In 1896, with the support of her employer Gaumont, Guy released a short fiction film entitled *La Fée aux Choux* (*The Cabbage Patch Fairy*), a humorous tale of a woman finding children in her vegetable patch. Following the success of this film, Guy became the head of production for Gaumont, a role she would continue to hold until 1906 producing a regular stable of dance and travel films, often combining the two disciplines into a narrative storyline. In 1906, Guy directed an epic film, one of the highest production films of the era, *The Life of Christ,* casting over 300 extras. Her keen skills as a creative, technical and financial manager with Gaumont Chronophone paralleled the success of the Lumière brothers whose films were in strong demand globally. In 1907, her husband and production manager Herbert Blaché, was appointed to Gaumont's U.S. operation and Guy resigned her position to follow him. After a successful run of films that she had directed, Guy-Blaché and her husband partnered George A. Magie to establish The Solax Company in New York. This new venture proved financially lucrative and soon the studio moved to more advanced facilities in New Jersey, the early birthplace of American film. In 1914, and after the birth of her second child, Guy-Blaché stepped down as the president of Solax to concentrate on writing and directing. Amidst rumours of her husband's poor investment decisions and infidelity, the company went into bankruptcy and the couple divorced in 1922. Guy returned to France and effectively retired from filmmaking.

Indeed, the contributions of Alice Guy-Blaché[2] were largely un-reported until historian Alison McMahan published her dissertation, *Alice Guy-Blaché: Lost Visionary of Cinema* in 2002. McMahan clearly evidences that Guy 'was almost solely responsible for every detail that appeared in front of the camera in the films she made at the Gaumont Company before the film studio was built in 1905' and by 1910, while at Solax, 'she had complete control over every film from scripting to art direction and editing, and directed the majority of them herself' (2002, xxxvi-vii). Indeed, McMahan talks about the painstaking research process required to differentiate the films

2. Alice Guy-Blache's career and contributions are detailed in *Slide.* 1996, 15-28.

Guy directed from those that she had other creative, financial and technical control over:

> Whether Guy directed every film made at Gaumont until 1905 or not, we know that she did produce them. According to her memoirs … she was pretty much left alone to shoulder all the responsibilities of production, writing and directing the Gaumont story-films. (2002, xxix)

While Guy's films demonstrate the advantages of a female producer to create narratives popular with general audiences, it was American writer-director Lois Weber who was the first female producer to actively produce narratives for and about women, reflecting the feminist voice in the silent era.

Lois Weber

Lois Weber commenced her career as a scenario writer and director also in Gaumont's U.S. studio in 1908. She went on to write and direct films that supported the legalization of birth control, dramatizing it in several films, including *Where Are My Children?* (1916) and *The Hand That Rocks the Cradle* (1917). Historian Anthony Slide believes that Weber was a true producer of the silent era:

> Along with D. W. Griffith, Lois Weber was the American cinema's first genuine auteur, a filmmaker involved in all aspects of production and one who utilized the motion picture to put across her own ideas and philosophies. (1996, 29)

Weber's contribution to early silent cinema was hugely influential, and her dominant roles as a writer, director and actress positioned her not only as a producer, but as an advocate for feminism who was able to mobilise production houses to champion her stories. In 1914, Weber moved from Gaumont to the boutique Bosworth company, which was run by Julia Crawford-Ivers, who was the first woman general manager of a film studio (Seger 2003, 8). Here, Weber produced, wrote and directed the film *Hypocrites* (1915), a moralistic drama brazenly presenting female nudity on celluloid. Weber's position as the film's producer was controversial; the film sparked riots in New York and it was banned in some parts of the United States (Mahar 2006, 96). While Weber continued to have an illustrious career as a film director with other studios, unfortunately *Hypocrites* was the last film she made for Bosworth. Supposedly, her contract was not renewed because Weber failed to fully adapt to the 'modern' morality mandated by Lasky's box-office formula (Mahar 2006, 148). In other words, her contentious feminist films were too financially risky for the commercial studios.

Julia Crawford Ivers

Julia Crawford Ivers was another divisive producer who claimed to be the only woman to direct a film from the Lasky Lot, thereby usurping Weber's notoriety and credits. Although there are conflicting reports about how Julia Crawford Ivers commenced her film career, it appears she began writing un-credited scenarios for Garbutt's Pallas Pictures in 1910, a studio for which her second husband Oliver Ivers was a partner (Wollstein 2015). Ivers reported that she had a range of film production roles during her early years, having 'done almost everything around a studio but sweep the floor' (cited in Miller 2013). Seger (2003), Mahar (2006) and Miller (2013) report Ivers was production supervisor at Bosworth Studios between 1915 and 1917, until the studio was sold to Pallas Pictures-Morosco Photoplay under the umbrella of Paramount Pictures. Screen credits reveal that she effectively worked as a producer at Pallas Pictures on at least two films including the five-reel *Lost in Transit* (1917) (Miller 2013):

> There are conflicting reports on authorship of a number of Ivers' films. AFI lists Maclyn Arbuckle and Edgar A. Guest as screenwriters on *The Reform Candidate*, while Spehr lists her as screenwriter. AFI lists Alice von Saxmar as a screenwriter on *The Stronger Love*, while Spehr again lists Ivers as screenwriter. FIAF lists Ivers as the producer on *The Bond Between, A Kiss for Susie*, and *Lost in*

> *Transit,* while AFI only lists her as the copyright holder.
> Finally, *The Call of the Cumberlands* (1916) is believed to
> be directed by Ivers, but is sometimes ascribed to Frank
> Lloyd. (Miller 2013)

According to Wollstein (2015), Ivers continued to work with
Garbutt at the Oliver Morosco Photoplay Company over
the next few years, with her films successfully distributed by
Paramount Pictures. Soon after, she was a senior manager of
the Famous Players-Lasky/Paramount Studio where she wrote,
directed, edited and supervised production in the post-war era
(Miller 2013). In 1922, Ivers directed her last film, *The White
Flower* (1923). Miller (2013) believes her fierce independence
on this film contributed to her departure from the major
studios shortly afterwards.

> I wrote the story… with a genuine love and affection
> for the islands, and will produce it in the same way. No
> 'roughneck' of a director will have a chance to squeeze
> the fragrance out of the plot, for I am going to direct the
> action myself," she says. However, Ivers follows up this
> confident statement by dutifully crediting her powers to
> Jesse Lasky's largess: "Mr. Lasky permitted me to select my
> own cast and to choose my technical force, camera man,
> art director and all. I am in full charge and I have every
> confidence in my company. (Ivers cited in Miller 2013)

Ivers resigned her position with Lasky shortly after *The White
Flower* was released to work as a 'freelance writer'. During this
period, Ivers continued to work closely with actor and director
William Desmond Taylor, a collaboration that resulted in the
production of approximately twenty films with a range of
studios. The arrangement ended abruptly with Taylor's 1922
murder, in which she was implicated as a suspect, although the
murder was never solved. (Miller 2013)

June Mathis

June Mathis, who is credited with discovering silent screen
legend Rudolph Valentino, followed a similar but more robustly

documented trajectory to Ivers, as a production supervisor and executive producer. As well as a recognised co-writer of adaptations and star vehicle scripts. Mathis was also a production executive working for Goldwyn Pictures, Metro Pictures and Famous Players-Lasky Film Corporation as an artistic supervisor and editorial director, 'overseeing the development of motion picture scripts, supervising activities on the set, and presiding over the editing process, duties studio producers commonly assumed in the 1930s' (Wright Wexman 2013). Appointed head of the scenario department at Metro in 1918 when she was only twenty-seven years old, Mathis was the first woman to occupy such an executive rank (Stamp 2012, 6). Mathis cast unknown Valentino in the lead role in *The Four Horsemen of the Apocalypse* in 1921 and continued to mentor Valentino until his marriage with costume designer, Natacha Rambova in 1924. Producing a series of films with Metro, she was also responsible for catapulting Russian actress Alla Nazimova's career and lauded for 'her talent in the careful pre-preparation of the shooting script along with the director, cutting out waste in production while at the same time sharpening narrative continuity' (Hill 2009). Following the success of her screenplay for Valentino's *Four Horsemen,* Mathis was headhunted to Famous Players-Lasky before she moved onto the role of the Head of Studio at Goldwyn in 1923. The new role was reportedly a 'large step up the corporate ladder' and 'she had been tempted by the huge salary and the offers of autonomous control' (Hill 2009). Despite her previous successes, Mathis was heavily criticized as a supervising producer for the failure of the epic *Ben-Hur* on location in Italy in 1924 (Wright Wexman 2013). The derailment of *Ben-Hur* and the subsequent merger of Metro-Goldywn-Mayer in 1924, coincided with the decline of Mathis' career. She continued to write for a series of lesser-known studios until her death in 1927.

Star-Name Companies and Niche Film Houses
World War I would change the silent film industry across the world. The number, and significance, of women in the U.S.

film industry increased dramatically. The role of producer became more distinct than in the early years of film. Gaines and Vatsal describe a post-war 'epidemic' of too many women in the film industry. Star-name companies used the brand names of female actresses not as a means for increased creative control for women, rather as a commodification, which male studio heads leveraged to promote films. The Women Film Pioneers Project[3] (2013) lists close to fifty actresses who are also credited as producers of movies during this period. The filmographies of these star-name producers are difficult to verify. The sheer number of star-name studios and the reels of films that they produced make it close to impossible to substantiate the credibility of producers within the scope of this chapter. Indeed, the frenzy of branding studios with the names of leading actresses often served to cloud the dedicated work of women such as Mathis, Ivers and Guy and muddy the already ambiguous term 'producer.'

In addition to the star-name frenzy, numerous smaller studios were established within the Hollywood giants in the period during World War I, with women serving in the roles of production executive or head of production. These niche production houses were often as short-lived as the success of the films they produced. For example, Victor Company, started by Florence Lawrence and Harry Solter in 1912 was one of the small companies that was integrated into Universal Studios in 1914 and quickly phased out in 1917 (Slide 1996, 221). The phenomenon was dubbed the 'Universal Women', a collection of female senior employees, accommodated in new large studio lots sprouting up in Los Angeles:

> …the layout of the new Universal City lot completed
> in 1915 in Los Angeles, it created a kind of 'laboratory

3 For a listing of star-name studios see Jane Gaines and Radha Vatsal (2013) web entry, 'How Women Worked in the U.S. Silent Film Industry.' In Jane Gaines, Radha Vatsal, and Monica Dall'Asta, eds. Women Film Pioneers Project. Center for Digital Research and Scholarship. New York, NY: Columbia University Libraries at https://wfpp.cdrs. columbia.edu/essay/how-women-worked-in-the-us-silent-film-industry/

for gender experiment' facilitated by 'physical mobility' on the set in contrast to the New York office hierarchy (Cooper 2010, 63). These conditions produced the phenomenon we call the 'Universal Women', the largest concentration of women who worked as directors, sometimes also as writers, actresses, and producers, from 1916 to 1921: Ruth Ann Baldwin, Grace Cunard, Eugenie Magnus Ingleton, Cleo Madison, Ida May Park, Ruth Stonehouse, Lule Warrenton, Lois Weber, and Elsie Jane Wilson. (Gaines and Vastal 2013)

While these star-name companies and female production executives seemingly endorsed the presence of the female producer in Hollywood during the final decades of the silent film, few of these women assumed the full responsibilities of a film producer. Projects initiated by Mary Pickford and Clara Kimball Young, for example, were largely seen as independent or experimental, and therefore a greater financial risk. There are many examples of failed ventures. In 1922, Alla Nazimova, after securing a partnership with United Artists, produced *Salomé* (1923) with her own capital, but when it faltered at the box office, she was left bankrupt. Similarly, Margery Wilson and Vera McCord Productions suffered losses with the studios' first films, leading to the closure of the studios or a takeover by larger corporates who were gearing up for 'talkies'. By the time talkies came to Hollywood, the handful of women producers operating within the United States and the remaining female-led studios in Poverty Row Hollywood, were squeezed out by larger studios and the vertical integration of the industry. Simultaneously, the major studios, Goldwyn Pictures, Metro Pictures, and Famous Players-Lasky Film Corporation discontinued labels such as production executive, artistic supervisor, head of production, etc. Miller (2013) confirms that 'such positions ceased to exist in the years that followed; but as far as one can tell, they involved overseeing the development of motion picture scripts, supervising activities on the set, and presiding over the editing process, duties studio producers commonly assumed during the 1930s.'

Women's voices outside of Hollywood: Australia and New Zealand

Australia's silent film industry serves as an example to illuminate the unrecognised contribution of women producers in the thriving cinema environment at the turn of the century. Despite the lack of recognition, these women paved a strong feminist voice in Australian cinema (Aquilia 2014). Jan Chapman, whose filmography is considered one of the finest of any Australian contemporary producer, eloquently honored these women pioneers in her 2002 Longford Lyell Lecture, paralleling her own personal experience with that of her forebear, the nation's first silent film star, Lottie Lyell:

> I imagine Lottie Lyell became a producer for much the same reason I did – that she wanted to ensure that an idea would really become a feature film. For it is the producer who is ultimately prepared to take responsibility for a film – to find the money for a script to be written and to support the writing of it, to find the budget needed to actually make it, to employ the director, the actors and the crew and to be there at the end to make sure the film finds a distributor so it can be seen in theatres. Lottie Lyell Cox (1890–1925) along with her acknowledged acting talents was a filmmaker. (Chapman 2002)

Indeed, Chapman retrospectively dedicates the title of producer to a series of women whose skills as screenwriter, art-director, producer and director were often downplayed in the press and in industry circles as 'helping' or 'assisting' a male counterpart or collaborator. Lottie Lyell, with her partner Raymond Longford, produced at least twenty-eight silent movies between 1911 and 1925. Indeed, Lyell's collaboration with Longford was only formally recognised with the establishment of Longford-Lyell Australian Picture Productions Company in 1922, more than a decade after her first role in the film industry. As a creative producer, Lyell furnished a voice to women's issues in film at a formative time – shortly after all women in Australia earned the right to vote and an increasing number of women were migrating to the cities to work in the booming industrial revolution. Lyell's films often 'challenged social conventions by presenting issues from a woman's point of view' (Lyell, Lottie Edith 2014). The themes of her films include gender inequity and domestic violence as in *The Woman Suffers* (1917) or countered public perception of the female stereotype, specifically the 'immoral' single working girl as in *The Sentimental Bloke* (1919). As a consequence of its contemporary feminist voice, Lyell's *The Sentimental Bloke* enjoyed international theatrical distribution, applauded for its humour, pathos and authenticity. (Lyell, Lottie Edith 2014)

Australian women film pioneers continued to promote the increasing economic independence of women after World War I and challenged the increasing public criticism against women's choosing to work over marriage and family. In 1924, Louise Lovely, who had forged a successful career in Hollywood since 1915, returned to Australia with her husband Wilton Welsh to produce films specifically endorsing women's roles and issues. Together, the couple wrote and directed the feature film, *Jewelled Nights* (1925), based on the novel of the same name, following a young woman's escape from a repressed marriage by posing as a male coal miner to support herself. Lovely became a spokesperson for women's rights and advocated for the economic independence of women, 'not as an alternative to marriage and raising a family but as a necessary fall back post war and to make their lives more interesting.' (Chapman 2002)

The McDonagh Sisters

In the mid-1920s, the McDonagh sisters established Australia's first entirely female-run film company, releasing four films. The three siblings, Isabel, Paulette and Phyllis formed a production company using a colonial mansion in the suburb Drummoyne as their house, and a bequest of £1,000 from their father's will to produce a feature film. The result was a romance film, *Those Who Love* (1926), about lovers thwarted by 'parental and class differences' (Shirley 2015). The commercial success of *Those Who Love* helped raise the £2,000 budget for the sisters' second film *The Far Paradise* (1928). The women were praised for their cleverness, courage, 'vim and enthusiasm' (Chapman 2002). In their capacities as co-producers, leading actor (Isabel), director-writer (Paulette) and art director-publicist (Phyllis), the sisters generated this initial success by making films that were Australian variations of popular Hollywood melodramas (Chapman 2002). Reporting to the 1927 Royal Commission into the Moving Picture Industry in Australia, Isabel argued for an Australian film quota system against the predominance of imported films in cinemas, explaining how as independent filmmakers they maintained control of their own films:

> My sister and I were responsible. We engaged Mr Reshner as director, my other sister Miss Paulette McDonagh wrote the scenario. We started against great opposition. All our friends advised us not to proceed with the venture but having confidence in ourselves we persisted and I think succeeded (cited in Chapman 2002).

The sisters continued to make a third feature, *The Cheaters* (1930) which incorporated the story of a woman who discovers her parents are involved in criminal activities when she falls in love with the son of a law-abiding father. Unfortunately, the film was unable to find a distributor due to the rising tide of Hollywood films flooding the Australian cinemas and the novelty surrounding the emergence of the talkies. Despite attempts to release partial sound versions of the film, the sisters shifted to producing short documentaries. Shirley (2015) cites interviews with Paulette who attributes the failure of their feature film business to inexperience, fear of moving to Hollywood and their often brazen style of negotiation. In the ensuing thirty years of the sound film, only a handful of Australian women are credited for their roles as either associate or co-producers, with this dearth only shifting with the women's movement of the 1960s and 1970s, which allowed more opportunities for women in the film industry. Today, 30% of all Australian producers are women. (Barber 2013)

In New Zealand, the course of history virtually erased the important contributions that women made towards the production of silent films. It has only been through the painstaking work of film historians who have collated letters, diaries, interviews and other archival resources to reconstitute the exact role women played in New Zealand's early cinema. Diane Pivac, in her article 'New Zealand Film Pioneer' (2015), recounts how Hilda Hayward, together with her famous husband Rudall Hayward (considered 'The Grandfather' of NZ film), produced twenty-eight films but remained un-credited for her numerous roles as producer, manager, location scout, publicist, make-up artiste, costume designer, photographer and editor:

> According to her son-in-law, Neil Boak, Hilda had a very good eye, and he attributes the beautiful scenery in some of the films to her, she 'had an eye for picking up, for converting a scene to a picture'. Beyond that, Boak states that Hilda was a filmmaker in her own right, and on at least one occasion when he was away, Hayward phoned Hilda with a message to get the camera and get to town – there was a riot in central Auckland that he wanted filmed. (Pivac 2015)

Aside from five feature films, Hayward was integral to the production of twenty-three community films in various New Zealand towns, 'based on a format that had proven successful in the United States and Australia' (Pivac 2015). Hilda Hayward designed publicity banners and distributed flyers to recruit talent in the locales she and her husband visited, arranged the locations, helped with the photography, quickly edited the footage, and while 'interest and excitement was still hot' organised 'world premieres' of the films in nearby picture theatres (Pivac 2015). This clever enterprise allowed Duckett and Potter (2015) not only to lament this 'historical forgetting of Hilda Hayward's contributions to the films credited to Rudall Hayward as director, but also the contemporary contexts in which Hilda's behind-the-scenes roles were suppressed or failed to be recognized.' Ironically, another unknown New Zealand female producer of the silent era was also named Hilda, the wife of Greymouth-based filmmaker, Lawrie Inkster. The Inksters were prolific makers of home movies and newsreels. Their films document family and social life, leisure activities and public events in the region during the 1920s (Pullar 2015). The NZ Film archive notes the important role Hilda Inkster played 'carrying equipment, helping in the darkroom and starring in home movies. Artistic Hilda made the beautiful inter-titles for the films and judging by how often Inkster appears in his own productions, she also spent her fair share of time behind the camera.' (The Film Archive Press Release 2005)

United Kingdom

In Britain, women struggled to make the number and calibre of films of their male counterparts. In the first two decades of the century, British women garnered little acknowledgment for their role as producers in the film industry, with many examples of women producing a single film after a long career as an actress. Ivy Close was one of the first actresses in the U.K. to set up her own film production company in London in 1914, but it was her husband Elwin Neames who was credited as the producer of most of the studio's short comedies. In 1917, Jane Denison produced the single film, *All Clear and No Need to Take Cover,* and in 1919 actress Mary Marsh produced her only film *Forgive Us Our Trespasses*, in which Mary starred alongside her husband. In 1920, Lucy Heys Thompson produced the short comedy, *Trotter on the Trot,* without any follow-up credits.

One of the most successful women producers of the silent era in the U.K. was actress Violet Hopson who in 1921 'completed the biggest deal yet attempted by a woman in

British film land [selling the rights of her films for the next two years to Butchers]' (cited in WSBC 2015). Hopson was reportedly renowned for 'her keen business sense', which firmly cements her veracity as a film producer as we know it today (WSBC 2015). Again, while her production company banked on Hopson's brand name as an actress, it was Walter West who was credited as producer on her films (IMDB 2015). In 1922, Peggy Hyland wrote, produced, directed and starred in *With Father's Help*. She continued as an actress and director in Hollywood, but there are no reports of further producing credits (WSBC 2015). Perhaps the most established female producer of the era was director Dinah Shurey whose production credits include *Afraid of Love* (1925), *Second to None* (1926), *Every Mother's Son* (1926), *Carry On!* (1927), and *The Last Post* (1929) (WSBC 2015). Gledhill (2007) believes the later films, with their militaristic and patriotic themes, 'often confused reviewers' expectations of female producers.' Shurey established her own production company in 1923, but the company folded in 1932 largely due to financial losses incurred by a failed venture in film distribution, leaving her bankrupt. (WSBC 2015)

Towards the end of the silent era, greater numbers of women were involved in production in Britain, many making the career switch from related fields. In the late 1920s, poet and journal editor, Hilda Doolittle, together with Kenneth MacPherson and her lover Annie Winifred Ellerman (known as Bryher) formed Pool Films, producing three films: *Foothills* (1927), *Wingbeat* (1927) and *Borderline* (1930). Connor reveals that the films were made using an inheritance from Bryher's mother (2004, 19). Although Doolittle is credited for writing and performing in the films, there is little evidence of her role as a producer in the contemporary sense. In 1927, educationalist Mary Field produced the long-running natural history films, *Secrets of Nature*, with the cinematographer Percy Smith, being one of the few women working on the talkies (Easen 2014). In summary, the involvement of women in the British film industry was less significant than that of the English language industries in other parts of the world, hampered by a lack of financial investment and the lack of large studio systems in the U.K. as compared to the U.S.. It was difficult for women to find backing beyond the single film and, as a result, despite the strength of the women's movement in London, film did not prove to be a medium in which to express feminist issues.

Europe

In Europe, following the decline of the mainstream industries in Italy and France during World War I, women largely worked more successfully in experimental film. Germaine Dulac was a French filmmaker who produced impressionistic films. Elvira Notari was an Italian filmmaker who ran her own production company, Dora Films, which was recognised for its feminist films that challenged censorship with their sexual undertones and strong language use. Danish actress Asta Nielsen founded her own film studio in Berlin during the 1920s along with her husband, director Urban Gad and German film producer Paul Davidson. She became one of the earliest international film stars, starring in over seventy films and earning over $80,000 a year (Film Star Postcards 2013). Due to the introduction of sound movies and the rise of Nazism in Germany she retired from the film industry, and returned to Denmark where she wrote her autobiography and became an artist.

Of special note, Elvira Notari made over sixty feature films in addition to a catalogue of hundreds of shorts and actualities, making her production house, Dora Films, one of the leading production houses in Naples. By 1912, the company had a studio set and Elvira had started an acting school where she encouraged women to feature in starring roles. Her films were often adapted from novels, melodramas featuring central *femmes fatales* of dubious morality, appealing to middle-class women (*Il nano rosso* 1917; *Rosa la Pazza* 1919). Her mid-career films were realistic city films featuring working women. The female leads in '*Nfama!* (1924) and *A Piedigrotta* (1920) are strong, unruly characters who struggled against adversity (Bruno 1993, 416). Her films often focused on the female body and female fantasy. Other films explored sexual and emotional desire and examined women's power over men through their sexuality. Notari's films were increasingly censored, and with the rise of Fascism, Notari diverted to making more commercial Neapolitan musicals, *scenegiatte,* that appealed to the growing Italian diaspora.

French producer/director Germaine Dulac, was often regarded as the first feminist of the *avant garde* era. Starting her career as a journalist on a feminist magazine, she established a film company D. H. Films (with the help of her husband who remained a silent partner and writer Irene Hillel-Erlanger), directing films which are noted for their impressionistic and surrealistic artistic expression: *La Souriante Madame Beudet* (*The Smiling Madam Beudet* 1922/23), and her Surrealist experiment, *La Coquille et le Clergyman* (*The Seashell and the Clergyman* 1928) (Williams 2007). These films pre-dated the legendary *Un Chien Andalou* (*An Andalusian Dog* 1929) by Luis Buñuel and Salvador Dalí. Dulac's interest in experimental film was piqued by a visit to the Film D'Arte Production House in Italy prior to 1914 with her friend and actress Stacia Naperkowska. The production house was renowned for its 'focus on contemporary stories, the dramas of economic and emotional catastrophes, the ruination of families, adulteries, and destructive passions' (Brunetta 2009, 25). In the early 1900s through the late 1920s, Dulac frequently opposed the modernity of the French capital to the provincial nature of rural France, a common dichotomy in her films. Soon after her return to France she decided to start a film company. Her films included *Les soeurs ennemies* (1915/16; Dulac's first film: *The Enemy Sisters*), *Vénus Victrix, ou Dans l'ouragan de la vie* (*Venus Victorious,* or *In the Hurricane of Life* 1917), *Géo, le mystérieux/La vraie richesse* (*Geo, the mysterious/True wealth* 1916) (Williams 2007). With the rise of

Fascism in the 1930s, Dulac made an increasing number of socialist films and was actively involved in the nationalisation of the French film industry in an attempt to keep cinema free from the limitations of commercialisation and rising Fascism. (Williams 2007, 292–300)

Notari and Dulac were not the only European women producers faced with the growing tide of radical politics in Europe. Danish actress Asta Nielsen, who had become an international success portraying determined, erotic *femmes fatales,* moved to the German film industry. After a decade of acting, and disappointed with the female character roles on offer, Nielsen founded her own studio in Berlin, where she set about making a film version of *Hamlet*, adapting the role of the Prince of Denmark to that of a woman:

> Where Garbo had to compromise her androgynous sex appeal, Nielsen enjoyed greater autonomy. Look no further than *The ABCs of Love,* a comedy that looks astoundingly modern a century on. Nielsen's character is a seemingly naïve country girl who sizes up a prospective fiancé, deciding to teach him to be a 'real' man. This involves her in cross-dressing and a trip to Paris (where else?). In *The Eskimo Baby* (also 1916), an outdated farce about a 'native' girl from Greenland who is brought to Denmark as a human souvenir [sic], her shoplifting spree in a big city department store is a small surreal jewel of a performance. (Librizzi 2015)

Despite the fact that Nielsen was a known Jewish sympathiser, she was offered her own studio by Nazi propaganda minister Joseph Goebbels and was invited to tea with Adolf Hitler, who tried to convince her to return to film, explaining the political power of her on-screen presence (Jensen 2010, 88–91). However, she left Germany in 1936 to return to Denmark where she retired from the film industry to be remembered for her naturalistic style of acting and her portrayal of a wide spectrum of female characters of different psychologies and social classes.

Germany was one of the most influential film industries of the silent era, attracting talented artists and filmmakers from all over Europe, including a number of women such as Aud Egede-Nissen, a Norwegian actress who starred in the Danish films popular in Germany before World War I. Egede-Nissen was the daughter of Norwegian politician, Adam Egede-Nissen, and her younger siblings were also involved in the silent cinema. After 1914, the German restriction on the importation and screening of foreign films made by the Allies, including French films, resulted in the need for more home-grown German films. Egede-Nissen quickly became a screen sensation in Germany and abroad. By 1916, she was able to her run her own production company, Egede-Nissen Films, together with her husband and director, Georg Alexander, and her sisters, Gerd and Ada. For the next few years, Egede-Nissen produced, and starred in, more than one film per month. The company was renowned for producing the world's first female detective serial featuring her sister Ada van Ehlers (Film Star Postcards 2013). The Egede-Nissen studio was able to survive the partial nationalization of the German cinema in 1917 due to the public demand for light entertainment films, mainly to counter the insurgence of German propaganda films. Germany was now the largest film industry in Europe and, in these boom years, Egede-Nissen garnered some thirty screen credits as a producer. However, the increasing machinations of nationalism soon made it difficult for smaller studios such as Egede-Nissen's to compete. As a result, Egede-Nissen Films' last production, *The Idea of Dr. Pax*, was released in 1921. That same year, Egede-Nissen starred alongside Austrian idol, Paul Richter, in a feature film, *The Night of the Burglar*, produced in Munich by a major studio, Münchner Lichtspielkunst AG (IMDB 2015). Egede-Nissen and Richter continued to star in movies together until 1926. In 1924, Egede-Nissen divorced Alexander to marry Richter. By the end of the decade, the rise of Hitler's

Nationalist-Socialist party led to greater scrutiny of national films and demonstrations against film screenings that negatively portrayed Germany's involvement in the war, for example Hollywood's *All Quiet on the Western Front* (Giessen 2003, 3). By 1931, Egede-Nissen and Richter divorced and she left Germany before Hitler's seizure of power. By 1933, hundreds of German filmmakers and artistes fled the radical policies and anti-Semitism of Nazi Germany (Giessen 2003, 7), including legendary director Fritz Lang who Richter and Egede-Nissen had both worked with. Egede-Nissen continued to produce films in Norway, including *A Happy Boy* (1932) and *Sinners Summertime* (1934) (Film Star Postcards 2013). In retrospect, the rise of Nazism and its ensuing subjugation of the medium, made it increasingly difficult for female star producers, especially those who were not German and whose backgrounds were melodrama and popular entertainment, to conform to the politics of propaganda filmmaking.

Conclusion

This chapter abounds in the seemingly unlimited cross-over of women producers who combined their roles as creative filmmakers with the professions of acting, writing, directing and editing. These women created important niches of film production in diverse cities and studio centres around the world. Often supported, and sometimes hindered, by the male-centric commercial studios and financiers, these pioneering women forged new characterisations and styles of performances that appealed to international audiences. Despite remaining un-credited and often unacknowledged for the creative, technical and financial expertise they lent to silent film production, the impact of female producers was definitely integral to the non-sound cinema era, 1880–1930. From the scarcity of numbers of women producers in the British, European and Australian industries to the phenomenon of too many star-name companies and Universal Women in the United States, this chapter shows that while women strove to be film producers, they were often hampered by institutionalised sexism within both the wider society, within the corporate studio system, or overlooked in the tide of radical politics sweeping the globe during the war years. Regardless, their impact in creating strong female characters, storylines and themes was fundamental to attracting early cinema audiences. Their portrayals of *femmes fatales* and socialist realist feminisations have influenced the course of cinema history and survive in both the method and style of performances on-screen today. Their courage and conviction to work behind the scenes and under the cloak of their male counterparts has paved the way for contemporary female producers to seek better representation and recognition of their skills to artistically, technically, and financially shape the film industry today.

Author Biography: Dr Pieter Aquilia

Pieter is a Conjoint Associate Professor at University of Newcastle, Australia. She is a former Associate Dean and Associate Arts Professor for NYU Tisch School of the Arts, and has held academic positions at UNSW Asia, Nanyang Technological University, Singapore, and Macquarie University, Sydney, and Edith Cowan University, Perth. She is a scriptwriter, script editor and director of television drama who graduated from the Australian Film Television and Radio School in 1988. Her research areas include the Media in Asia, International Television Drama, Screen Studies and the Globalisation of Screen Education.

References

Aquilia, Pieter. 'Brilliant Careers: Three Waves of Australian, New Zealand and Indigenous Women Film Directors', *Celluloid Ceiling: Women Film Directors Breaking Through*. Gabrielle Kelly and Cheryl Robson, Eds. London, Supernova, 2014, 255–271.
Barber, Lynden. 'Women directors are cracking the glass camera in the world of film', *The Australian*. March 30, 2013. http://www.theaustralian.com.au/arts/review/women-directors-are-cracking-the-glass-camera-in-the-world-of-film/story-fn9n8gph-1226608278247
Brunetta, Gian Pietro. *The History of Italian Cinema: A Guide to Italian Film from Its Origins to the Twenty-First Century*. Jeremy Parzen, Trans. Princeton, New Jersey, Princeton UP, 2009.
Bruno, Giuliana. *Streetwalking on a Ruined Map*. Princeton, New Jersey, Princeton UP, 1993.
Chapman, Helen. 'Some Significant Women in Australian Film – A Celebration and a

THE SILENT PRODUCER

Cautionary Tale', annual Longford Lyell Lecture, printed in *Senses of Cinema*. October 22, 2002. http://sensesofcinema.com/2002/australian-women/chapman/

Connor, Rachel. *H.D. and the Image*. Manchester, Manchester University Press, 2004.

Cooper, Mark Garrett.
Universal Women: Filmmaking and Institutional Change in Early Hollywood. Urbana/Chicago, University of Illinois Press, 2010.

De Winter, H. 'What I Really Want to do is Produce?', *Top Producers Talk Movies and Money*. London, Faber & Faber, 2006.

Dooley, Marilyn Sue. *Women of the Silent Era – Virgins, Vamps and Heroines: selections from Australian film 1896–1930* (documentary, 83 mins.). Australia, Canberra, National Film and Sound Archive, 1997.

Duckett, Victoria and Susan Potter. 'Introduction: Women and the Silent Screen', *Screening the Past: Special Dossier Women and the Silent Screen*. 40. 2015. http://www.screeningthepast.com/issue-40/

Easen, Sarah. 'Field, Mary (1896–1968)', BFI Screen Online. 2014. http://www.screenonline.org.uk/people/id/581940/

The Film Archive Press Release. 'Laurie Inkster: Films from the Wild West Coast', *Scoop Independent News*. August 11, 2005. http://www.scoop.co.nz/stories/CU0508/S00093.htm

Film Star Postcards. 'Aud Egede-Nissen.' August 9, 2013. http://filmstarpostcards.blogspot.com.au/2013/08/aud-egede-nissen.html

Gaines, Jane and Radha Vatsal. 'How Women Worked in the U.S. Silent Film Industry', *Women Film Pioneers Project, Center for Digital Research and Scholarship*. Jane Gaines, Radha Vatsal, and Monica Dall'Asta, Eds. New York, Columbia University Libraries, November 18, 2013. https://wfpp.cdrs.columbia.edu/essay/how-women-worked-in-the-us-silent-film-industry/

Gledhill, Christine. 'Reframing Women in 1920s British Cinema: the Case of Violet Hopson and Dinah Shurey', *Journal of British Cinema and Television*. 4 (1). 2007, 1–17.

Giessen, Rolf. *Nazi Propaganda Films: A History and Filmography*. Jefferson, North Carolina, McFarland Press, 2003.

Hill, Donna. 'It began with a tango – June Mathis and her unique friendship with Rudolph Valentino', *Strictly Vintage Hollywood*. 2009. http://strictly-vintage-hollywood.blogspot.com.au/2009/06/it-all-began-with-tango-june-mathis-and.html

IMDB. Walter West. 2015. http://www.imdb.com/name/nm0922386/?ref_=fn_al_nm_1

IMDB. Violet Hopson: Biography. 2015. http://www.imdb.com/name/nm0394472/bio?ref_=nm_ov_bio_sm

IMDB. *Die Nacht der Einbrecher* (1921). 2015. http://www.imdb.com/title/tt0012495/fullcredits?ref_ˉtt_ov_st_sm

Jensen, Jytte. 'Asta Nielsen'. *Modern Women: Women Artists at the Museum of Modern Art*. Cornelia H. Butler, Ed. New York, The Museum of Modern Art, 2010, 88–91.

Librizzi, Jane. *Asta Nielsen: The Woman Who Played Hamlet,* The Blue Lantern. 2015. http://thebluelantern.blogspot.com.au/2015/07/asta-nielsen-woman-who-played-hamlet.html

Lyell, Lottie Edith. *The Encyclopedia of Women and Leadership in Twentieth-Century Australia*. Canberra, ACT, Australian Women's Archives Project, 2014. Accessed http://www.womenaustralia.info/leaders/biogs/WLE0420b.htm

Mahar, Karen Ward. *Women Filmmakers in Early Hollywood*. Baltimore, Johns Hopkins University Press, 2006.

McMahan, Alison. *Alice Guy-Blaché: Lost Visionary of the Cinema*. New York, Continuum

International, 2002.

Miller, April. 'Julia Crawford Ivers' Women Film Pioneers Project, Center for Digital Research and Scholarship. Jane Gaines, Radha Vatsal, and Monica Dall'Asta, Eds. New York, Columbia University Libraries, September 27, 2013. https://wfpp.cdrs.columbia.edu/pioneer/ccp-julia-crawford-ivers/

Newey, Katherine. 'Women and Early British Film: Finding a Screen of Her Own', *Moving Performance: British Stage and Screen 1890s–1920s*. Linda Fitzsimmons and Sarah Street, Eds. Trowbridge, Flicks Books, 2000, 151–165.

Pardo, Alejandro. 'The Film Producer as a Creative Force.' Widescreen 2 (2). 2010. http://widescreenjournal.org

Pivac, Diane. 'New Zealand film pioneer: Hilda Maud Hayward (1898–1970)', *Screening the Past: Special Dossier Women and the Silent Screen*. 40. 2015. http://www.screeningthepast.com/issue-40/

Pullar, Ellen. 'Ice Cream and the Great Kiwi Summer' *Gauge*. January 20, 2015. http://www.ngataonga.org.nz/blog/film/icecream-and-the-great-kiwi-summer/#more-2095

Selznick, David. O. 'The Functions of the Producer and the Making of Feature Films', *Memo from David O. Selznick*. R. Behlme, ed. Los Angeles, Samuel French, 1937; 1988, 473–74.

Shirley, Graham. 'The McDonagh Sisters', *Australian Screen*. Canberra, National Film and Sound Archive Australia, 2015.

Slide, Anthony. *The Silent Feminists: America's First Women Directors*. Lanham, Maryland, Scarecrow Press, 1996.

Stamp, Shelley. 'Women and the Silent Screen', *The Wiley-Blackwell History of American Film*. Cynthia Lucia, Roy Grundmann, and Art Simon, Eds. 1st Ed. Oxford, Blackwell Publishing, 2012, 1–26.

Thomas, Bob. *Thalberg: Life and Legend*. Garden City, NY, Doubleday, 1969.

Toulmin, Vanessa. 'Women Bioscope Proprietors – Before the First World War', *Celebrating 1895: The Centenary of Cinema*. John Fullerton, Ed. Sydney, John Libbey, 1998, 55–65.

Wollstein, Hans J. 'Overview: Julia Crawford Ivers.' AllMovie.com. 2015. http://www.allmovie.com/artist/julia-crawford-ivers-p185273

Women and Silent British Cinema (WSBC). 2015. https://womenandsilentbritishcinema.wordpress.com

Wright Wexman, Virginia. 'June Mathis', Women Film Pioneers Project, Center for Digital Research and Scholarship Jane Gaines, Radha Vatsal, and Monica Dall'Asta, Eds. New York, Columbia University Libraries, September 27, 2013. https://wfpp.cdrs.columbia.edu/pioneer/ccp-june-mathis/

Williams, Tami. *Germaine Dulac: A Cinema of Sensations*. Champaign, Illinois, University of Illinois Press, 2007.

4. WOMEN WERE WRITING: Beyond Melodrama and Hot House Romances

Patricia Di Risio

> Until recently, the first world map of cinema history imagined large portions of the world in which there were no women filmmakers in the silent era. (Gaines 2004,117)

More recent feminist studies have shown that the gradual industrialisation of the film industry during the silent era provided a unique opportunity for women to contribute to the formation of creative professions within the film industry. During the silent era scriptwriting was still in its infancy, and the art of writing scripts emerged from the ability not just to employ cinematic language but also to invent stories that could be easily translated to the screen. For writers in general, film became the latest medium in which to practice their craft.

> Scenario writers in the silent era also read and evaluated story material from outside sources (much like the contemporary work of script reading and assessment known as "coverage") and early writers undertook multiple roles within the company they were contracted to. (Conor 2014,15)

The ability to invent stories with popular appeal was the way many writers were able to make a name for themselves. The scenario writer was almost an invisible figure in the rapidly growing and lucrative enterprise of filmmaking and there is significant evidence to suggest that during the silent era, between the years of 1896–1930, these scenario writers were predominantly women. (Mahar 2006)

Nowadays professional scriptwriting for the film industry is dominated by men. Reports by both government and industry bodies in several English-speaking countries have released statistics which show that women scriptwriters are frequently outnumbered by men, have less work opportunities, and that less faith is placed in the profitability of scripts written by women.[4] It is hard to imagine women being allowed to figure prominently in a professional sphere that is today considered to be men's work. Research shows that during the silent era this was, in fact, the case.

Unlike other male dominated professions such as business, engineering, politics, the military or medicine, where women have historically not been permitted to work, the early days of the film industry was populated by vivid examples of successful female filmmakers. This is especially true when considering the way women contributed to the industry as writers. 'Women did not struggle to be a part of the growing industry of the scenario writing in its early days, for women dominated the industry, and women like Marion, Loos, Mathis and Macpherson were among the most successful scenarists (male or female) in film history' (Casella 2006, 217). More recent studies of the silent era also demonstrate that the female scriptwriter was deliberately and systematically excluded from Hollywood filmmaking, and subsequently erased from its history. Women began to be marginalised by perpetuating the image of the female writer as more suited to subject matter that reiterated traditional Victorian notions of femininity. This was more a product of the demands of the studios who believed that women '...were

4 In the report 'Scoping Study into the Lack of Women Screenwriters in the U.K.', presented to the U.K. Film Council, the authors stated that, 'While little research has been conducted in the UK, international research shows a marked imbalance in the number of women working as screenwriters in a number of countries, including the US, Australia and Denmark. (Sinclair, Pollard, Wolfe 2006, 7) The Hollywood Writers Guild Report 2014 also showed the women writers continue to be significantly outnumbered by men and that television offers more opportunities for women than film.

more attuned than men to turning out the kitsch melodramas and hot-house romances…' (Carey 1970–71, 51). Writing romantic comedies and moralistic melodramas often provided the female scenario writer with the opportunity to break into the industry but this was by no means the only genre where women were able to exert their talent and imagination. The silent era offers vibrant examples of gifted women writers who were interested in questioning gender roles, and challenging traditional understandings of women and femininity, both on- and off-screen. Thus, their work can easily be considered to be operating in a feminist vein. Who were some of these leading women? What were they writing about? What genres and characters were drawn from this female imagination? And to what extent did they reflect the behind the scenes reality of industrialised filmmaking?

Perhaps the most famous female scenarist of the silent era is Frances Marion (1888–1973). Marion has been credited with the writing of 300 scripts and producing over 130 films. Like many other scenarists, Marion did not work strictly as a writer and her talents included directing, producing and acting. In the silent era, particularly before the introduction of sound, these roles were less distinct than they tend to be in contemporary commercial contexts. Marion's career even survived the transition to sound and in 1930 she became the first female to win an Academy Award for Best Adapted Screenplay for the film *The Big House* (Hill 1930). This film is set in an overcrowded and demoralising prison and depicts the personal and amorous tribulations of Kent Marlowe (Robert Montgomery). Marlowe is an unlikely criminal who ends up in prison for drunk driving which results in manslaughter. The film gives a frank account of how he must contend with the fellow hardened inmates and their power structures in order to survive. In 1932, Marion received the Academy Award for Best Story for *The Champ* (Vidor 1931). This canonical boxing film depicts the life of the fictional character Andy Purcell (Wallace Beery), an ageing boxer whose career has faded. He lives alone with his son and struggles with financial difficulties and alcoholism. Purcell's wife abandoned him and their son only to return years later (after marrying a more successful man) to reclaim their child. Marion was actually most acknowledged for material which seems far removed from the lighter subject matter she is more popularly associated with.

> She wrote Pickford as the beguiling fairy girl of the woods in *Fanchon the Cricket* (1915), as the spunky female in *Johanna Enlists* (1918), and the sweet girlchild in adaptations of *Rebecca of Sunnybrook Farm* and *The Little Princess* (1917) *Anne of Green Gables* (1919) and *Pollyanna* (1920). (Casella 2006, 230)

In her memoir *Off With Their Heads* (1972) Marion shows she was clearly fond of her working relationship with Mary Pickford. However, she bemoaned the restrictive nature of the kinds of portrayals of Pickford that the industry demanded. Marion states that both she and Pickford were disgusted by the emphasis on this 'sweet girl-child' stereotype and she resented having to yield to these demands in order to maintain the momentum of her employment. Other writers such as June Mathis, Alice Guy-Blaché and Lois Weber, who also worked as directors or even had their own studios, were also interested in producing a diverse range of portrayals of women. 'These women were powerful in Hollywood because they held multiple positions in the industry… allowing them to bring their ideas about filmmaking to the screen with little opposition from studio executives' (Casella 2006, 232). History shows us there was no shortage of women whose work can be defined by a feminist agenda.

Gene Gauntier (1885–1966) was a writer, director and actress in films from early 1906 to 1920. A prolific filmmaker of her time, she wrote thirty-one screenplays and performed in twenty-eight films. In 1928 she published her memoir, appropriately titled *Blazing the Trail*, which chronicles how women were virtually leading the industry in all aspects of filmmaking in the silent era. Gauntier started out as an actress and quickly turned her hand to writing as a means of supplementing her income. She worked at length for the production company Kalem and played an instrumental role in developing the conventions of scriptwriting.

> The birth of the screenplay as we know it today can be traced to Gauntier's work at Kalem. She wrote straight for the screen scenarios, and included technical language in scenarios that in her hands were something more than one-page summaries.' (Casella 2006, 220)

Her ability to adapt literary texts thoroughly and accurately to the screen resulted in the first copyright infringement case for the film *Ben Hur* (Olcott 1907). Kalem, together with Gauntier, faced a suit by Harper and Brothers and the author's estate (General Lew Wallace). The case worked its way through the court system for years before the United States Supreme Court finally ruled in favour of the plaintiffs. This landmark case established the conventions that would govern the acceptable process for adapting literary works to the screen.

Over time as specific roles eventually emerged in the film industry they became more defined and institutionalised, especially with the introduction of sound and the formation of the vertically integrated studio system. These off-screen professional roles, such as scriptwriting, were forged and defined by the groundbreaking work of figures such as Gauntier. Moreover, the protagonists that she conceived for the screen were aligned with the spirit of irreverence these scenario writers were enacting as professional working women. Many of their characters were far removed from the more conventional representations of women that had gained popularity and dominated the studio demand. Unfortunately, this popularity resulted in dictating the genre and styles that women would gradually be steered into. However, the more unconventional ways these women scenario writers envisaged femininity on-screen also enjoyed a great deal of popularity with audiences.

> The girl adventure films featured spunky women in
> daring, often death defying roles outside the domestic
> sphere. (Casella 2006, 227)

Gauntier's contribution to this tradition, albeit sketchily
recorded, was also significant. She devised *The Girl Spy* series
which was produced between 1908 and 1911. Titles in the
series include: *The Girl Spy: An Incident of the Civil War* (1909),
The Further Adventures of the Girl Spy (1910), *The Girl Spy Before
Vicksburg* (1910). In these films, Gauntier portrays Nan, a
young girl spy who works on behalf of the Confederates.
Nan is left motherless in infancy and loses her father and
brother to the civil war. Embittered by her misfortune she
devotes her life to working against the Union army. The
series revolves around her escapades in both espionage and
romance. 'Gauntier eventually married her off at the end of
the war, but the public demanded more and she brought her
back to the screen.' (Casella 2006, 228) The scene breakdown
of *The Girl Spy: An Incident of the Civil War* suggests that
Gauntier devised and performed one of the earliest examples
of the action heroine in Hollywood; 'Scene 1: Nan Receives
Her Orders. Scene 2: The Wires are Tapped. Scene 3: Nan
Escapes with the Tapped Dispatches. Scene 4: Nan Eludes
Her Pursuers. A Clever Ruse. Scene 5: Nan's Horse Found.
Again Suspected. Scene 6: Nan is joined by Her Confederate
and They Escape. Scene 7: The Pursuit. Scene 8: The
Dispatches Delivered.' [5]

Gauntier was employed at Universal in 1915 but left shortly
afterwards clearly unable to work in the new industrialised
context and her film career drew to a close by 1920. However,
Gauntier's writing career continued unabated; in 1919 she
began working as the film and drama critic at the Kansas
City Post.

---

5 http://www.imdb.com/title/tt0233795/plotsummary?ref_=tt_ov_pl

> The demand for girl adventure stories was not all that
> surprising. These stories served as a form of escapism,
> temporarily transporting the female audience out of the
> home or out of the workplace. The on-screen female
> characters were pro-active – within bounds – and they
> enticed rather than challenged the men they encountered.
> (Casella 2006, 228)

I would argue that these female characters both enticed and
challenged men and, as a result, the women who created them
were eventually ushered out of the important creative and
decision-making roles in Hollywood.

Grace Cunard, who collaborated extensively with John
Ford's elder brother Francis, also furnished the screen with
numerous strong female leads.[6] The women she devised and
portrayed engaged in 'action-packed' adventures and their
stories were so popular that they became serialised. 'After
Cunard and Ford had made several successful one- and two-
reelers, Universal chose their unit to develop the studio's answer
to Pathé's instantly successful *Perils of Pauline*. Cunard and Ford
revamped a two-reel Western *Lucille Love, Girl of Mystery* and
turned it into a fifteen-chapter installment play.' (Mahar 2006,
114) As a team they became a leading box office draw and
their most famous collaborative effort *The Broken Coin* (1915)
engendered the character Kitty Gray. Cunard devised her as a
reaction to what she saw as the more commonly 'insipid' roles
available to women (Mahar 2006, 115). The treatment that
Cunard wrote for the film is an example of her fertile feminist
imagination and the tendency to create characters who were an
extension of her own real life persona:

> Kitty Gray, an American newspaper woman and
> star reporter on a popular newspaper, finds, in

---

6 John Ford later became famous for his work in the Western genre and directed the
canonical Western *Stagecoach* (1939) which featured Claire Trevor as the protagonist.
Trevor played Dallas, a former prostitute, who couples with another society outsider
Ring Kid (John Wayne). Trevor was actually cast as the lead character, was paid a
higher fee than her co-star and exhibits a variety of unconventional female traits
throughout the film. (Kitses 2004, 49)

an old curiosity shop, half of a broken coin. On this half of the coin is inscribed several words in Latin, which, when translated, read as follows: Underneath/flagstone f/north corner/torture cham/be found/treasures/valuables/the kingd/Gretzhoffen/Mi.

Her curiosity aroused by the word 'Gretzhoffen,' Kitty goes home and looks up an old article of hers written some time ago regarding the kingdom of Gretzhoffen and its threatened bankruptcy. Thinking she has material for a good story, she sees the editor of the paper and wagers one year's salary with him: if she does not come back with a good story regarding the hidden treasures of the Kingdom of Gretzhoffen, he can donate her salary to charity… (Birchard 1993, 80)

Cunard and Ford's last successful collaboration was *The Purple Mask* (1916). In this series Cunard plays Patricia Montez who disguises herself as 'The Queen of the Apaches' and acts like a modern day Robin Hood. She is pursued by her antithesis, detective Phil Kelly (Francis Ford), who also leads a double life as the leader of a strange gang. In episode nine of the series, she disguises herself as a man to gain employment in a factory belonging to Robert Jackson, a wealthy corrupt manufacturer of high speed motors. She, along with her 'Apache' gang, investigates Jackson who is apparently plotting against his employees.[7] Cunard invented stories and characters that placed women well and truly outside of the domestic sphere and right in the thick of complex and dangerous intrigues. Her tendency to create flippant characters, who were prone to notoriety, produced the jewel thief, 'Lady Raffles' for the films *The Mysterious Leopard Lady* and *The Mystery of the White Car* both released in 1914. Her stories were set in various locations and the behaviour of the women has been fittingly described as 'zany' and 'intrepid'. Cunard, like Gauntier, also portrayed these characters on-screen, and sometimes caused halts in

7 http://www.silentfilmstillarchive.com/purple_mask.htm, http://www.allmovie.com/movie/v148973

production because she sustained injuries while performing physically challenging stunts (Bean 2013). Thus the female imagination was prone to inventing physically daring characters as well as experimenting with ways they could actually perform some of their fantastical feats.

Clara Beranger was a scenario writer who also conjured up some very enduring unconventional female figures. She turned to filmmaking from a career in journalism and she frequently enunciated her feminism in a manner which was atypical for female filmmakers of the period. Her writing background also made her particularly skillful in adapting literary works as well as creating original stories that could be successfully staged for film. She is well known for her adaptations of classic novels and brought *Anna Karenina* (1915) and *Dr Jekyll and Mr Hyde* (1920) to the screen. Beranger worked for most of the major studios of her time; Edison, Vitagraph and Kalem and was eventually appointed as a writer for both Fox Film Corporation and Pathé. She had a longstanding working relationship with screenwriter and director William de Mille (the older brother of the more famous Cecil B. DeMille) with whom she was also romantically involved. Her script for the film *The Bedroom Window* (1924) provides one of the most important early examples of a story that 'featured a strong female in dangerous professions' (Casella 2006, 228) Matilda Jones (aka Rufus Rome), is a successful female mystery writer who also solves crimes in real life. She saves her nephew, Ricardo Cortez, from the electric chair by identifying the real culprit of the murder he is wrongly accused of committing. This is a narrative staple, which was to become one of the favourites in the murder mystery genre, and is clearly a precursor to Miss Marple who first appeared in Agatha Christie's short story *The Tuesday Night Club* (1926). However, Beranger was not always able to successfully bring feminist heroines to the screen. In her 1921 adaptation of Zona Gale's play *Miss Lulu Bett* she was forced, by popular demand, to alter the ending and make her female protagonist more conventional. In the original story

Lulu rebels against societal pressure and prefers to live an independent life. The film version yields to the more traditional expectations of the time and Beranger writes a more romantic ending where her heroine finds love with a man. Like many other women scenario writers, Beranger did not end her career as a scriptwriter but continued working in a related profession.

> After Clara Beranger retired from motion picture work, she taught screenwriting at the University of Southern California and, along with de Mille, was one of the original faculty of the USC School of Cinema-Television. Beranger continued to promote both the art and technique of motion pictures in Writing for the Screen, published in 1950 when Beranger was sixty-four years old.' (Rossiter 2013)

In an era where little had been recorded about the work of female filmmakers Clara Beranger also made her mark as an outspoken feminist. There is ample evidence of Beranger's support and promotion of women working in the film industry. According to Beranger, quoted in 'Moving Picture World' in 1918, women were dominating the industry as scenario writers not simply because they were more suited to melodramatic material but because they were more adept at dealing with stories that had emotional depth.

> It needs no cursory glance at the current releases and those of even six months ago to prove there are more writers among the feminine sex than the male persuasion. The heart throb, the human interest note, child life, domestic scenes and even the eternal triangle is more ably handled by women than men because of the thorough understanding our sex has of these matters.[8]

The article is being deliberately provocative in its headline; '*Are Women the Better Script Writers? Clara Beranger Perhaps Starts an Argument When in Some Detail She Tells Why She Thinks So.*' In an article in the same publication in 1919 Beranger points out that

8 'Are Women Writers the Better Script Writers?', *Moving Picture World*. 24th August, 1918, 1128. http://archive.org/stream/movwor37chal#page/1128/mode/2up

women have also 'scored as directors'. In 1920 Moving Picture World journalist, Edward Weitzel, interviewed her in her home in New York. He reported that she was successfully combining a career as a 'scenario expert' with her role of wife and mother with 'seeming effortlessness'. Beranger's consistent public comments in favour of women scenario writers 'diffused criticism of women in the work force' (Rossiter 2013) and the film industry increasingly provided exciting employment opportunities. This is in stark contrast to the situation in contemporary screen based industries. The issue of balancing a career in the high risk and precarious employment conditions, typical of creative industries, with the demands of family life remains one of the major obstacles for many women (French 2014, 190). Today film and television is much more limited in the opportunities it provides for women to thrive as writers (or in other creative and leadership roles). 'As a number of film critics and historians have pointed out … there was no overt 'feminist' political agenda among women filmmakers of the period, despite the fact that the suffragist movement was well under way by World War I' (Casella 2006, 231). Thus, Beranger stands out from most of her female counterparts who were equally strident in their pursuit of a career and supportive of fellow female filmmakers but, perhaps, less eager to brand themselves as feminists.

The contribution of women scriptwriters to the silent film era is also evident in the availability of books providing guidelines to their craft. Frances Marion, was author of *How to Write and Sell Film Stories* (1937) Such titles were part of what Conor (2014, 82) describes as a 'selling and marketing subgenre' and both men and women were writing these manuals. Louella O. Parsons wrote *How to Write for the 'Movies'* (1915), and John Emerson and Anita Loos co-authored *How to Write Photoplays* (1920). In 1921 Grace Lytton wrote *Scenario Writing Today* (1921) and Jeanie Macpherson wrote *The Market for Scenarios*. Clara Beranger wrote a similar book much later in her career and, as many of these titles suggest, these women were also covering the entrepreneurial aspects of scriptwriting, not just the artistic or structural aspects such as plot and character development. Women scenario writers were equally capable of giving business insights into the way the story ideas could be marketed for success. As the studios became larger and more male dominated many of these women found working in the new industrialised context unsuitable to the more maverick, inventive approach that the silent era was able to offer. Women were such a large part of the landscape of the silent era there was fear that they may take over the industry altogether. 'It is not surprising that historical accounts of early women screenwriters are also tinged with fears about female contamination. A number of references are made to the perceived "tyranny of the woman writer" in the Hollywood studios in the 1930s…' (Connor 2014, 117). This lends weight to the suggestion that women were systematically marginalised from the film industry, not merely to gain control of what was developing into a lucrative enterprise, but also to ensure that the kind of material that women excelled in would not be fuelling popular demand. Since the introduction of sound, women filmmakers have struggled to make their mark in the more commercial spheres of the film industry, especially at the level of creative control and instigation, a situation that appears to be becoming worse rather than improving.[9] The stories of the daring and inventiveness of pioneers such as Marion, Gauntier, Cunard and Beranger are inspirational. In 2013, independent filmmaker, Lucy Hay, complained that the sexist belief that women 'write too much about childbirth and losing your virginity' has become rife within the industry.[10] Contrary to this narrow minded attitude, these early female filmmakers show that women have always been interested in the potential of film to question and expand cultural understandings of

9 Women accounted for 11% of writers working on the top 250 films of 2014. This represents an increase of 1 percentage point from 2013 and a decrease of 2 percentage points from 1998. 79% of the films had no female writers. (*The Celluloid Ceiling: Behind-the-Scenes Employment of Women on the Top 250 Films of 2014* by Martha M. Lauzen, PhD)
10 Lucy Hay, novelist, script editor and blogger and one of the organisers of London Screenwriters Festival laments this tendency: http://www.londonscreenwritersfestival.com/its-not-sexism-damn-right-it-is-by-lucy-v-hay/

gender. It is no coincidence that this early experimental period of Hollywood history, which provided rare encouragement and support for female writing talents, led to nurturing new and fresh ideas about the image of women and femininity.

The reasons behind women's gradual exclusion from film industry at the time often centre around the need to protect powerful economic interests. Film production is an expensive enterprise requiring large amounts of borrowed capital and financiers were less likely to invest in projects where women were seen to be in control of the creative output. However, this merely reiterates the role of rising social pressure to confine women to domestic spheres and to place them in a position of disadvantage where they were increasingly daring to compete with men. This tendency can also be seen in policies such as the implementation of the Hays Production Code (1930–1968), which had very strict and conservative moral guidelines around the way women could be represented on screen; women seen 'selling their virtue' was forbidden and the institution of marriage was to be portrayed in a positive light. The opportunities for women writers to sustain their involvement in film was also hampered by technological advancements. The introduction of sound and more sophisticated engineering and equipment in film production required the kind of specialised training that was predominantly available to men. These factors suggest that the success of women scenario writers in the silent era, and the more liberal notions of femininity that their work often promoted, were perceived as a threat to male privilege. The recent studies examining the alarming gender imbalance both on and off-screen, especially in popular cinema, is evidence that such sexist attitudes created a legacy that continues to blight the more commercial aspects of the industry even today.

I would like to acknowledge the invaluable work of the Women Film Pioneers Project: https://wfpp.cdrs.columbia.edu. This vast and beautifully presented resource documents the enormous contribution of women to silent film and enables detailed discussion and reflection on their work.

Author Biography: Patricia Di Risio

Patricia is a PhD candidate in Screen Studies at the University of Melbourne. Her thesis has a particular focus on the representation of women in late-twentieth-century-Hollywood cinema and explores the interplay between gender and genre. Patricia has been a teacher in film and theatre studies at secondary and tertiary level in Australia, Italy and the U.K. and is currently a sessional teacher and research assistant in Screen Studies at the University of Melbourne.

References

Bean, Jennifer M. 'Grace Cunard', Women Film Pioneers Project, Center for Digital Research and Scholarship. Jane Gaines, Radha Vatsal, and Monica Dall'Asta, Eds. New York, Columbia University Libraries, September 27, 2013. https://wfpp.cdrs. columbia.edu/pioneer/ccp-grace-cunard

Birchard, Robert. 'The Adventures of Francis Ford and Grace Cunard', *American Cinematographer*. July, 1993, 77–82.

Bisplinghoff, Gretchen. 'Gene Gauntier.', Women Film Pioneers Project, Center for Digital Research and Scholarship. Jane Gaines, Radha Vatsal, and Monica Dall'Asta, Eds. New York, Columbia University Libraries, September 27, 2013. https://wfpp. cdrs.columbia.edu/pioneer/ccp-gene-gauntier

Gary Carey. 'Written on the Screen: Anita Loos', *Film Comment*. 6, no. 4. Winter, 1970–71), 51.

Casella, Donna, R. 'Feminism and the Female Author: The Not So Silent Career of the Woman Scenarist in Hollywood – 1896–1930', *Quarterly Review of Film and Video*. 23:3. 2006, 217–235.

Conor, Bridget. *Screenwriting. Creative labor and professional practice*. London and New York, Routledge, 2014.

Gaines, Jane, M. 'Film History and then Two Presents of Feminist Film Theory', *Cinema Journal*. 44, No.1, 113–119.

French, Lisa. 'Gender then, gender now: surveying women's participation in Australian film and television industries', *Continuum: Journal of Media & Cultural Studies*, 28:2, 2014, 188–200.

Mahar, Karen Ward. *Women Filmmakers in Early Hollywood*. Baltimore, The John Hopkins University Press, 2006.

Rossiter, Lori. 'Clara Beranger', Women Film Pioneers Project, Center for Digital Research and Scholarship. Jane Gaines, Radha Vatsal, and Monica Dall'Asta, Eds. New York, Columbia University Libraries, September 27, 2013. https://wfpp.cdrs. columbia.edu/pioneer/ccp-clara-beranger

Ruvoli, JoAnne. 'Frances Marion', Women Film Pioneers Project, Center for Digital Research and Scholarship. Jane Gaines, Radha Vatsal, and Monica Dall'Asta, Eds. New York, Columbia University Libraries, September 27, 2013.

5. DOING IT ALL: Women's On- and Off-screen Contributions to European Silent Film

Julie K. Allen

When people think about the movie industry, Hollywood is often the first (and sometimes the only) place that comes to mind. Although American production companies and American films came to dominate the global cinema market in the 1920s and continue to do so, the U.S. was just one of many vibrant developing film markets in the early twentieth century. On the American side of the Atlantic, George Eastman invented Kodak film in 1889 in New York and Thomas Edison developed the Kinetograph camera in 1891. On the European side, the Lumière brothers in France transformed Edison's heavy, horse-drawn, battery-powered contraption into a portable machine called a *cinématographe* that could both record, print and project films, thereby moving film from the amusement arcade to the art house. Many film histories cite the Lumières' initial public screening on 28th December 1895[1] as the beginning of motion-picture history, while others credit the Edison Company's kinetoscope premiere in New York City in April 1896.

A narrative privileging only American film history misses an important part of the story of early cinema, in particular the ways in which European silent cinema challenged and inspired American film culture and vice versa. Several film moguls dominated the early European silent film marketplace, including Pathé Frères and Gaumont in France, Nordisk in Denmark, and Cines in Italy, but many other smaller production and distribution companies also vied quite successfully for market share. This competitive situation led to innovative developments that enabled European companies to break into the American market prior to World War I. Robert Pearson explains that the dominant European companies, particularly Pathé and Nordisk, were 'forced into aggressive expansion by relatively small domestic demand.'[2] The fact that, in 1907, for example, only 400 of the 1200 films released in the U.S. were domestic products[3] confirms the efficacy of this strategy, at least in the short term. This European dominance was not uncontested, however, and the establishment of the Motion Picture Patents Company in the U.S. in January 1909 can be seen as the opening salvo of a 'ferocious struggle for control of the booming film industry,'[4] not just in the U.S., but around the globe.

Just as an exclusively American history of cinema would be incomplete, so too would any silent film history that ignored the significant role played by women, both in front of and behind the camera, as well as in the areas of scriptwriting, costuming and marketing, to name just a few. Unsurprisingly, most of the major figures of the early European silent film industry were men – notably the producers Charles and Emile Pathé, Léon Gaumont, Ole Olsen and Paul Davidson, who employed hundreds of male actors, screenwriters, cameramen, etc., but quite a few women were involved from the very beginning as well. The most reknowned of these was Alice Guy (later Guy-Blaché), who was working as Gaumont's secretary when he allowed her to make some of the demonstration films used for marketing his motion-picture cameras. Although Gaumont initially stipulated that she must not allow her filmmaking to disrupt her secretarial duties, Guy made films of enough commercial value that Gaumont eventually promoted her to the position of 'directrice du Service des théâtres de prises de vues' (director of the department of cinematography), in which capacity she not only directed films, but also oversaw story development, costumes, scenery, and casting.[5] Ephraim Katz describes her as 'the world's first woman director and possibly the first director of either sex to bring a story-film to the screen.'[6] Unfortunately for the European film industry, Guy emigrated to the U.S. in 1907 together with her new husband, Herbert Blaché, who had been tasked with establishing a Gaumont franchise there, and worked for the rest of her long and eventful career in American film.[7]

Competition between the American and European silent film industries, particularly in the years leading up to World War I, gave European women astonishingly diverse opportunities for hands-on involvement in all aspects of cinema production. As the American cinema market expanded rapidly in the early decades of the twentieth century on its way to becoming the largest in the world, the necessity for European film companies to find ways to compete with the massive output of single-reel films from U.S. production companies created spaces for creative innovation within the industry itself. The American film industry relied on a strict division of labour between specialists (scriptwriters, wardrobe mistresses, etc.), whereas many European film companies allowed talented employees to involve themselves in a range of production activities. The particular working conditions in the European silent film industry not only inspired such innovations as the multi-reel film but also facilitated the rise of the monopoly film distribution system and the film star. Although Richard Abel identifies the rise of the film star as a barrier to the success of European films abroad,[8] it also created a power dynamic that gave female film stars unprecedented (and to a certain degree unparalleled since) freedom to participate in the largely male-dominated film industry in many different capacities – not only in front of the camera, but also behind the scenes, as producers, directors, editors, screenwriters, studio owners, costume designers, technicians, etc.), particularly in the years prior to World War I. By the 1920s, the economic dominance of American film had had a repressive effect on European film companies, leading to greater industry standardisation, a shift to a director-centric system, and a correspondingly inhibiting effect on the freedom of female stars to influence multiple aspects of film production.

To a certain extent, then, the early silent film industry was a blank slate that allowed for a high degree of experimentation and creativity on the part of not only directors and producers, but also actors and actresses. The European silent film community in particular was tremendously enriched by the work of dozens of resourceful, creative women in many different countries. The dramatic innovations of actresses like Lyda Borelli (1884–1959) and Asta Nielsen (1881–1972) have been well documented by film scholars, but European women's off-screen work is less well known. A few examples of female European director/producers include Caroline van Dommelen[9] (1874–1957) in the Netherlands, one of only two female directors in Dutch silent film history; Thea Červenková[10] (1882–1961), who worked as a director, screenwriter, inter-title translator, journalist and entrepreneur in Czechoslovakia before emigrating to Brazil in 1923; and Carmen Cartellieri (1891–1953), a Hungarian actress who co-founded the Cartellieri Film company with her husband Mano Ziffer-Teschenbruck in Vienna in 1920 and made such commercially successful films as the comedy *Skifahren* (*Carmen Learns to Ski*) (Ziffer-Teschenbruck, 1920) and the crime drama *Die Würghand* (*The Hand of the Devil*) (Cornelius Hintner, 1920).[11] Even if they didn't direct films, many female European stars, such as Henny Porten (1890–1960) in Germany, ran their own production companies and involved themselves in film production, marketing and distribution.

Despite the fact that 'women might be said to have virtually controlled the film industry' in the silent era, as Anthony Slide asserts,[14] relatively little has been published about most of these European women in English, although the Women Film Pioneers Project at Columbia University in New York City has made great strides toward recovering some of their histories. Even less has been written about how these women's contributions shaped the silent film industry in their home countries, Europe, and the world. This chapter strives to make a start at stimulating this conversation by outlining and contextualising, albeit briefly, the impressively versatile, pioneering contributions to filmmaking made by some of the brightest female stars of the European silent cinema firmament. Given space constraints, this account cannot be exhaustive, but will focus instead on a few exemplary women who both acted and directed/produced films during the silent film era in Europe. These women, represented here by Asta Nielsen, Francesca Bertini, Aud Egede-Nissen, and Musidora, shattered perceived gender boundaries in the silent film industry by 'doing it all', both on-screen and off, and left a significant legacy that deserves to be acknowledged.

The Danish Prima Donna: Asta Nielsen

While Alice Guy-Blaché worked exclusively behind the camera, one of the earliest female European silent cinema pioneers to work both in front of and behind the camera was the Danish theatre actress Asta Nielsen (1881–1972). She burst on to the global cinema market with her debut film *Afgrunden* (*The Abyss;* Urban Gad, 1910). In this film, Nielsen introduced the world to her minimalistic acting style, which contrasted sharply with the histrionics of other early film actresses, as well as to her remarkably expressive eyes and sensuality, which featured prominently in the film's extended erotic gaucho dance sequence. Denmark had a thriving, innovative silent film industry in the early twentieth century, led (rather tyrannically) by Ole Olsen at Nordisk, but it relied heavily on exports, as the domestic market for film was quite small and fiercely territorial. The reaction from Danish film companies to Nielsen's independent film was tepid, but when *Afgrunden* proved to be a huge success abroad, Nielsen was recruited to work in Germany, where she soon became one of the most successful and aggressively marketed film stars of the period. In an era when actors and actresses were rarely credited on-screen for their roles, Nielsen's global fame and the commercial success of her films gave her the necessary leverage to demand an active role in the production of her own films. Prior to World War I, the German film industry was fairly small and heavily reliant on imports, primarily from France, Denmark, Italy and the U.S., but the production of films in Germany, for both domestic consumption and export, increased exponentially from the 15% market share it commanded in 1910[12] to 67.6% by 1925.[13] A major factor in this shift was the emergence in Germany in 1911–12 of the monopoly film distribution system, which was based on selling exclusive distribution rights to a series of feature-length films to particular cinemas in a given country. This new business model infused new funds into the German film industry and created a peculiarly favourable climate for an ambitious, creative individual like Asta Nielsen to become a major player in the industry. *The Abyss* was the first film to be distributed in Germany on this basis and its tremendous financial success instantly made Nielsen a valuable commodity.

After having spent a decade struggling to make her name in the Danish theatre world, Nielsen became an international celebrity with both wealth and influence. She made a few more films in Denmark, for Fotorama and Nordisk, as well as a series of films for Deutsche Bioscop in Berlin, for increasingly high salaries, but without influence over the production process. In the summer of 1911, Austrian film distributor Christoph Mülleneisen orchestrated an agreement among several German film production companies, including Paul Davidson's Projektions – AG Union (PAGU) and Carl Schleussner's Deutsche Bioscop, to establish a new monopoly distribution company, Internationale Film-Vertriebs-GmbH, based in Vienna and headed by Davidson, which would distribute thirty-two Asta-Nielsen films over the next four years. Although still under contract in Denmark, Nielsen seized the opportunity, which brought with it an annual salary of 80,000 German marks, 33.3% of the revenues generated by her films, full artistic freedom in choosing her screenplays, costumes, and supporting actors, and, perhaps most importantly, the right to be directed exclusively by her soon-to-be husband Urban Gad.[14]

As a result of these favourable contractual terms, Nielsen was able to be intimately involved in the creation of both her films and her public persona, unlike many Hollywood stars whose image was dictated by the studios. Working closely with Gad on each year's Asta Nielsen Series, a collection of eight to ten films that had been presold to distributors around the globe, Nielsen exercised a degree of control over her work on an artistic, technical and economic level that was extraordinary for a woman at the time. Heide Schlüpmann explains, 'Under the sign of the Asta Nielsen series, Nielsen worked with a producer and director in a contractually secured constellation in which all of the freedom was hers.'[15] Some of this freedom may have been due to her close, collaborative relationship with Gad, with whom she made the majority of her (and his) most commercially successful films over a four year period. Although, as Stephan Michael Schroeder documents, Gad provided detailed scripts for his wife's roles, Nielsen claimed much of the credit for the authorship of the films she made with Gad.[16] Gad is credited as both director and screenwriter on most of their joint films, but Nielsen, in an interview with Danish film historian Marguerite Engberg, described his scripts as partially-completed canvases that left her considerable room for improvisation and dismissed his contribution as primarily concerned with 'coming up with good roles for me.'[17]

'Doing it all' was thus a central part of Nielsen's professional image. According to her published memoirs and frequent newspaper interviews over her long life, Nielsen had a hand in the pre- and post-production phases of all of the films she made, from choosing the screenplays and making her own costumes to splicing the negatives and helping to market the final product. Her film *Die Filmprimadonna* (*The Film Prima Donna;* Gad, 1914) even offers meta-cinematic commentary on this state of affairs. According to Schlüpmann, *Die Filmprimadonna*:

...grants a look at the ways in which this star does not merely play a role, but rather influences the entire creation of a film. She selects the script, she chooses her partner, she controls the shooting and discussions with the camera people, she controls the darkroom to look on while the film is developed ... Nielsen, as we read in her autobiography, also picked out the fabrics and patterns of her costumes herself.[18]

During World War I, Nielsen formed her own production company, Neutral Film, which brought her into direct competition with the heavily male-dominated German film production industry, represented by men like Davidson and Schleussner. The films Nielsen made with Neutral, including *Das Eskimo Baby* (*The Eskimo Baby;* Heinz Schall) and *Die Börsenkönigin* (*Queen of the Stock Market*; Edmund Edel) are clever and bold, but their circulation was inhibited by wartime conditions. Most were not released until 1918 and many of the originals were destroyed in a warehouse fire in Berlin. After the war, in 1920, she launched another production company in Berlin, Art-Film GmbH, under the auspices of which she made such ground-breaking films as her *Hamlet* film (Svend Gade, 1921), in which she plays a cross-dressing female Hamlet. The increasingly director-centric production conditions in Germany after 1918 meant, however, that Nielsen could no longer exercise the same degree of influence over her films as before the war. As her highly publicised disagreement with Ernst Lubitsch over the making of *Rausch* (*Intoxication;* 1919) revealed, she refused to accommodate directors' insistence on their ownership of the films they made and their authority over the actresses who played in them.[19] She continued making films in Berlin until 1932 – her final film, *Unmögliche Liebe* (*Impossible Love*; Erich Waschneck, 1932) was also her only sound film – but she found herself increasingly excluded from the off-screen elements of filmmaking she had once handled with such finesse. She returned to Denmark in 1937, where she lived in quiet obscurity as 'Fru Nielsen' – except for her sensational love match at the age of eighty-eight with an art dealer eighteen years her junior that made headlines across Germany and Denmark – until her death in Copenhagen in 1972.

The Italian Diva: Francesca Bertini

Asta Nielsen's star persona and realistic acting style is often cited as a decisive influence on the development of the Italian diva film, which flourished between approximately 1910 and 1917. Angela Dalle Vache explains that the 'diva-film genre re-elaborated the traits of a phenomenon – stardom – that came to Italy from Denmark and which was discussed in the trade film journals of the period, not only in relation to Northern Europe but also with strong awareness of the Hollywood star system.'[20] Although Italian film in the early 1910s was widely distributed internationally, particularly in Germany, the U.K., and the U.S., the Italian silent film industry was highly regional and lacked both an undisputed capital of film production – a function that Valby, Babelsberg, and Hollywood came to provide for Denmark, Germany and the U.S., respectively – and vertical integration of production, distribution and exhibition that would allow the industry to generate consistent, significant profits. This ad hoc system would eventually lead to bankruptcy for much of the Italian film industry at the end of World War I, but in its early years, the cinema offered a range of job opportunities for Italian women, primarily behind the scenes, as seamstresses, typists, assistants, milliners and costume designers, but also in front of the camera as actresses. The most innovative and influential Italian film actresses of the early silent period came to be known as divas, following the operatic tradition.

While Nielsen's films were often criticised for either their sensuality, such as the gaucho dance sequence in *Afgrunden,* or their irreverence, for example her performance in *Engelein* (1914) – as a thirty-two-year-old – of an eighteen-year-old girl dressed as a twelve-year-old lying in a child-sized bed smoking, with her feet sticking out over the railing, the Italian diva personified a more serious, melancholy character type, 'a combination of the Catholic *mater dolorosa,* of the femme fatale of Northern European literature and painting, and of the new, modern woman.'[21] Italian diva films could be escapist adventures or melodramatic romances, but they often dealt with real problems faced by Italian women, including 'out-of-wedlock pregnancy, child custody, abandonment, shame, adultery, divorce, prostitution and financial ruin.'[22] Many of these topics also appeared in German and Danish melodramas, including many of Nielsen's films, but the difference in Italian diva films is the extent to which the characters played by Italian divas – 'the betrayed woman, or the independent woman, or the female orphan, or the naïve daughter' – are blamed for their own misfortunes and punished at the end of the films.[23] In their desperation, Italian film divas' characters often resort to murder, but are redeemed, Dalle Vacche explains, by their beauty, which was 'a positive value in a culture sensitive to an ancient aesthetic practice at odds with the glitches and rough spots of mechanical reproduction.'[27] The development of the silent film industry in Italy was influenced by the strong presence of the Catholic Church in the Italian peninsula. In addition to enforcing conservative gender norms, for example by limiting women's options for independence by banning divorce, the Church's fear that the cinema would corrupt its viewers led to strict rules about where and how films could be screened. No screenings were allowed in religious buildings, for example, and any screenings for minors had to be segregated by gender. Dalle Vacche suggests, therefore, that the 'phenomenon of the diva … is symptomatic of Italian women's tightrope-walking act between tradition and rebellion.'[24]

One of the most prominent representatives of the Italian diva tradition was Francesca Bertini (1892–1985), who vied with Lyda Borelli for pre-eminence as the first Italian film diva. Unlike Borelli, who came from a prominent theatre family, Bertini was a self-made woman, stigmatised by her illegitimate birth, who taught herself to act. She worked her way up, first in sporadic appearances on stage, and then on film, from the *film d'art* to the short film to the diva film, in a variety of genres, from short melodramas to feature-length comedies. In contrast to Borelli's more studied, theatrical acting style, which emulated the beloved Italian stage actress Eleonora Duse and has been immortalised in the Italian verb *borelleggiare,* Bertini's acting was intuitive, realistic and measured. In 1914, the Italian film critic Cesare Naretto explained, 'Francesca Bertini does not pursue an unrealistic ideal through an artificial deployment of poses; instead she conveys reality through spontaneous facial expressions and natural gestures... She is not a model who strikes a sculpture-like pose, she is, rather, a woman of the real world.'[25] Bertini's naturalistic style closely resembles Nielsen's Danish example, which, in Dalle Vacche's opinion, may be one reason that Italian film scholars have tended to favour Borelli as the banner carrier for the Italian diva film.[26]

Bertini was first marketed as a 'diva' by the film company Celio in connection with the film *Sangue bleu* (*Blue Blood;* Nino Oxilia, 1914), in which, as Lea Jacobs notes, her character is forced to dance a '"tango of death" ... on a variety stage [that] is almost an exact copy (with identically dressed cowboy partner) of the dance that Nielsen ['s character] was similarly forced to perform in *Afgrunden*.'[27] Despite the many similarities between the two films and their female protagonists, the outcome is quite different. Whereas Nielsen's character stabs her former lover and is taken off, stonc-faced, to jail in the film's memorable final scene, Bertini's character stabs herself. Jacobs concludes,

> The Nielsen heroine is much more clearly following her own desire, one which leads her to reject the option of a respectable marriage, while the Bertini character is undone by the force of circumstances beyond her control: divorcing a husband who no longer loves her, she loses her daughter to the former husband when she is falsely accused of having a lover. In general, the diva

plays someone who belongs to, or joins, a cosmopolitan aristocracy, and she is more likely to be a passive victim than the active heroine typical of Nielsen's parts.[28]

What is striking about the Italian diva film, however, is the weakness and relatively 'wooden' performance of the male characters, which Jacobs attributes to the absence of the male equivalent of the diva, the 'divo'. She explains 'the diva may move her hands about her face and flutter about in her chair and strike tortuous attitudes in ways that no male film star ... any longer dared to attempt.'[29] Francesco Pitassio agrees 'no male actors could compete with the diva in terms of narrative and performative significance.'[30] Despite the limitations on women's options in Italian society, this example illustrates that silent film gave women like Bertini and Borelli the opportunity to dominate the screen.

As a film pioneer who 'did it all', Bertini was far more engaged in all aspects of the film industry than Borelli and much more innovative. She rebelled against the stuffy operatic roles of Italian *film d'art* and broke new ground in Italian film by playing a cross-dressing role in *Histoire d'un Pierrot* (*Pierrot the Prodigal*, 1913). Although Bertini was only eighteen at the time, she should also be considered a co-director/co-producer of that film, as the director who is credited for the film, Baldassare Negroni, walked off the set halfway through the film, leaving Bertini and her colleague Emilio Ghione to finish the job under the supervision of Baron Alberto Fassini at Celio Film, which was a branch of Cines in Rome.[31] In 1915, Bertini starred in, co-wrote, and co-directed a film version of Salvatore di Giacomo's 1909 play *Assunta Spina,* known outside of Italy as *Sangue Napolitano* (*Neapolitan Blood*). She played the lead in such successful films as *Il processo Clémenceau* (*The Clemenceau Trial,* Caesar Film, 1917) and *Il nodo* (*The Knot,* Caesar Film/ Bertini Film, 1921). Even in minor films, her acting and her impeccable costuming stand out – she was known to prefer Worth's in Paris as her dressmaker.[32]

Bertini's influence in the Italian film industry dwindled after World War I, for a number of reasons. Not only was the Italian film industry bankrupt and threatened by a dramatic increase in U.S. film imports, but Italian directors, like their counterparts in the U.S. and Germany, increasingly came to regard actors and actresses as raw material to be manipulated, rather than co-creators of their own films. Like Nielsen and many other star actresses who struggled to retain a foothold in an industry that increasingly relegated them to the far side of the camera at the end of the 1910s, Bertini founded her own production company, Bertini Film, in order to retain more creative control over her roles and their execution. Together with Caesar Films, Bertini Films produced such films as *La Lussuria* (*Luxury*, 1919), *La Piovra* (*The Octopus*, 1919), *La Contessa Sara* (*Countess Sara*, 1919), and *Mariute* (1918). The latter is a highly self-referential film, reminiscent of Nielsen's *Die Filmprimadonna,* that depicts Bertini herself at home and in the studio, 'first parodying herself with all of her star caprice, then establishing herself as a dramatic actress in a wartime drama to raise war bonds.'[33] Bertini also wrote at least one film scenario using the pseudonym Frank Bert,[34] and co-directed at least one more film, *La Tosca* in 1918. She was, allegedly, recruited by Fox Films in Hollywood in 1920,[35] but instead she married the Swiss banker Paul Cartier and largely retired from the screen. She appeared sporadically in films in the 1930s and 40s, however, and even allowed herself to be persuaded to appear in Bertolucci's *Novecento* (1900), filmed in 1976, and was the subject of the documentary *L'Ultima Diva* (*The Last Diva*; 1982), when she was ninety years old. She died in a grand hotel in Rome in 1985, at the age of ninety-three, receiving admirers and well wishers in a luxurious salon until the end.[36]

The Norwegian Entrepreneur: Aud Egede-Nissen

Although Norway was not as involved in the silent cinema market as its Nordic neighbours Denmark and Sweden, it was not because of any delayed appreciation for the cinematic spectacle. The first film exhibition in Norway took place just a few months after both the Lumière Brothers' public projection in Paris and Max and Emil Skladanowsky's presentation of Bioscop films at the Wintergarten in Berlin. The director of the Circus Varieté in Kristiania (as Oslo was known from 1624 to 1925) arranged to have the Skladanowsky brothers include their 'living pictures' in a performance on 7th April 1896, in Tivoli.[37] After several years of itinerant cinema exhibitions, the first permanent cinema was opened in Kristiania in November 1904. By 1915, Kristiania had twenty-one cinemas with a gross income of 1.2 million Norwegian crowns, which testifies to the popularity of the cinema as a popular urban entertainment in Norway at the time.[38]

Most of the films shown in Norway in the silent period were, however, French, Italian, Danish, British or American, while domestic production was very limited. This was due in large part to municipal control of local cinemas, which severely constrained the availability of production capital. Only seventeen feature films were made in Norway between 1906 and 1919, one of which was filmed in a Danish studio, and none at all were produced between 1913 and 1917. This state of affairs was, according to Gunnar Iversen, due to a 'combination of uncertainty about the role of films in Norway and the massive drain of creative talent' to Danish, Swedish and German cinema.[39] Under these circumstances, it is perhaps not surprising that Norway's greatest female pioneer of the silent film era, Aud Egede-Nissen, made only two films in her home country, both of them in the 1940s.

One of the radical Norwegian politician and mayor of Stavanger Adam Egede-Nissen's eleven children, Aud Egede-Nissen (1893–1974) came from a political family, but she and six of her siblings (four sisters and two brothers) chose to make a career of acting instead.[40] She began appearing in theatres in Trondheim in 1911 but soon joined her sister Gerd in Copenhagen in order to make the leap to film, under the auspices of Dania Biofilm. In Copenhagen, Egede-Nissen met director Bjørn Bjørnson, son of the celebrated Norwegian author Bjørnstjerne Bjørnson, and made her film debut in his 1913 film *Scenens børn* (*The Children of the Stage*). She followed Bjørnson to Berlin the next year, where she began working in the German film industry. She appeared in nearly twenty German films between 1914 and 1916,[41] including Otto Rippert's science-fiction serial *Homunculus* (1916), alongside the Danish actor Olaf Fønss, and *Das Phantom der Oper* (*Phantom of the Opera;* Ernst Matray, 1916).

Seeing an opportunity in Germany's economically isolated situation during World War I, which had disrupted the customary importation of films from France, Britain, and the U.S., Aud, together with her sisters Gerd and Ada and Aud's new husband, the German actor and director Georg Alexander, launched their own Berlin-based film production company, Egede-Nissen-Film Compagni GmbH, with Alexander as managing director.[42] With a Norwegian distribution arm called Egede Nissen Filmsbyraa A/S,[43] the German Egede-Nissen Film Company produced thirty feature films between 1917 and 1930, which starred the Egede-Nissen sisters in three different series (though never together) – the Ada van Ehlers series, starring Ada Egede-Nissen; the Gerd Nissen Meister-Cyklus, starring Gerd Egede-Nissen; and the Egede-Nissen series, starring Aud Egede-Nissen, who also produced all thirty films.[44] The combination of control over production and exclusive on-screen access to the Egede-Nissen actresses gave the new company an edge in a rapidly expanding domestic German film market, and allowed Aud Egede-Nissen to attain unprecedented influence in the industry. In a 1918 article in *Ukens revy,* the Norwegian journalist, Jonas Lie, Jr., son of the prominent author Jonas Lie, described the company as entirely controlled by 'die schöne Egede-Nissen' (the beautiful Egede-Nissen).[45] Unfortunately for modern audiences and scholars, all but one of the films she produced have been lost. The lone exception is *Erblich belastet* (*A Tainted Inheritance*; Georg Alexander), from either 1917 or 1919, which Iversen describes as both formulaic and innovative, particularly in terms of its exploration of stylistic expressivity.[46]

Facing the rise of the German film giant Universum Film AG, commonly known as UFA, and the consolidation of the German film industry in the wake of World War I, the Egede-Nissen film company ceased production in 1920. The two younger Egede-Nissen sisters abandoned both film and Germany, choosing to return to Norway in 1921, while Aud Egede-Nissen divorced Georg Alexander and married the Austrian actor Paul Richter in 1924, with whom she lived in Berlin until their divorce in 1931. She had a productive career as an actress in at least thirty-seven German films of the 1920s, including supporting roles in two Ernst Lubitsch films made in 1920: as Haidee in *Sumurun,* alongside Pola Negri, and as Jane Seymour in *Anna Boleyn,* starring Henny Porten. She also played Cara Carozza in Fritz Lang's *Dr. Mabuse, der Spieler* (*Dr. Mabuse, the Gambler*; 1922) and had major roles in Karl Grune's *Die Strasse* (*The Street*; 1923), F. W. Murnau's *Phantom* (1922) and *Die Austreibung* (*The Expulsion;* 1923). Like Asta Nielsen, she made one sound film in the early 1930s, *Zwischen Nacht und Morgen* (*Between Night and Dawn;* Gerhard Lamprecht, 1931), before turning her back on German film for the rest of her life and returning to Norway. She worked in the Norwegian theatre as a director for several decades, but she did appear in a supporting role in two Norwegian wartime films: *Hansen og Hansen* (Carsten Winger, 1941) and *Trysil-Knut* (Rasmus Breistein, 1942), and was reportedly involved with some small film projects as late as 1962.[47] She died in Oslo in in 1974 at the age of eighty-one.

The Versatile French Vamp: Musidora

Given that France was an early and dominant force in the European silent film industry, as well as in the international cinema market, it is surprising that there were relatively few female actresses/producers in the silent era in France. After the Lumière brothers' first public film screening in 1895, the cinema rapidly attained a position of importance in French society as both a popular form of entertainment and an economically significant industry, in which many women were involved in a variety of capacities, including the pioneering director/producer Alice Guy-Blaché. The number of cinemas in Paris increased dramatically, from only ten in 1906 to eighty-seven by the end of 1908.[48] Pathé, which had pioneered the vertical monopoly organisation, opened an American distribution office in 1904 and soon controlled a significant share of the U.S. market at the beginning of the twentieth century. In fact, Pathé was the largest single supplier of films for the American market in 1908.[49] This trend was, however, reversed in the decade following World War I, when American films began flooding European markets. Charles Drazin explains that in 1910, about 60% of all films distributed worldwide were made in France, but by 1920, French film companies controlled just 10% of the domestic French market.[50] While France had been forced to cut back on film production during the war, the American film industry had integrated itself vertically, controlling all aspects of production and distribution to an unprecedented degree. As Asta Nielsen experienced in Germany, the trend toward rigid compartmentalisation of tasks within the industry made it much more difficult for actresses to make the leap to directing and producing, or vice versa.

There are exceptions to every rule, however, and one of the French women who bridged the on-screen/off-screen gap most successfully in the silent film era was the actress Jeanne Roques (1889–1957), best known by her stage name Musidora. From performing in revues at music halls and cabarets, such as the Folies Bergère and La Cigale,[51] she went on to act in more than fifty films between 1914 and 1926. Her first film was *Les Misères de l'Aiguille* (*The Miseries of the Needle*; Raphäel Clamour, 1914), but her most famous roles were the product of her collaboration with French director Louis Feuillade on the serial crime films *Les vampires* (*The Vampires*; 1915–16) and *Judex* (1917). Her performance, particularly as the black silk bodysuit-clad Irma Vep in the former, established her as a *femme fatale* or 'vamp', whose exotic, dark sensuality contrasted with the 'virginal' blond appeal of heroines such as Pearl White in the American serial *The Perils of Pauline* (Louis Gasnier, 1914). Even more important in terms of her pioneering contributions to cinema, however, is Musidora's absolute centrality to the film's project and narrative. Far from being simply decorative or sexually objectified, Musidora's character is simultaneously an object of desire and the uncanny double of the master criminal, Fantômas. Vicki Callahan argues that

> Musidora's centrality to these [Feuillade's] films is due not only to her placement in the literal center of the films (she's the one unambiguous force of evil across two of Feuillade's most popular serials) but also to the relentless efforts, through a multiplicity of strategies, to contain her threat... Both of the two serials that feature Musidora end with her death. But in each instance, there is something that eludes the control of male authority. Beyond her star persona and thematic control of the films, the image of Musidora represents another layer of resistance to social and cultural order.[52]

Although Musidora was not involved in the production of these films, both the actress herself and her powerful female characters were integral to their narratives and aesthetics in fundamental ways.

While the political changes that took place across Europe in the wake of World War I had a disruptive effect on many aspects of the European silent film industry, they also provided an opportunity for some people, including both Aud Egede-Nissen and Musidora, to attain greater influence and commercial success in the film industry. With Feuillade as her mentor, Musidora became increasingly involved in other, off-screen aspects of filmmaking toward the end of World War I. Between 1916 and 1926, she wrote, adapted, directed and/or produced nearly a dozen films. It can be quite difficult to determine exactly what Musidora's involvement with each film was, since she almost always acted in her own films and often worked with a co-director. For her first directorial attempt, which does not seem to have ever been released, she collaborated with the novelist Colette in 1916 on a screenplay adaptation of the latter's novel, *Minne* (1904). Her breakthrough film as a producer was *La Vagabonde* (*The Vagabond*; 1918), for which Colette wrote the scenario. Musidora adapted it together with director Eugenio Perego and played the leading role.[53] In 1919, she starred in *Vincenta,* for which she also wrote the screenplay. Although she was initially only credited in them as an actress, she later claimed to have co-directed three films that had been produced by her company Société des Films Musidora, established in 1918: *La flamme cachée* (*The Hidden Flame*; Roger Lion, 1918), which involved another collaboration with Colette on the script; *Pour Don Carlos* (1921); and *Soleil et Ombre* (*Sun and Shadow*; 1922), both co-directed with Jacques Lasseyne.[54] She filmed and starred in another of her own screenplays, *La Terre des Taureaux*/*La Tierra de los Toros* (*The Land of the Bulls*), with Antonio Cañero in 1924 on location in Spain, where she lived in the early 1920s, as well as *Le Berceau de Dieu* (*The Sheep of God*; 1926). The last film she directed, *La Magique Image* (*The Magical Image;* 1950), made after nearly a quarter-century absence from the film industry, featured a compilation of clips from her early films.

Musidora was not, however, widely recognised as a screen-writer, director and producer, roles which she herself downplayed until relatively late in life. Annette Förster suggests that Musidora's 'reluctance to claim the screenwriting and directorial credits on her own productions may … be partly explained by her status as a film star and a revue celebrity. From the point of view of publicity her fame as an actress was a bigger asset than her name as a director or a producer.'[59] Förster also suggests that an alternative reason that Musidora chose to foreground the better-known names of the literary authors, in particular Colette, on whose works several of her films were based, was as a marketing strategy. Her films do not appear to have been commercially successful, however, despite generally positive press reviews. In a 1946 interview with Renée Sylvaire,

Musidora complained that she lost money on all of the films she produced, due to the unfavourable terms of her contract.[60] Musidora retired from the screen in 1926, turning her attention back to the stage, as well as to journalism, fiction, and poetry. From 1946 until her death in Paris in 1957, she occasionally worked at the ticket booth of the Cinémathéque Française, thereby mastering yet another facet of the film industry.[55]

Conclusion

The many unique stories of women's contributions to European silent cinema have only just begun to be told. The goal of this chapter has been to illustrate several representative cases of how individual women were able to involve themselves in many different aspects of filmmaking during the silent film era in Europe, despite widely varying national contexts, shifting socio-cultural mores and the devastating impact of global events like World War I. Both on- and off-screen, creative, ambitious, talented women like Asta Nielsen, Francesca Bertini, Aud Egede-Nissen and Musidora played a vitally important role in silent film's maturation into an artistically refined, economically significant component of global culture. The ravages of time, war and weather on fragile nitrate prints have combined with the ever-increasing speed and volume of cultural production in the twentieth and twenty-first centuries to render many of the women pioneers of the cinema virtually invisible and largely forgotten, but their individual histories are just as worthy of restoration as the images of their bodies on film.

Author Biography: Julie K. Allen

Julie is the Paul and Renate Madsen Professor of Danish at the University of Wisconsin-Madison in the United States, where she has taught since 2006. She received her PhD in Germanic Languages and Literatures from Harvard University in 2005. Her primary research interests deal with the dissemination of models of national and cultural identity, primarily in Germany and Denmark, through film, literature and popular culture. She is the author of *Icons of Danish Modernity: Georg Brandes and Asta Nielsen* (2010) and *Danish but not*

Lutheran: The Impact of Mormonism on Danish Cultural Identity, 1850–1915 (2016). In addition to her work on European silent film, she has published on topics including Danish-American autobiography, the stories of Hans Christian Andersen, and the philosopher Søren Kierkegaard. She is also the editor of *The Bridge,* journal of the Danish American Heritage Society.

Endnotes

1. Robinson, David. *World Cinema: A Short History* 2nd edition. London, Eyre Methuen, 1981, 1.

2. Pearson, Roberta. 'Transitional Cinema', *The Oxford History of World Cinema.* Geoffrey Nowell-Smith, Ed. Oxford, Oxford University Press, 1996, 23.

3. Pearson. 'Transitional Cinema'. 24.

4. Robinson. *World Cinema.* 29.

5. Drazin, Charles. *French Cinema.* New York, Faber and Faber, Inc., 2011, 3.

6. Katz, Ephraim. *The Film Encyclopedia* 3rd edition. Revised by Fred Klein and Ronald Dean Nolen. New York, Harper Perennial, 1998, 575.

7. Guy-Blaché, Alice. *Autobiographie d'une pionnière du cinema, 1873–1968.* Paris, Denoël/Gonthier, 1976.

8. Abel, Richard. *The Red Rooster Scare: Making Cinema American 1900–1910.* Berkeley, UC Press, 1999, 150.

9. Slide, Anthony. *Early Women Directors.* New York, A.S. Barnes, 1977, 9.

10. Jelavich, Peter. '"Am I Allowed to Amuse Myself Here?" The German Bourgeoisie Confronts Early Film', *Germany at the Fin de Siècle. Culture, Politics, and Ideas.* Suzanne Marchand and David Lindenfeld, Eds. Baton Rouge, Louisiana State University Press, 2004, 235.

11. Garncarz, Joseph. 'Art and Industry. German cinema of the 1920s', *The Silent Cinema Reader.* Lee Grieveson and Peter Krämer, Eds. London, Routledge, 2004, 390.

12. Hansert, Andreas. *Asta Nielsen und die Filmstadt Babelsberg, Das Engagement Carl Schleussners in der Deutschen Filmindustrie.* Petersburg, Germany, Michael Imhof Verlag, 2007, 48.

13. Schlüpmann, Heide. '27th May 1911: Asta Nielsen Secures Unprecedented Artistic Control', *A New History of German Cinema.* Jennifer M. Kapczynski and Michael D. Richardson, Eds. Rochester, NY, Camden House, 2012, 47.

14. Schroeder, Stephan Michael. 'Und Urban Gad? Zur Frage der Autorschaft in den Filmen bis 1914', *Unmögliche Liebe. Asta Nielsen, ihr Kino.* Heide Schlüpmann et. al., Eds. Vienna, Verlag Filmarchiv Austria, 2009, 194–210.

15. Engberg, Marguerite. *Asta Nielsen.* Copenhagen, 1966.

16. Schlüpmann. '27th May 1911'. 45.

17. Schlüpmann. '27th May 1911'. 48.

18. Vacche, Angela Dalle. 'The Diva-Film: Context, Actresses, Issues', *Italian Silent Cinema: A Reader.* Giorgio Bertellini, Ed. New Barnet, U.K., John Libbey Publishing, 2013, 188.

19. Dalle Vacche. 'The Diva-Film'. 186.

20. Dalle Vacche. 'The Diva-Film'. 187.

21. Dalle Vacche. 'The Diva-Film'. 188.

22. Dalle Vacche. 'The Diva-Film'. 187.

23. Dalle Vacche. 'The Diva-Film'. 186.

SILENT WOMEN

24. Naretto, Césare. 'Francesca Bertini', *Il maggese cinematografico* 2, nr. 30th December 1914. 10. Qtd. in Francesco Pitassio, 'Famous Actors, Famous Actresses: Notes on Acting Style in Italian Silent Films,' *Italian Silent Cinema: A Reader,* ed. by Giorgio Bertellini (New Barnet, U.K.: John Libbey Publishing, 2013), 258.

25. Vacche, Dalle. 'The Diva-Film'. 192.

26. Jacobs, Lea. 'Naturalism and the Diva: Francesca Bertini in *Assunta Spina*,' http://uwfilmies.pbworks.com/w/page/4660017/Bertini

26. Jacobs. 'Naturalism'.

27. Jacobs. 'Naturalism'.

28. Pitassio, Francesco. 'Famous Actors, Famous Actresses: Notes on Acting Style in Italian Silent Films', *Italian Silent Cinema: A Reader*. Giorgio Bertellini, Ed. New Barnet, U.K., John Libbey Publishing, 2013, 258.

29. Vacche, Dalle. 'The Diva-Film'. 191.

30. Vacche, Dalle. 'The Diva-Film'. 1.

31. Blom, Ivo. 'All the Same or Strategies of Difference: Early Italian Comedy in International Perspective', *Italian Silent Cinema: A Reader*. Giorgio Bertellini, Ed. New Barnet, U.K., John Libbey Publishing, 2013, 181.

32. Vacche, Dalle. 'The Diva-Film'. 190.

33. Katz. *Film Dictionary*. 125.

34. Böhm Volker. 'Francesca Bertini'. http://www.imdb.com/name/nm0078116/bio?ref_=nm_ov_bio_sm

35. Evensmo, Sigurd. *Det store Tivoli. Film og kino i Norge* 2nd edition. Oslo, Gyldendal Norsk Forlag, 1992, 9.

36. Evensmo. *Tivoli*. 112.

37. Iversen, Gunnar. 'Sisters of Cinema: Three Norwegian Actors and their German Film Company, 1917–1920', *Nordic Explorations: Film Before 1930*. John Fullerton and Jan Olsson, Eds. Stockholm Studies in Cinema. Sydney, Australia, John Libbey & Co., 1999, 94.

38. Svendsen, Trond Olav. 'Aud Richter', *Norsk biografisk leksikon*. 13th February, 2009. https://nbl.snl.no/Aud_Richter

39. Iversen. 'Sisters'. 94.

40. Qtd. in Iversen. 'Sisters'. 98. Original source: Jonas Lie, Jr. 'Aud Egede Nissen – Norsk Kunstnerliv i Berlin II, *Ukens revy*. 1918.

41. Iversen. 'Sisters'. 99.

42. Iversen. 'Sisters'. 100.

43. Peason. 'Transitional Cinema'. 27.

44. Vasey. 'Spread'. 53.

45. Drazin. *French Cinema*. 29.

46. Förster, Annette. 'Musidora', Women Film Pioneers Project, Center for Digital Research and Scholarship. Jane Gaines, Radha Vatsal, and Monica Dall'Asta, Eds. New York, Columbia University Libraries, 2013. Web. https://wfpp.cdrs.columbia.edu/pioneer/ccp-musidora

47. Callahan, Vicki. *Zones of Anxiety: Movement, Musidora, and the Crime Serials of Louis Feuillade*. Detroit, Wayne State University Press, 2005, 44.

48. Felando, Cynthia. 'Musidora Biography'. http://www.filmdirectorssite.com/musidora

49. Förster. 'Musidora'.

50. Förster. 'Musidora'.

51. Förster. 'Musidora'.

52. Katz. *Film Encyclopedia*. 995.

6. FEMALE LEGENDS OF THE SILVER SCREEN

Melody Bridges

While the comic mastery of Charlie Chaplin is still much appreciated on-screen by modern audiences, few of the screen goddesses of the silent era have passed into popular culture as household names.

However, the influence of the female legends of the silent screen on the development of cinema is both significant and long lasting. They not only discovered how to mesmerise audiences with their luminous acting but also how to enthrall men and women with their erotic sexual magnetism. It was the attraction of these motion picture idols that sold millions of cinema tickets internationally and enabled the motion picture industry to grow into the successful multinational business that it has become today. Fan clubs developed as the appetite to know as much as possible about their favourite stars became insatiable. The costumes worn by the actors influenced fashion as the fans sought to emulate their idols. Trends in hair and make-up too were often sparked by a star's 'look'. Newspapers and magazines soon employed women to write about fashion, review films or relate celebrity gossip to sell copies to this new community of movie-goers. Cinema took over from the music halls and theatres as the main platform for popular culture and reflected how technology was shaping the modern world.

In this chapter, we rediscover some of the fascinating

female legends from both the silent movie era and the early days of the 'talkies'.

Legendary Lillian Gish (1893–1993)

Lillian Gish is credited by many as one of the greatest actors of the silent film era. Born on 14th October 1893 she was a stage performer and friend of Gladys Smith (later renamed Mary Pickford) who introduced Lillian and her sister Dorothy to director D. W. Griffith in New York. Lillian and her sister appeared in their first film, *An Unseen Enemy*, in 1912 and Lillian continued to work as an actress for eighty-five years until her final film, *The Whales of August*, in 1987 (also starring Bette Davis and Vincent Price).

Her waif-like performance on-screen evoked a sense of fragility and vulnerability which led her to be described by author Ally Acker as 'D. W. Griffith's virginal, ethereal muse'.

Her powerful intensity on-screen made her the pre-eminent actress of the silent era, appearing in Griffith's classic film *Broken Blossoms* (1919), she expressed terror as her drunken father breaks open the door to the closet in which she is hiding. Breaking with traditional acting styles, she gave nuanced performances in *Birth of a Nation* (1915) and *Intolerance* (1916) and a brilliant performance in the popular melodrama *Way Down East* (1920). During World War I, Griffith went to Europe to make propaganda films, and Gish followed. Henry Sartov, who was a photographer on Griffith's *Hearts of the World* (1918) and later became a cinematographer, invented a special lens to film Lillian Gish in soft focus.

Gish also directed her sister Dorothy in a 1920 movie, *Remodelling her Husband*, but this was a solo project and she did not direct again. She did act as a producer, investing her own money in two successful films which were made in Italy – *The White Sister* (1923) and *Romola* (1924).

She was a consummate actress who joined MGM in 1924 inking a contract which paid her $1 million for six films. She successfully transitioned to sound films in the 1930 talkie *One*

Romantic Night but the fashion for vamps and sexy harlots was at odds with Gish's image as the long-suffering child-like heroine. She returned to the stage in the 1930s then worked on radio and television.

She received an honorary Academy Award in 1971 and a lifetime achievement award from the American Film Institute in 1984. She also received the D.W. Griffith Lifetime Achievement Award and is regarded as a true pioneer of cinema.

'It Girl' Clara Bow (1905–1965)

The word 'legend' seems too small to encompass someone who meant so much to so many. Clara Bow's name alone was enough to sell out movie theatres and she received mountains of fan mail during both her silent screen and talking movie career. Born in Brookyln, New York on 29th July 1905 she had a terrible family life with two siblings dying young, an abusive father and a mother who was psychologically unwell. The story goes that Bow would sneak out to the cinema to seek refuge from her unhappy home. She dropped out of school and won a beauty contest before winning a small part in her first film, *Beyond the Rainbow* (1922) – although her part was later cut. She continued to find movie work in New York and then in Los Angeles in films such as *Down to the Sea in Ships* (1922) and *Dancing Mothers* (1926) but it was really with her 1927 movie *It* that she became the famous 'It' girl. She called herself 'The real jazz girl' and was well known for her vivacious energy and stunning looks. She was a style icon – with women across the country copying her look and wanting to emulate her glamour. Producer B. P. Schulberg promoted her as 'the hottest jazz baby on film' and her star looked set in the ascendent. But studio bosses kept lending her money to gamble and she fell into heavy debt. The one person whom she trusted to keep her finances straight – secretary Daisy DeVoe – was convicted of theft for stealing from Bow in 1931. (Although it must be stated that later academics, including Hans Sherrer, have stated that this conviction was wrongful). The scandalous trial that brought Bow and DeVoe to the courtrooms rocked Hollywood and sent newspaper sales out of control. The vivid, energetic fun-loving girl that the public had fallen in love with was now dragged through the gutter. The public heard sordid secrets from Clara Bow's private life – including gambling, drinking and numerous lovers. This ruined her reputation and even though she tried to make a comeback, she ended up retiring from the screen at the age of twenty-eight. Clara Bow said: 'I've had enough. A sex symbol is a heavy load to handle when you're tired, hurt and bewildered.' The toll of working hard for so long, to make so many films, had worn her out and she suffered the first of many breakdowns.

The famous actress Louise Brooks stated, in this fascinating documentary – *Silent Hollywood Clara Bow 'The It Girl'* that of course Clara Bow had a breakdown when the movie studios didn't want her any more:

> (She) didn't' really exist; she didn't exist off the screen. She manufactured this whole person.

Louise Brooks: From stage dancer to Cabaret (1906–1985)

In the public consciousness – if you've heard of her at all – you may connect Louise Brooks with the bobbed haircut that she made so famous. This wonderful 'flapper' look is central to our concept of 1920s fashion – and Brooks was the woman that made this so. Born on 14th November 1906 as Mary Louise Brooks, she became a dancer and then an actress. She is most well known as playing the lead in three feature films, *Pandora's Box* (1929), *Diary of a Lost Girl* (1929) and *Prix de Beauté* (1930). She worked her way up from chorus girl to dancer in the Ziegfeld Follies, a lavish revue produced on Broadway. She gained a five-year contract with Paramount Pictures where she came to the attention of Charlie Chaplin (with whom she had an affair). She mixed with the rich and famous of the time, and was lucky enough to be a guest at San Simeon – the castle-like mansion owned by newspaper magnate William Randolph

Hearst. After Paramount denied her an expected raise, she left Hollywood behind and worked in Europe making the films for which she is best known. The legendary role of 'Lulu' in the movie, *Pandora's Box* was perhaps infamous due to its frank exploration of sexual desire and included the first on-screen lesbian kiss. Returning to the U.S. she discovered that she was blacklisted by Hollywood and broke. She became a 'shop girl' at Saks department store in Fifth Avenue and had a number of dalliances with wealthy men. Some view this as a tragic end to a too-short screen career. She retired in 1933 – after making seventeen silent films and eight 'talkies' – but she was 'rediscovered' in the 1970s and made a number of brilliant appearances in documentaries relating tales of the early days of cinema, which can be viewed on the internet. She is less well known – although some argue that she should be more so – as an author. Her legendary 'look' lives on in the celebrated 1972 film *Cabaret*:

> I went to my father [film director Vincente Minnelli], and asked him, what can you tell me about thirties glamour? Should I be emulating Marlene Dietrich or something? And he said no, I should study everything I can about Louise Brooks. – *Liza Minnelli, Inside the Actors Studio*, on preparing for the role of 'Sally Bowles' in *Cabaret*

Mary Pickford: 'America's Sweetheart' (1892–1979)

Pickford was born in 1892 in Toronto, Ontario, Canada as Gladys Mary Smith. Perhaps best known for her golden ringlets and innocent smile, these masked a brilliant mind and sharp wit. An early break – at the age of seven – found her onstage in Toronto and subsequently her siblings and mother started touring too. As a teenager she made her debut in a Broadway play called The *Warrens of Virginia* before being talent-spotted by D. W. Griffith (for the Biograph company) who immediately offered to pay her double the going rate that other actors were being paid. He later said of her:

The thing that most attracted me the day I first saw her
was the intelligence that shone in her face.

By 1909, she was working with D. W. Griffith on dozens of
short films before following him to California where the film
industry was developing. Some of her best performances
were in his films, such as *Friends*, *The Mender of Nets*, *Just Like a
Woman*, and *The Female of the Species* (all released in 1912). The
first issue of *Photoplay* magazine (1912) featured twenty-year-
old Mary dressed as Little Red Riding Hood and she often
played the roles of girls or teenagers in films such as *The Little
Princess* (1917), *Rebecca of Sunnybrook Farm* (1917) and *Poor Little
Rich Girl* (1917), adapted by her friend Frances Marion.

By the age of twenty-four, she was earning around a million
dollars a year and few studios wanted to pay her the huge fees
she demanded. She joined with D. W. Griffith, Charlie Chaplin
and Douglas Fairbanks to form the United Artists production
company in 1919. The studios were opposed to the idea,
commenting that 'The inmates have taken over the asylum'.

Divorcing husband Owen Moore, she married Douglas
Fairbanks in 1920. The new couple became even more popular
and the media treated them as Hollywood royalty. Pickford
successfully made the transition to sound movies and won a
Best Actress Academy Award for her first 'talkie,' *Coquette* in
1929, in the role of the flirtatious Norma Besant.

Seeking more control over her work, Pickford had become
a creative producer at an early age, initially with Famous
Players-Lasky Studios (later Paramount Pictures), then as a
board member of United Artists. Following her final film as
an actress, *Secrets* (1933), she continued to work until 1950
as a producer on many films such as *Sleep My Love* (1948)
directed by Douglas Sirk. She also helped found the Society of
Independent Motion Picture Producers in 1941.

Pickford was an early advocate of archiving and film
preservation and a founder of the Academy of Motion Picture
Arts and Sciences. Throughout her life, she devoted her time and

energy to many charities. She received an honorary Academy Award for her contribution to motion pictures in 1976.

Olive Thomas: the first Hollywood hell-raiser (1894–1920)

A number of scandals rocked Hollywood in the 1920s and one of the first of these was the mysterious death of Olive Thomas, which took place while she was staying in Paris. A beautiful and accomplished actress and writer, Thomas was found naked and dead on 10th September 1920 in the Ritz Hotel in Paris. The scandalised rumour-mongers mused: Did she commit suicide or was she murdered by her husband? After a dizzying ascent from shop-girl to Ziegfeld's Follies, to Selznick studios, her career seemed unstoppable. Her appearance in the 1920 movie, *The Flapper* seemed only to assure her new status as a star. With the news of her sad death at the age of only twenty-five the newspapers had a field day. Her death was used as a cautionary tale, a warning of the decadence of Hollywood.

A year later, in 1921, another young starlet by the name of Virginia Rappe died mysteriously at a three-day drinking party in San Francisco. Comedy legend Roscoe 'Fatty' Arbuckle, who had recently signed a contract with Paramount for $1 million, was charged with rape and murder but over the course of three trials he was subsequently acquitted. The 'Arbuckle' case was said by William Hearst to have sold more newspapers than the sinking of the Lusitania in 1915. By 1930, with continuing scandals rocking Hollywood, Motion Picture producers and distributors agreed to censor and control the moral content of films. They outlawed nudity, rape, profanity and obscenity as well as forbidding mixed race relationships or anything that glorified criminal actions to be shown on-screen. This became known as the 'Hays Production Code.' Today Olive Thomas is a footnote in the Hollywood story, and her tragedy serves as an emblem of the many ruined lives of those caught up in the Hollywood dream.

The Sapphic Circle: Garbo, Dietrich and Mercedes

What's fascinating about these scandals and the introduction of the Hays Production Code in the 1930s is that in the earlier days of cinema, films were much more permissive and liberal than we might imagine. There were films that explored sexual orientation, cross dressing, birth control, abortion and even nudity.

Several major Hollywood players – Marlene Dietrich, Tallulah Bankhead, Greta Garbo included – were involved in unconventional relationships which we now understand as lesbian or bisexual. Born on 18th September 1905, Greta Lovisa Gustafsson left Sweden behind her and become an international star in Hollywood under the name Greta Garbo. Nominated three times for Academy Awards, and winning numerous accolades in her own lifetime she was star spotted by Louis B. Mayer (chief executive of MGM) in 1925 and flew out to Hollywood straight away. She made twenty-eight films in the U.S. between 1926 and 1941, after which she retired early at the age of thirty-five. Whilst many actresses were left behind with the advent of sound in movies, the marketers made a celebration of her first film with dialogue – the 1930 film *Anna Christie*. 'Garbo talks' became the phrase of the day. She revelled in parties, glamour and a decadent lifestyle,

> The thing I like best about Hollywood is that here is one place in the world where you can live as you live and nobody will say anything about it, no matter what you do!

In Diana McLellan's book *The Girls* (2000) she carefully lays out the case for a love affair between Dietrich and Garbo. For decades they denied any knowledge of each other, let alone an affair, but there was evidence that they both appeared in the 1925 silent film, *The Joyless Street*. Despite sharing well known lovers – such as the intriguing writer Mercedes de Acosta (whose glamorous life deserves its own screenplay) – they kept each other at a professional distance.

German-born Marlene Dietrich (1901–1992) had minor

roles in seventeen films before she became a huge name after her turn as Lola-Lola in the German/American co-production *The Blue Angel* (1930). The film was directed by Josef von Sternberg and it led to Dietrich gaining a contract with Paramount Pictures and becoming one of Hollywood's highest earning stars. She had worked extensively in theatre before her cinematic breakthrough. The song she performed in *The Blue Angel* 'Falling in Love Again' became synonymous with Dietrich for the rest of her life. She worked with von Sternberg on several other movies, in which he used 'butterfly lighting' to enhance her performance and establish her character as a new kind of sex symbol – the *femme fatale*. The most successful of these films was *Shanghai Express* (1932). Dietrich seemed comfortable dressing in men's attire; her fantastic top hat and tails performance in the movie *Morocco* (1930) for which she was nominated for an Academy Award, has inspired female stars to wear men's clothing ever since (including Katharine Hepburn and Diane Keaton). Her appearance as the lesbian Swedish monarch in the title role of *Queen Christina* only added to her stardom. 'I have no intention of dying an old maid, on the contrary, I shall die a bachelor!' (line from the movie). Although her singing ability was limited, her voicing and phrasing compensated for it. Her 'exotic' looks and glamorous persona made up for any shortcomings she had as an actress and she was one of the first stars to manipulate her image by continually re-inventing herself. Pitted against each other by their rival studios (Garbo – MGM, and Dietrich – Paramount) their stories inevitably became interwoven and their legendary style, poise and glamour were the envy of the world.

Dietrich's contract with Paramount was cancelled in 1937 following a number of flops. She entertained the troops as a singer during the war and then revived her career, performing in numerous movies, with directors such as Billy Wilder and Alfred Hitchcock, as well as singing internationally. She was nominated for a Golden Globe Award for the film *Witness for the Prosecution* (1958). Her last film was *Just a Gigolo* (1978). France gave Dietrich the Legion d'Honneur in 1950 and she was honoured on a German postage stamp in 1997. In 1999, belatedly, the American Film Institute included her in the top ten female film stars of classic Hollywood cinema.

Reputedly a 'friend' to both of these stars, Tallulah Bankhead (1902–1968) was a larger than life personality and noted wit. She was famous for parties where 'anything goes' – where it was said that she performed a cartwheel in a skirt, whilst wearing no underwear, and offered canapés in the nude. She became a successful star on the London stage for eight years before she landed a contract with Paramount Pictures earning her $50,000 per film. Her first few films did badly at the box office and she disliked living in Hollywood. Her promiscuity and wild parties were notorious and she gave a frank interview to *Motion Picture* magazine in 1932, saying:

> I'm serious about love… I haven't had an affair for six
> months… If there's anything the matter with me now,
> it's not Hollywood or Hollywood's state of mind … the
> matter with me is – I want a man! Six months is a long,
> long while. I want a man!

Bankhead fell foul of Hollywood's new conservatism with these candid remarks and earned the disapproval of Will Hays. She was known to be sexually attracted to both men and women and enjoyed drinking and partying which lead to her eventual demise.

Her 1932 film, *Devil and the Deep* is notable not just as a classic film starring Gary Cooper, Charles Laughton and Cary Grant, but also because her name was given star billing over all of theirs. She made one more film called *Faithless* (1932) which flopped before returning to the New York stage. A brief marriage with actor John Emery followed. She finally achieved success in Lillian Hellman's play *The Little Foxes* in 1939 but fell out with Hellman over political affiliations.

It was not until 1943 that she returned to films in what

became her best known role as Constance Porter in Hitchcock's 1944 film *Lifeboat*. When collecting her New York Film Critics Circle Award for the film, she acknowledged the audience with a smile, 'Dahlings, I was wonderful!'

I'm No Angel: Mae West (1893–1980)

Like many an enterprising actress, when Mae West couldn't find suitable parts, she decided to write her own plays under the name Jane Mast. Her first starring role was in a Broadway play that she had written, directed and produced. The play, entitled *Sex* caused quite a scandal in 1926, and perhaps not surprisingly, did well at the box office. West was arrested and accused of 'corrupting the morals of youth' and sentenced to a brief time in jail. The ensuing publicity helped her career, and later she quipped that she was a great believer in censorship: 'I made a fortune out of it.' Undeterred, her next play was called *Drag*, exploring homosexuality, but this too was banned.

Mae West should be celebrated, not only as a performer, but also as an incredible writer – as her plays, *The Wicked Age*, *Pleasure Man* and *The Constant Sinner* were well received and always drew controversy. Packed houses were filled with eager audiences enjoying her stage persona, risqué lines and double-entendres. Nowhere was this more true than in West's 1928 play, *Diamond Lil* which became a huge Broadway hit. Not only did this cement her popularity but she would return to this character throughout her long career.

At the age of thirty-eight, Hollywood came knocking, in the form of a contract with Paramount Pictures and she took it by storm, playing the sexy harlot character she had become famous for, notably in the 1933 film *She Done Him Wrong*.

West is credited with talent spotting Cary Grant – yelling to a director, 'If he can talk, I'll take him!' – and immensely improving the script of any film she was working on. One of her biggest successes was the 1933 movie *I'm No Angel* which she also wrote. Her wise-cracking dialogue and saucy double-entendres, made her a household name.

Extract from *I'm No Angel* (1933, Paramount Pictures):

JACK (played by Cary Grant): You were wonderful tonight.

TIRA (played by West): Yeah, I'm always wonderful at night.

JACK: Tonight you were especially good.

TIRA: Well, when I'm good, I'm very good. But when I'm bad, I'm better.

However, it wasn't long before West's scripts fell foul of the Hays Production Code and from 1934 they were heavily censored. West also suffered from adverse press and media, with William Randolph Hearst refusing to carry any adverts or reviews in his newspapers or magazines for her film *Klondike Annie* (1936) about a woman accused of murder switching identities with a missionary sister. Despite this, and suffering a ban in Georgia, the film was popular at the box office.

As her film career waned, West returned to the stage and later, found success on television. Her later films *Myra Breckinridge* (1970) and *Sextette* (1978) found an audience on the cult film circuit where Mae West is still celebrated as the 'queen of camp.'

Conclusion

Look to the actors – Hamlet (Shakespeare, Act 2, Scene 2) tells us for they are the 'abstract and brief chronicles of the time'. This chapter gives us insight not only into the lives of these pioneering female performers but also of the times in which they lived and the challenges they had to face. Reading this book, we hope that you will go on to enjoy some of the great performances which the silent films and early 'talkies' offer.

Ever since the dawn of cinema, women have sought to express themselves in a wide variety of roles from courtesans to queens, to avoid being stereotyped as the loyal wives, devoted mothers and whores with a heart of gold which have littered so many scripts. Films made in the silent movie era featured women in a wide variety of roles – from child-like heroines, to adventurous risk-takers. The 'talkies' featured sassy, wise-cracking independent women and sexy *femmes fatales*. During the 1930s, there was an attempt to rein in the kind of roles that women could play and to cover up female flesh on-screen. This kind of censorship hampered the open expression of women's stories. Paradoxically, although the films now had sound, the ability of women, such as Mae West, to speak out in their films, was increasingly limited.

In 1924 *Variety* stated:

> …Clara Bow lingers in the eye, long after the picture has gone.

However, in the public's consciousness today, names such as Clara Bow, Lillian Gish and Mary Pickford have faded. Sometimes their films have been lost, their work has been uncredited, and their lasting contribution to cinema history has been ignored.

The studio system created female stars to help feed the demand for celebrity news and pictures by the fan magazines of the day. They expected their stars to emulate their carefully manufactured screen goddess images in public. But the media images were often at odds with the performers themselves, and the pressure of keeping up the pretense, and trying to win box office success, drove many of them to alcohol, drugs and suicide.

Today, we are better able to understand that the many pressures on performers in the fickle entertainment industry can be too much to bear. There have been so many (too many) tragic early deaths as evidence of this: Marilyn Monroe, James Dean, Judy Garland, and more recently Heath Ledger and Philip Seymour Hoffman.

The women who starred in the silent age of cinema and the early days of the 'talkies' not only gave brave, original performances which broke new ground as actors, they helped to build the motion picture industry by winning fans and selling tickets. Many pushed the boundaries by depicting women's sexual desire in their erotic portrayals of *femmes fatales*, vamps and adulteresses. Others challenged the system, set up their own studios or wrote their own material in an effort to play more interesting roles.

Today, with more than a century of cinematic history to draw on, it is shocking to report that the representation of women on-screen is as unequal as ever. The Geena Davis Institute on Gender in Media has reported that in a study of crowd scenes in films, women only feature 17% of the time despite making up 51% of the population. Only one in five screen roles are written for women. As Jennifer Lawrence, the star of *The Hunger Games* Trilogy has recently commented, movie actresses are still fighting for equal pay, and equal billing with their co-stars. There are signs of hope with complex characters on TV such as Olivia Benson in *Law and Order: Special Victims Unit* and on film with exciting heroines like Beatrice Prior in the *Divergent* Series and Charlize Theron as Furiosa in *Mad Max: Fury Road*. Charlize Theron said of the film:

> George [Miller] just showed the truth of who we are as women, and that's even more powerful. Women thrive in being many things. We can be just as dark and light as men. We're more than just nurturers, more than just breeders, we're just as conflicted. (*Guardian*, May 15, 2015)

But there is still a paucity of interesting roles for women over thirty-five to play, and few films are being made which have central female characters. Movie star George Clooney has suggested one remedy is to cast women in parts written originally for men and as an example of this, Sandra Bullock is playing a role which was originally written for Clooney in the political drama *Our Brand is Crisis* by David Gordon Green. Meryl Streep has launched a programme for women screenwriters to help remedy the lack of decent roles for women. All too often there is only one role in a film for a woman and that's as the male protagonist's love interest. We look forward to a time when sassy, complex, sexy women characters are no longer a novelty but a mainstay of cinema today – and we remember the intensity and wit of the great female screen legends who once graced the cinema screens and captured our hearts and minds.

Author Biography: Melody Bridges

Melody is an award winning writer-director with over fifteen years' experience in theatre, television and film. She has directed numerous television series and stage shows, and has written for both stage and screen. Bridges lectures regularly on Women in Media, and supports emerging writers and creatives through a number of initiatives including running an annual arts festival in Sussex. You can find out more about her here:

www.melodybridges.com

Further research:

On Lillian Gish:

Gish, Lillian and Ann Pinchot. *Lillian Gish: The Movies, Mr. Griffith, and Me.* Englewood Cliffs, Prentice-Hall, 1969.

Gish, Lillian. 'In Defense of the Silent Film.' *Revolt of the Arts.* Oliver M. Sayler, Ed. New York, Bretano's, 1930. 225–30.

Acker, Ally. *Reel Women: Pioneers of the Cinema, 1896 to the Present.* New York, Continuum, 1991.

On Clara Bow:

Stenn, David. *Clara Bow: Runnin' Wild.* Cooper Square Press, NY, 2000.

Quote from review of *Grit, Variety,* 29th February 1924.

On Louise Brooks:

http://www.pandorasbox.com/#

On Olive Thomas:

http://www.silentsaregolden.com/articles/lpolivethomasdeath.html

References:

http://www.post-gazette.com/life/lifestyle/2010/09/26/Olive-Thomas-the-original-Flapper-and-a-Mon-Valley-native-still-fascinates/stories/201009260258

https://www.youtube.com/watch?v=XAgVeTW7hNA

http://jeffreykauffman.net/francesfarmer/sheddinglight.html

McLellan, Diana. *Sappho Goes to Hollywood: The Girls. Robson Books Ltd.* 2001.

Farmer, Frances. *Will There Really Be a Morning?* HarperCollins Publishers Ltd, 1983.

Tiffin, Georges. *All the Best Lines.* Head of Zeus, 2014, 191.

Shiach, Don. *Movie Classics.* Hermes Books, 2003.

Robb, Brian J. *Silent Cinema.* Kamera Books, 2010.

Gronowicz, Antoni. *Garbo: Her Story.* Simon & Schuster Ltd, 1990.

7. DIRECTORS FROM THE DAWN
OF HOLLYWOOD

Francesca Stephens

A century of near obscurity has passed, yet many filmgoers do not know that there were any women directors in the early days of cinema. It takes some searching out to find them, but they're there, and in fact women's contribution to the beginnings of cinema was groundbreaking – and brave. Delve deeper into film history, and it becomes evident that women have been making movies since the very inception of the moving picture. This helps us to understand that the history of film is much more diverse than commonly acknowledged. There are many female directors hidden in the archives such as Ida May Park, Vera McCord, Leontine Sagan, Wanda Tuchock, Germaine Dulac, Lotte Reiniger, Esfir Shub, Lucie Derain, Jacqueline Logan, Elizabeth Pickett and Dorothy Davenport. Few people realise that German-born director, Lotte Reiniger invented silhouette animation, and made the first feature length animated film in 1926, *The Adventures of Prince Achmed*, using colour-tinted film, ten years before Walt Disney. In particular to note are three female directors who made an extremely significant impact on the beginnings of the motion picture industry and Hollywood. Alice Guy-Blaché (neé Guy), ignited the flame, when she made the first narrative film in Paris in 1896, and subsequently took this know-how to New York. Lois Weber ran alongside her, carrying the flame to California, and in 1916 was the highest paid director in Hollywood. Dorothy Arzner, kept the flame burning, as she emerged through the ranks of the studio system of Hollywood and became a top director, making major studio productions until 1943, ushering in the Golden Age of Hollywood. Each of these women have substantial filmographies – they made stars, made money, and were well-known for making great films. These women weren't on the periphery of the film industry; they were *bona fide* movers and shakers, making films, making deals and calling the shots! In the journals, fanzines and trade papers of the day, their names appear along with all the stars' names we recognise today. Yet Alice Guy-Blaché, Lois Weber and Dorothy Arzner are not so easily recognised. History has done them a disservice and all but obliterated their cinematic efforts. Thankfully, the female pioneers of early cinema are getting more recognition and more exposure through the research of Cari Beauchamp, Ally Acker, Alison McMahan, Claire Johnston, Judith Mayne, Shelley Stamp, Karyn Kay, Gerald Peary, Anthony Slide and many others.

Alice Guy-Blaché (1873–1968)

A French national, Marie Clotilde Franceline Guy, voyaged seven weeks by boat from Chile to France, determined to have her fifth child on French soil. Alicé Ida Antoinette Guy was born, 1ˢᵗ July 1873, in Saint Mande, France. Guy's entrance to the world was dramatic and intriguing, as was her film career, and omission from cinema history. In 1894 she secured a job as a secretary in a stills photography company with Leon Gaumont, which began her adventure with film and led her to become one of the first French pioneers in cinema. She associated with the greatest minds in Paris, including Gustave Eiffel, Louis and Auguste Lumière, and Georges Méliès, to mention a few. Her memoirs begin:

> I have no pretense to making a work of literature, but simply to amuse, to interest the reader by anecdotes and personal memories concerning their great friend

the cinema, at whose birth I assisted.[11]

This is no exaggeration, she certainly did assist the birth of cinema. In December 1895 Alice Guy and Leon Gaumont were invited to attend a showing of *La Sortie De L'Usine* which was the Lumière Brothers first film. Sparking her interest in the moving picture, she thought:

'…one could do better than the early demonstration films.'[12]

She asked permission to make some short films, or shots as they were known, with the moving camera. Gaumont agreed, as long as it did not interfere with her secretarial duties. So with might, determination and creative flair Guy began to make shots in her spare time. From 1896 to 1907 she made hundreds of reels of film. Beginning with *The Cabbage Patch Fairy* (1896), which was based on a fairytale of how babies come into the world. It has a fresh and joyful feel and is now considered to be one of the first film narratives. Guy would ask friends, circus performers, musicians, opera singers and popular artists of the day to help tell all sorts of stories. She played around with ideas, techniques, camera angles and tricks, working with and developing early significant cinematic discoveries, which she would later take to America.

Her prolific output of shots led her to become Head of Production at Gaumont Pictures in 1897, when she was only twenty-three. The resulting filmography is rich, diverse and astonishingly original. Ranging from comedies like *Wonderful Absinthe* (1899) where a man gets blind drunk, to literary adaptations like *Faust and Mephistopheles* (1903) which utilised cutting techniques to create the illusion of images appearing and disappearing and transportation from place to place in an instant. There's the amusing and observational *The Consequences of Feminism* (1906) a light-hearted look at gender roles, in which a group of men act effeminately doing all the womanly chores,

---

11 Slide, Anthony, Ed. *The Memoirs of Alice Guy-Blaché*. Roberta and Simone Blaché, Trans. The Scarecrow Press, 1996, 1.
12 Slide. *The Memoirs of Alice Guy-Blaché*. 26–27.

while the women act like men, drinking, smoking and fighting before finally, in the end the roles revert back to normal. *Madam's Fancies* (1907) dramatises the ravenous cravings of a pregnant lady, in which comedy is derived from the man having trouble controlling her, and one of the earliest use of close-ups heightened the bizarre nature of the woman's cravings. Guy also made an early biblical epic, *The Life of Christ* (1906), featuring 300 extras. It is important to note the role of women in these early shots, as they are neither simply sex objects, nor victims. Guy gives us another dimension to the female image on film. We can thank Alison McMahan for one of the most comprehensive studies of Guy's life and work: *Alice Guy-Blaché: Lost Visionary of the Cinema* in which she details Guy's truly groundbreaking work. She also went on to restore some of her previously lost films.

Guy was also one of the first to experiment with sound and the moving image. She made over a hundred phono-scenes of popular musical artists of the day singing and dancing, which she recorded with Gaumont's invention of a synchronised sound system – the chronophone. The chronophone was instrumental in bringing together Alice Guy and a young cameraman from England, Herbert Blaché, who worked for Gaumont Pictures. Some Germans had bought a chronophone, and Herbert Blaché was sent to help them. He was struggling, so Gaumont sent Guy to explain the technicalities of the chronophone to the Germans, whilst Herbert Blaché translated. It was in Berlin that their love grew, and they were married when they returned to Paris.

Shortly after their marriage, Herbert Blaché was asked to take the chronophone to America, and Guy left Gaumont in Paris to travel with her husband. A stranger in a foreign land, Alice Guy-Blaché had no intention of making movies. She settled into life as Madame Blaché, whilst Herbert headed up Gaumont Pictures in New York and their first child Simone was born in 1908. After a couple of years in America, Guy-Blaché saw the potential of some underused studio space, and hiring the Gaumont studios in Flushing, New York, the couple founded a production company called Solax on 7th September 1910, with Mme Blaché as president. Solax subsequently joined the Motion Picture Patents Company (MPPC), or the Movie Trust which offered distribution to many of the big independent film companies such as Essaynay, Vitagraph and Biograph. It was set up to challenge the domination of foreign films in American movie theatres. It standardised distribution and rental agreements but also limited members to using Eastman Kodak film stock and Edison camera equipment and tried to maintain control of the motion picture industry by licensing use of its patents. However, it was vital to Solax productions to get their films shown in the New York movie theatres[13] as New York was a hub of entertainment at this time. Theatre, vaudeville, burlesque and the new medium of film co-existed as entertainment for the masses. There were numerous independent film companies operating at this time in and around New York but Solax gained popularity and prestige by producing high quality films with engaging and believable performances. Guy-Blaché headed up production for hundreds of early movies, making funny one-reel films like *Canned Harmony* (1912) and *Algie the Miner* (1912) along with more serious dramatic pieces like *Falling Leaves* (1912) and *A House Divided* (1913). She had a good relationship with her actors and often worked with the same crew and cast. She advised her actors to 'Be Natural'. A reporter describes Guy-Blaché working:

> …It seems magical, the closeness of understanding between her and the player who happens to be the centre of the story at any seemingly small part of an instant and it is marvellous that the effect she desires is obtained so easily.[14]

Guy-Blaché's contribution to early American cinema cannot be underestimated. Her technical knowledge would certainly have helped to advance the camera techniques being used in

---

13 Slide. *The Memoirs of Alice Guy-Blaché.* 67–68.
14 Slide. *The Memoirs of Alice Guy-Blaché.* 137.

New York. When working on one picture, her advice on how to create a certain special effect was invaluable:

> …their ignorance of certain procedures really astonished me. The first time that I asked a cameraman to get a special effect (on that occasion, a man walking on water) he told me that this was impossible. I had to assist and guide him, step by step, to obtain a result which filled him with admiration and earned me his respect.[15]

Solax was extremely successful and made enough money to enable Guy-Blaché to build her own studio … in Fort Lee, New Jersey. The studio was completed in 1912, the same year Guy-Blaché gave birth to her second child, Reginald. At its height, Solax was producing three reels a week, the same rate of output as D. W. Griffith, who was also filming in Fort Lee. Alice Guy-Blaché became a well-respected filmmaker and studio owner and was certainly one of the heavyweights in the early days of cinema in New York. On 17th February in 1912 she appears in *Motion Picture News* as one of the prominent Independent Film manufacturers, along with Carl Laemmle who went on to be head of Universal Pictures, and was important in Lois Weber's film career.[16] Interestingly, Carl Laemmle had formed Independent Moving Pictures (IMP) in 1909, a year before Solax was formed, but by merging with several other independents in 1912 and creating the Universal Film Manufacturing Company, he created one of the early consortiums.

Sadly, as quickly as Guy-Blaché's success grew, it disintegrated, and her place in cinema history disappeared almost altogether. Herbert Blaché took over the presidency of Solax, and his wife did not attend any more meetings:

> I would have embarrassed the men who wanted to smoke cigars and to spit at their ease while discussing business.[17]

The exclusion of women from business meetings allowed the studios to become even more male dominated over the

15 Slide. *The Memoirs of Alice Guy-Blaché.* 69.

16 *New York Clipper.* 17th February, 1912. mediahistoryproject.org

17 Slide, *The Memoirs of Alice Guy-Blaché.* 79.

coming decades. Some bad luck clouded 1919, as Guy-Blaché caught Spanish Influenza, a deadly flu that killed some of her colleagues and nearly killed her too. Herbert moved to California with his mistress, following a few bad business deals for Solax which depleted funds considerably. The film industry in New York was also suffering due to the turmoil created by World War I which had seriously reduced revenues from European markets. Many independents did not recover from the downturn while others moved to California for the warmer climate and longer hours of daylight, and to avoid the monopoly and restrictions of the MPPC. Unable to sustain production during this period of flux, Solax was auctioned in 1920.

By 1922, Alice Guy-Blaché was divorced and left with nothing. She attempted to resurrect her career and in 1927, to no avail, she tried to find her films, but she eventually returned to France, disheartened. Another blow for Guy-Blaché came in 1930 when Gaumont published a history of his film company, leaving out any production pre-1907. Upset by the omission of her work while at Gaumont, she wrote to get this corrected, which Leon Gaumont eventually did, but this was only published by his son Louis in 1954. In 1955, Guy-Blaché received the Légion d'Honneur for her contribution to cinema, the highest honour in France. Guy-Blaché was very aware of the omission of her rightful place in cinema history and towards the end of the 1940s she began to write her memoirs. A precious insight into her life and works, it is here we get the nuances of her career and some of the injustices, but mainly her brilliance, creativity, intelligence and technical prowess as a filmmaker. Guy-Blaché was without a doubt a formidable lady, and a force to be reckoned with in the early days of cinema. It took the Directors Guild of America one hundred years to recognise her incredible contribution and in 2012 she was posthumously awarded an American Lifetime Achievement Award, accorded by Martin Scorsese.

Lois Weber (1879–1939)

Lois Weber crossed paths with Guy-Blaché at the Gaumont studios, where Weber was working with Herbert Blaché as a singer and performer. It was here that Weber began to write and direct short scenarios. Guy-Blaché briefly, but not warmly, mentioned Weber in her memoirs:

> Herbert Blaché had directed, in the little Gaumont studio at Fort Lee, a singer named Lois Weber who recorded several songs for the chronophone. She had watched me direct the first little films and doubtless thought it was not difficult. She got a directing job and certain Americans pretend that she was the first woman director. My first film, of which I speak of in the first part of these memoirs, dated 1896.[18]

Weber's beginnings were quite different from Guy-Blaché's. Weber was born in Allegheny, Pennsylvania to a devoutly religious family, which had a profound effect on her view of life, and her films. Weber saw the potential of film as a way to express her ideals and possibly challenge commonly held beliefs. She was concerned with poverty and other social injustices possibly due to having had firsthand experience of extreme poverty, as she:

> …did missionary work in the slums of New York and on Blackwell Island, especially among poor girls. I know them and their problems, and not a few of my stories have been suggested by incidents recalled from those early experiences.[19]

Weber seemed drawn to give a voice to the voiceless. Class is of importance here too as it would be very unlikely at that time for a girl from the slums to be able to tell her story to a mass audience, but Weber could, and did. Weber's films were not pure entertainment, but commentaries on what she saw as the wrongs in society. A gifted musician, she was a professional concert pianist at sixteen, then a few years later she joined a

18 Slide. *The Memoirs of Alice Guy-Blaché*. 79.
19 'Lois Weber Talks Shop', *The Motion Picture News*, 1916. mediahistoryproject.org

couple of touring musical theatre companies as a singer and performer. This was where she met her first husband Phillips Smalley, a stage manager. They married and lived in New York. Interestingly, Weber was sometimes referred to as Mrs Smalley, but it appears that she was mainly referred to as Lois Weber, as she did keep her maiden name throughout her career. It was around 1908, when Weber ventured to Gaumont to work as a singer. Smalley was away on tour and later joined her when he returned. They continued as an acting and directing team for many of the independent film companies, with their time at Gaumont acting as the catalyst for their film career.

Lois Weber and Phillips Smalley had made the side step from theatre to film, as many performers did, and they had quickly become the *prima facie* heads of Rex Motion Picture Company[20] which would become part of The Universal Manufacturing Company, headed up by Carl Laemmle. In 1915, they moved to San Fernando, California. This led Weber to be part of the effervescent film industry taking root in California, along with other filmmakers, drawn by the year-long sun.

Weber's most cited film, *Suspense* (1913), was based on the play *Au Telephon* by André de Lourde, and earlier attributed to D. W. Griffith. As with many of her early films, she acted in, directed and wrote this captivating movie, which used sophisticated shots to draw the audience in, and build tension. It is well noted for the use of a triple split screen depicting action happening simultaneously in different locations. *Suspense* is now fully restored and has been exhibited at MOMA, and various film festivals. Some of these early films demonstrated Weber's literary competence, like her adaptation of Oscar Wilde's *The Picture of Dorian Gray* (1913) in which she starred, with Smalley as director. Weber also adapted, directed and acted in Shakespeare's *The Merchant of Venice* (1914). The film that brought notoriety and controversy was *Hypocrites* (1915), a story about hypocrisy in the Church, and generally in human nature, following a monk's journey to find truth. The film also

20 Slide, Anthony. *Lois Weber: The Director Who Lost Her Way.* 1996. 46.

examines what can come between a person and the truth. The controversy came from Weber's' choice of representing truth as a naked woman superimposed onto the film – literally, the naked truth. Some audiences responded with riots in New York; it was banned in Ohio and Cleveland would only show the film if the body had clothes painted on the negative. This controversy propelled the success of *Hypocrites*, which was shown in many other countries including England and Australia, with audiences watching in their thousands.

Weber was not afraid to tackle controversial issues, and was determined to tell stories in her own personal way. *Where Are My Children* (1916) addressed birth control, at first seemingly denouncing the poor, and blaming crime on the birth of unwanted babies born into poor households. The story twists its focus, to a married middle-class childless couple: the husband is a judge, and the wife is a lady that lunches, but it transpires that she and others have had illegal abortions so they can carry on enjoying their social life. The couple try to have a baby, but the wife can no longer conceive due to the abortions she had. This subject matter would even be controversial today and consequently the film was banned in some states. Poverty is the subject in *Shoes* (1916) and focuses on a girl who works at a 5 cent store. She is so poor that she cannot afford new shoes, and the ones she is wearing are worn completely through, so she resorts to prostituting herself to buy a new pair of shoes that she desperately needs. A review at the time describes the realism of the poverty portrayed:

> Lois Weber ... has gone a step too far in showing a close-up of the girl extracting splinters from the sole of the foot. She has gone too far in showing the girl scraping mud from her feet with a scissors. There is such a thing as being too realistic.[21]

The little known facts of Weber's life, and the storytelling of strong subjects, speaks of her pragmatic and independent

21 Milne, Peter. *Shoes* review, *Motion Picture News*. 24th June, 1916. mediahistoryproject.org

spirit. She always had clear ideas of the stories she wanted to produce. Weber, along with Guy-Blaché, could be described as early 'auteurs' as they had total control of the pictures they made. In an interview, Weber acknowledged the importance of controlling what she wanted to say through her films:

> I'll never be convinced that the general public does not want serious entertainment rather than frivolous… If I can sow a few helpful seeds in my pictures, which will appeal to some man or woman in my audience, I shall be satisfied. That is why I want to go on with this work, I want to present my ideas and again, that is the reason I cannot be happy to direct someone else's story – that would be only half a creation.[22]

It is estimated that Weber made nearly 200 films, including over forty feature films. Weber achieved fame and success in a few short years and by 1916, her wage as a director was higher than any other director at the time. She received critical acclaim as well as commercial success and went on to run her own company – Lois Weber Productions – in 1918.

Ill-health blighted the last years of Weber's life and she died in 1939 of a stomach ulcer. Weber's importance is reflected in the film journals and trade papers of the day. Unfortunately, Weber's memoirs are considered lost, as well as many of her films. Lois Weber is an iconic director, someone who stood up for her beliefs. Her views were often ahead of her time and she had a clear vision of what she wanted to say and how she wanted to say it.

Dorothy Arzner (1897–1979)

As Weber's film career was coming to an end, and Guy-Blaché had returned to France, B. P. Schulberg promoted Dorothy Arzner from editor to director at Players-Lasky, which later became Paramount Pictures. Arzner is one of the most referenced of early female directors, due to the fact that film

---

22 'The Muse of the Reel by Arline', *The Motion Picture Magazine*. March, 1921, 105. mediahistoryproject.org

was taken more seriously at that time. The studio system was in place and Arzner's career developed within this system. Feminist film theory from the 1970s has also contributed to raising Arzner's profile as an important figure in film history.

Dorothy Arzner was born in San Francisco. Her family then moved to Los Angeles, where her father Louis Arzner ran the Hoffman Café which was a popular hangout for many silent stars of the day, like Sara Bernhardt, Erich von Stroheim, Charlie Chaplin, Mack Sennett, D. W. Griffith, Douglas Fairbanks and James Cruze, who Arzner later worked for as an editor. This however, was not the stepping-stone to her career in Hollywood. Initially, her aspirations were to become a doctor and she studied at medical school, though she quickly became disenchanted with this idea as she found that people were: '…always talking about their troubles and their sicknesses and this was boring.'[23]

It was not until she visited the Players-Lasky Studios with the Ambulance Corp that Arzner saw the film studios for the first time: '…and when I first stood on a klieg-flooded set, I suddenly knew that my future was inside those studio gates.'[24]

Arzner was able to work successfully within the studio system, which is no mean feat in itself. Like Guy-Blaché, Arzner began working as a secretary at Players-Lasky, but unlike Guy-Blaché, Arzner was very clear that she wanted to be a film director, and every day she was working towards this aim. She negotiated her way through and up the ranks of the studio quickly to script girl, writer, and then editor. From 1920 to 1926 Arzner worked as a writer and editor for Paramount Pictures on over a dozen films. The first film Arzner was given to direct was *Fashions for Women* (1927), but this was only after Arzner had said she was leaving to direct elsewhere. She agreed to stay on one condition:

> …(if) I can be on set in two weeks with an A picture…

23 Mayne, Judith. *Directed by Dorothy Arzner*. Bloomington, 1994.
24 'Directed by Dorothy Arzner', *Screenland Magazine*. Builders inc., August, 1929. 70. mediahistoryproject.org

With that he (Schulberg) left, saying, "Wait here." He was back in a few minutes with a play in his hand. "Here. It's a French farce called *The Best Dressed Woman in Paris*. Start writing the script and get yourself on the set in two weeks. New York is sending Esther Ralston out to be starred. She had made such a hit in *Peter Pan* (1924), and it will be up to you." So, there I was a writer-director. It was announced in the papers the following day or so: "Lasky Names Woman Director."[25]

It is a common belief and boldly stated that Arzner was the only woman in Hollywood throughout her career. Though certainly the most prominent and prolific, Weber made her last film in 1934, and in the 1920s there were many other women writers, editors and directors working in Hollywood. Arzner herself often worked with female screenwriters such as Zoë Akins, Akins, Gertrude Purcell, Ethel Doherty, Mary C. McCall Jr., Doris Anderson, Tess Slesinger, Agnes Brand Leahy, Hope Loring, Vera Caspary and Winifred Lenihan. She also worked with many fine female editors: Marion Morgan (also Arzner's life partner), Viola Lawrence, Adrienne Fazan (an accomplished editor whose credits include *Singin' in the Rain*, and *Gigi*), and Jane Loring. It is true to say that from the mid-1930s to the mid-1940s Arzner was the only female director immersed in the Hollywood studio system and she was also the only female member of the Directors Guild of America.

Arzner was working in a film industry where many filming techniques had been perfected, the language of film had been formed and the business of filmmaking had taken shape. It was now talking pictures that were the latest technology. Arzner's second film featured the sensation at the time, silent star Clara Bow in her first talkie – *The Wild Party* (1929). If you watch Clara Bow's early silent film performances she is very lively and free spirited with a relaxed fluid way of moving. It

25 Interview with Dorothy Arzner Karyn Kay and Gerald Peary, originally published in *Cinema* (U.S.) in 1974, was reprinted in the 1975 British Film Institute pamphlet, *Dorothy Arzner: Towards a Feminist Cinema*.

was while working with Bow that Arzner invented the boom microphone, by attaching a microphone to a fishing rod to follow the actors, revolutionising the talking picture, and this gave Bow freedom of movement whilst acting out scenes. Arzner captures Bow's essence perfectly, and made Bow's debut talkie a roaring success. Previous to Arzner's invention, actors would need to be completely static for the sound to be clearly recorded.

Arzner made a stella amount of quality feature films under contract with Paramount Pictures from 1927–32, and then began directing independently for several of the other studios beginning with *Christopher Strong* (1933) starring Katharine Hepburn. Arzner made seven films as a freelance director in Hollywood until 1943. She was well renowned as a top director, and like Guy-Blaché and Weber, the trade magazines and fanzines of the day are full of praise and admiration for her work. It must be noted that Arzner's contemporaries were John Ford, Josef von Sternberg, Howard Hawks and Frank Capra, and she was as successful as these film legends in her day. Arzner also worked with many stars, and helped build their careers, including Katharine Hepburn, Cary Grant, Fredric March, Sylvia Sidney, Lucille Ball and Joan Crawford.

Merrily We Go To Hell (1932) was the last picture Arzner made under contract to Paramount Pictures. A highly naturalistic and funny film, the story focuses on a young wealthy girl who falls in love with an alcoholic journalist, and the difficulties that arise. They get engaged and her father throws a big announcement party, which Jerry is too drunk to attend. Joan is obviously distraught and drives off in tears, as her friend says, 'She'd be mad to marry him after that.' But, alas the next scene is of Joan and Jerry in the church getting married, and at the end of the scene it is revealed that the groom has used a bottle opener in place of the wedding ring which he has lost. The couple laugh, and this image perfectly captures the tragi-comedy of the scene. Arzner cleverly uses a humorous image to depict the possible tragic mistake of marrying an alcoholic. There is complexity and humour in the male/female relationships that Arzner captured on celluloid, which is strikingly different to most films of the time.

Despite being nearly a hundred years ago, some of the most natural and real scenes between women can be found in the films of Arzner. The female dynamic is depicted with ease. Arzner's sexuality is often noted as she was a lesbian, and has become a queer icon. As a lesbian one might assume that her view would be complicit with the *male gaze,* as described in Laura Mulvey's analysis of cinema.[26] The actuality is that Arzner offers up a more complex narrative, and other forms of the gaze. In *Working Girls* (1931) there is a series of shots of women dressing for work, or to go out. These are short quick shots depicting the functionality of clothes, very natural, clearly recognisable to a female audience, and not created to satisfy the male gaze. In *Dance, Girl, Dance* (1940), starring Lucille Ball, the audition scene offers an interesting commentary on the male gaze. At first a serious ballet dancer is auditioning for a male theatre owner who is not impressed at all, then Lucille Ball bounces in, throws her coat off, adjusts her skirt to reveal more of her figure, and proceeds with a sexy audition dance, to please the theatre owner. The dance teacher running the auditions and in control of the music, gives an approving smile to the sleazy theatre owner, but as he turns, her fake smile quickly turns to a disapproving glare. This adds layers to the scene, and demonstrates that all is not in the eye of the beholder, and succeeds in telling a few female stories simultaneously: the young girl retaining her dignity; the brazen girl playing the gaze to her own ends; and the older matriarch who is complicit with, yet acknowledges her discomfort with this scenario. This theme continues through the film, and is central to the film's narrative. The dance teacher in *Dance, Girl, Dance* has been referred to as a representation of Arzner, due to her masculine style of dressing. Could the disapproval from the dance teacher be a subtle clue as to Arzner's own

26 Mulvey, Laura. *Visual Pleasure in Narrative Cinema.* 1975.

disapproval of the male domination, and objectification of women? Often a glance can speak a thousand words. This kind of subtle messaging may be a means of vital communication between women, and another way for a female audience to engage with the film narrative. Arzner's films stand out as being female-centred in a heavily male-dominated Hollywood. Her films are focused around complex female characters and often have challenging female storylines.

Arzner left Hollywood in 1943, and it is not exactly clear why. We do know she had pneumonia for a year, and moved to La Quinta with Marion Morgan, her life partner, and the choreographer on *Dance, Girl, Dance*. At this point Arzner's career diversified. She made training films for the army, along with training some women in the army to cut and edit the films. She then went on to start the first filmmaking course at the Pasadena Playhouse on a non-existent budget, instructing her students with a single camera and tape recorder. She made Pepsi-Cola commercials for her old friend Joan Crawford and she taught filmmaking at UCLA for four years in the 1960s, where she taught Francis Ford Coppola. Arzner died in 1979 leaving a rich body of work, and is now considered an icon of the LGBT community.

It could be argued that all three of these women, as directors and early auteurs, helped to build the foundations of the American film industry, artistically, technically and financially. Their influence on film has been profound. Guy-Blaché was one of the first to use the medium of film for storytelling. She experimented with sound, editing and special effects and introduced a more natural acting style to moving pictures. Weber introduced a social conscience to Hollywood, created powerful stories that were seen globally and helped build Hollywood's international status. Arzner brought in huge revenue for the studios, helped create the success of talking pictures and her invention of the boom microphone is still used to this day. Unfortunately, many of their films have been lost, and there is more work to do to reclaim our female heritage. It is true to say that Alice Guy-Blaché, Lois Weber and Dorothy Arzner were forces to be reckoned with – and truly great cinematic pioneers.

Author Biography: Francesca Stevens

Francesca lives and works in West London, with her two teenage children. She studied Drama and Theatre Arts BA (Hons) at Goldsmiths College, University of London. She has written and directed fringe theatre performances in London, Edinburgh and New York, and taught drama at a local Youth Theatre. She currently dabbles in filmmaking, writing screenplays, as well as contributing to various blogs: A Girl Named Frank, Women in Film and Television History Network, and Women Make Waves.

Her first childhood memories are of being engrossed in the black and white movies of early cinema, showing on a tiny TV. From a very early age she was completely enchanted by the silver screen. She loved film then, she loves film now. The strong presence of women behind the camera in the early days of cinema is a recent discovery for her and she has wondered why she had not known of these women sooner. It pulls into question the history that is represented to us, and how strongly this can form opinion.

Writer/Filmmaker
Zora Neale Hurston
ca. 1915, U.S.

Photo: Carl Van
Vechten (left)

Eslanda Goode Robeson, wife and manager of the Actor/Singer
Paul Robeson, performing with her husband in the film *Big Fella,* 1937.
Photo: Hammer Films, U.K. (below)

Nell Shipman Actress/Writer/Director/Producer Publicity shot, 1919. Photo: Boise State University, U.S.

Nell Shipman on location in Idaho, U.S., 1922.
Photo: Boise State University.

The first narrative
filmmaker:
Alice Guy-
Blaché.

Photo: Apeda
Studio, New
York, 1913. Solax
Collection.

Marion Wong,
the first
Chinese-American
Actress/Writer/
Director/Producer
ca. 1916 when her film
The Curse of Quon Gwon
was produced.
Photo: Violet and
Marion Wong
Collection, U.S.

Mary Pickford Producer/Actress/Co-founder United Artists ca. 1916.
Photo: Library of Congress.

Alla Nazimova,
Russian Actress.
As Maguerite
Gautier in *Camille*,
1921, U.S.
Photo:
Arthur Rice
(right)

Glass slide advertisement for
The Hand That Rocks The Cradle,
1917, U.S. Photo: Shelley
Stamp collection (left)

Director Lois Weber at work on the set of *The Angel of
Broadway*, 1927 with cinematographer Arthur C. Miller.
Photo: British Film Institute.

Frances Marion, screenwriter. Photo: *Photoplay* Magazine 1918, U.S.

Lillian Gish Actress/Producer. Photo: *The Wind,* 1928, U.S.
Directed by Victor Sjöström, adapted by Frances Marion from
the novel by Dorothy Scarborough.

Margaret Booth, Supervising Film Editor at MGM where she worked from 1924 until 1969.

Four-time Oscar nominee, Film Editor, Dorothy Spencer. She began as a cutter in 1926 and achieved 75 feature film credits before retiring in 1979.

Anne Bauchens, Film Editor with Cecil B. DeMille. She worked as his film editor from 1918 to 1956.

Louise Brooks
Actress/Dancer
as Lulu in
Pandora's Box,
1929, with
Gustav Diessl as
Jack the Ripper.
Photo: Kino
International,
Germany.

Mae West,
Writer/Actress
Photo: *She Done
Him Wrong* 1933.
Paramount
Pictures, U.S.

Actress, Clara
Bow, the original
'It Girl'.
Nude scene
from *Hula* 1929.
Photo: Paramount
Pictures, U.S. (left)

Greta Garbo with John Gilbert in *Flesh and the Devil*, 1926, U.S. Publicity photo, MGM (above) Movie poster for *Flesh and the Devil*, 1926 (left)

Marlene
Dietrich
Singer/Actress
often dressed
in men's clothes
on and off set.

Publicity photo
for *Morocco*
1930,
Paramount
Pictures, U.S.

Francesca Bertini, Actress in many silent films including *Assunta Spina* 1915, Italy. She is credited with co-writing and co-directing the film with Gustavo Serena.

Elizaveta Svilova, Film Editor and Co-founder of Cinema Eye, 1920, Russia.

Photo: from *Man with a Movie Camera,* 1929, directed by Dziga Vertov, Soviet Union.

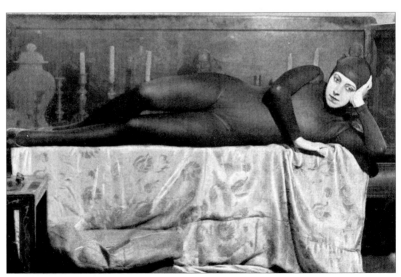

Musidora in *Les Vampires* 1915–1916, directed by Louis Feuillade, France.

Actress/Producer Aud Egede-Nissen and Paul Richter in *Peter The Pirate* 1925, directed by Arthur Robison, UFA, Germany. Photo: Postcard produced by Ross Verlag, Berlin 1927.

Leni Riefenstahl, Actress/Director, at work in Germany, 1936. Photo: German Federal Archives.

The McDonagh Sisters near a ship's gangway, Sydney, Australia
in the late 1920s. Photo: NFSA, Australia.

George Albert Smith and his wife Laura (née) Bayley who were early
filmmakers in Brighton, U.K. Photo: *A Kiss in* the *Tunnel,* 1899.

Alma Reville advising husband Alfred Hitchcock on a script
ca. 1964. Photo: Philip Stern.

Lydia Hayward (right), Actress and Screenwriter of over 30 films.
The Pillars of Society is a 1920 British silent adaptation of Ibsen's play
filmed in Norway. With Pamela Neville and Charles Ashton.
Photo: National Library of Norway.

Gene Gauntier, Actress/
Writer/Director, U.S.
With actor/husband
Jack J. Clark
on location in Ireland
filming
You Remember Ellen,
1912.

Classroom teachers,
most of whom
were women, began
incorporating films
into their lessons in the
1910s.

Asta Nielsen
Actress/
Producer on
the set of
The Black Dream
Photo: Bain
News 1911,
Denmark.

Josephine Lovett,
Screenwriter, U.S.
Photo: Paramount
Pictures, 1933 /
Academy Film Archive.
(left)

Elvira Notari was the first Italian
woman Producer/Director. She
worked with her husband Nicolai
who was the cameraman on her
films ca. 1920, Italy. (right)

Ida Lupino, Actress/Writer/Director working on *Hard, Fast
and Beautiful* ca. 1950. Publicity photo: RKO U.S.

Dorothy Arzner,
Director.
Publicity Photo 1934,
U.S. (right)
Movie poster for
The Wild Party, 1929,
U.S. (below)

Dorothy Arzner, Director.
Photo: David Gill, 1977, U.S. (below)

8. INTERVIEW WITH DIRECTOR DOROTHY ARZNER

Kevin Brownlow

The date was 5th June 1977.

Kevin Brownlow – the British film historian and documentary director – approached Dorothy Arzner for an interview. At that time he worked regularly with David Gill as a filmmaker and fellow producer.

In Kevin Brownlow's own words:

'David Gill and I were very anxious to film an interview with Dorothy Arzner, and she refused point blank. We realised that it was probably because she felt she looked too old, so we suggested we simply recorded it on audio tape. She agreed to that and David, ever the optimist, brought a stills camera, and remarkably, she didn't mind being photographed in that way (see corresponding photograph).

Although I had interviewed her before (also on tape), I couldn't find where she had moved to. We found her thanks to Dr Paul Eldridge of the University of Nevada, in Reno.

We went to La Quinta, in the desert near Palm Springs, where she had shared a house with Marion Morgan. At the height of her fame she had a proper Hollywood-style house on Los Feliz, very near where Cecil B. DeMille lived (at 2,000 – deux mille! – DeMille Drive). But La Quinta had become a retirement colony for picture people – I met Sidney Franklin and Enid Bennett, Clarence Brown, Jackie Coogan, Frank Capra and Janet Gaynor down there, but somehow missed Charles Farrell, who ran a tennis club in the area.

Arzner was fascinating and she wasn't in the least intimidating. She loved those pioneering days, and she had obviously been a thoroughly reliable and dedicated colleague.

She died on the 1st of October 1979.'

*

Q: Your first contact with picture people occurred at a very early age, can you tell us about that?

A: Yes, it was at Paramount when I was a typist, I got a job as a typist. William de Mille gave me the job. It's a long story. Do you want long stories?

Q: I want an even earlier one, it was much, much earlier, you first met the great Mr Griffith and other people in a…

A: Oh, in my father's restaurant, yes. They had a round table and D. W. Griffith came in with Mary Pickford and Tom Moore and Owen Moore and all of them. I remember my dad telling me that Griffith always brought his company in there to eat until they finished the picture and it was sold and then he paid his bill. I don't know how old I was, pretty young, going to school. The first time I ever visited a set was the *Intolerance* set in the scene where they were pouring lead down upon the attacking side. Griffith was doing the real thing almost, having them pouring hot lead down onto the enemy, it was very exciting.

Q: A bit before that though can you tell us that lovely story about Wilton Lackaye?

A: They were stage actors, it was the Grand Opera House which was the first theatre in Los Angeles that my father had a restaurant in connection with and I used to go to the theatre, which ran sort of blood and thunder plays. Wilton Lackaye was the head. He would come into the restaurant when I was little and he'd pick me up and throw me up in the air and I'd come down whacking at him. I hated it because you know they always thought of little girls, you know four or five years old, as something to pick up and toss about and I didn't like it.

Q: When you finally made contact with Paramount, William de Mille challenged your ambition as a set dresser?

A: That's right. I was introduced by a rather important woman that he knew personally, who was gathering young people to drive ambulances and of course I applied. I wanted to go to France and drive an ambulance on the front line. I was too young to join the Red Cross, so I applied to her for this Los Angeles emergency drivers' scheme and then when the war was over I drove for the commander and the commander's wife invited me to dinner. I was saying, 'Where do I go from here?' I didn't want to go back to the university – I was going to USC. I was two years at USC and I didn't want to go back to school. I'd had a taste of being out in the world, so I said, 'Where do I go from here?' and she spoke up and said, 'Dorothy's a modern girl, I think she should be in a modern business, the motion picture business.' Apparently she was a motion picture buff, I mean she was very enthusiastic about motion pictures. She thought they were the coming thing, so she arranged an introduction for me and said, 'Now, you have an appointment with William de Mille and I'll drive you out.' She drove me there and dropped me off and left me and I can remember standing in the middle of Vine Street yelling at her, 'Don't leave me!' But anyway I went in because the appointment was made and that's when I met William de Mille. He said, 'Well, what would you like to do?' And I said, 'I don't know but I think I could dress sets,' and he said, 'What's the period of the furniture in this office?' and I didn't know and he said 'It's Franciscan', so I will never forget what period furniture is, and then later he told me to look around for a week, which I did, and he said, 'Why don't you talk to my secretary?' I talked with her but I looked around first and the first set I was interested in was Cecil DeMille's. He was making *Male and Female,* I believe, and I remember sitting there and saying to myself, 'Gee, he's the whole works; that's the thing to be if you're going to be in this business. Be the director and tell everybody what to do'. And then I talked to William de Mille's secretary, Mildred Bell and she told me the thing to do is to start typing scripts because that was the blueprint of motion pictures. So I typed scripts for three months. But very quickly I was ambitious to get out of typing scripts so I went over to the Nazimova Company and held script for Nazimova and that was an experience. The head of the scenery department said that Mr de Mille had said, 'What did you let her go for?' so I thought that's good, I can go back so I went back to Paramount and I held script on the set. Donald Crisp was the director on the first one we were making. It was during prohibition because the first picture, I remember, was called *The Six Best Cellars* where they had that home brew and everything started exploding in the basement.

Q: And this brought you into the cutting room?
A: Yes, it was Donald Crisp. Nan Heron was his cutter and I was interested in learning, so she let me watch her cut the first reel and then she watched me cut the second reel and on Sunday, I went into the studio and worked all day long, cutting the next reel myself and I saw that if you made mistakes you could correct them, you could get reprints. I saw that it wasn't any great tragedy if I made an error so I cut the whole reel on Sunday and showed it to her and she thought it was just fine and from then on I was a cutter. It was very quick.

Q: What was your attitude to editing?
A: I loved editing, just loved it. Nobody could bother you and you could do things with the actors, you could cut them off if they were no good and you could cut off their long draggy exits and cut through the other side into something else so that you'd get them out of the room. I used to love to do things

to the film that usually the director liked because he worried about certain things and if you could correct them, well, it was just fine. I did quite a number before I got to the point of *The Covered Wagon* – that was the big thing that began to have attention given to me as a top editor.

Q: But *Blood and Sand* had just brought attention to you…

A: *Blood and Sand* was the first, it was before *Covered Wagon*, yes, it was. I devised a method to show the bull fights and we were waiting for a process and they were having a convention of the salesmen at Paramount, a big banquet and they wanted to show *Blood and Sand*. So I went in and said I think I could cut the bull fights in if they'd let me have a bull tied to a stake and if Valentino would be willing to co-operate then I could match it into the stock footage of the Madrid arena, which I did. Valentino was wonderful, he thought it was such a good idea. They could show the picture then intact to the salesmen. It was an expensive picture and they were anxious to have the salesmen see it. I think it had something like three or four bull fights in it and also Valentino was killed in one. He was gored by the bull in the end and I had him in the Madrid bull arena stuff and I just matched frames.

I remember the first night I looked at it all because it was the real thing; the horses really were gored. I was ill to my stomach watching this stuff. After a while I could look at it without any reaction and then I had to start selecting what I could use and also I had to match the costumes with Valentino wearing the costume that would match. I'd show him the film and I'd tell him just how far he could go and we'd have the cowboys out there, with the bull tied to a stake and the bull would lunge and Valentino was marvellous. He'd lunge out and I'd cut to the long shot of the Madrid arena stock footage where this matched perfectly so that today if you look at *Blood and Sand*, that's the way it is, there's nothing more done, it was left like that and they called off their $50,000 process.

Q: And (director) James Cruze saw that?

A: Yes, we had two projection rooms side by side and you had to walk through one to go to the other and he was walking through when I was running *Blood and Sand* and I can remember him saying, 'My God, who cut that?' and I modestly said, 'I suppose I did' and he said, 'Would you cut *The Covered Wagon* for me? I'm about to do an epic picture,' and I said, 'Well, if you arrange it. It doesn't matter who I cut for.' So he did and that's how I went with him on *The Covered Wagon*.

Q: And what was the spirit on location for *The Covered Wagon?*

A: Well, it was a very tough location. We were eighty-five miles from the railroad in the wilds of Utah, living in tents at the wrong time of year, too… It was February because the snows came and we had to clear snow to get some of our shots. It was deep alkali dust, about two feet deep, it just cut into your face terribly and there was a lot of hardship to it and we had five tribes of Indians and cowboys and oxen broken to the yoke – and hundreds of horses – the whole wagon train was out there in the middle of the wilds of Utah.

Q: There was one occasion when Cruze tried to get everybody to stay on?

A: Oh, yes, because we ran into the snow and it was difficult to shoot. Paramount sent word that he should come back and shoot it on the Lasky lot. That's when he stood up with all the company out in the countryside and said if they'd stay with him, why he'd be able to finish the picture and see that they'd be paid. Then they all were willing to stay whether we were paid or not. We wanted to see the picture through, we'd been through so much and he'd been so great and he was really a fine man in every way, except that he drank a quart of liquor every night. But it never affected his work because he never drank in the day time.

Q: Can you tell us about the assistant on that picture?

A: Vernon Keays was the assistant, he was an excellent assistant and worked hard. I was with Jim Cruze pretty much but I know that Vernon Keays managed very difficult things, handling all the crew and the Indians.

Q: And the cameraman?
A: Karl Brown was the cameraman and I can still see him pick up the camera and almost run from one shot to another. He was strong. How he did it I don't know and he just lasted through the day. Everybody would be exhausted, it's hard work but he was unusually good and I don't ever remember a shot that wasn't good. He was an excellent cameraman. Of course, we had a lot of cameras there and when we put things like all the animals across the lake, which was supposed to be the river Platte, why, there were lots of cameras on it and the same way with gathering the long train, which was so thrilling to me when we finally gathered that long train and saw Charlie Ogle who was the older man that led the train. When he gave the word and the crack of the whip to start that train and you saw it slowly pull through this deep alkali dust, it was very thrilling, because it took so many hours to line it up. I don't know how many wagons we had. It was a great line almost to the horizon and then we had teams of animals behind, the oxen and the horses and men on horseback and all the rest of it. It was a thrilling thing. We had lots of cameras on that also on the side wheels that showed the alkali dust that they were going through. And all that cutting was interesting to me and I could dramatise all that. I had such an emotional feeling about it when I saw it.

You see, those days the cutter was on the set with the director; he was sort of the right hand. I used to line up the scenes to shoot even, you know, shoot this one first and that one second because I knew the order that they should be shot in and I think I had thousands of feet of film, two hundred and fifty thousand feet I think, to cut down to eleven reels, reams of film to go through with all the cameras on it. But Jim Cruze shot very fast. If he was just doing an ordinary scene of a picture he would cut right with the camera and that's what I learned from him, and so I did the same. No producer could ever do anything with my film; there wasn't a lot of extraneous film. Of course with things like *The Covered Wagon* there was, but it was mostly just shots that would fit in to the starting of the train or else to the swimming of the animals across the lake. Otherwise when Cruze did the dramatic scenes he cut with the camera. They hardly sat down until he picked them up the next minute, you know, just into the seat practically. Sometimes you'd wish you had a couple of frames more but your mind covered the space.

Q: *Get Your Man* — can you tell us that marvellous story about the waxworks?
A: Well, that's the one episode in *Get Your Man* that I liked and I can't remember too much what the story was … I think it was set in France and it was Madame Tussaud's waxworks. That was the whole comedy of Buddy Rogers and Clara Bow visiting the waxworks and being frightened of the skeletons and the famous murderers – and we recreated most of the famous groups that were in Madame Tussaud's. Marion Morgan used her dancers and there were no wax figures at all, they were all live figures. I did the Coronation of Napoleon, which was a big group, and we had one bust of the Spanish Infanta. I had the Infanta who was one of the dancers and just used the bust, and Clara Bow went up and touched her eyeball and Ben Schulberg, who was the big producer at Paramount at that time, bet $500 dollars that that was a wax figure. Of course the whole staff came down after seeing the rushes and asked where the Spanish Infanta was and I said, 'Right over there,' and she was sitting on a high stool laughing and talking to Buddy Rogers and so he said, 'You've just lost me $500 dollars!' But anyway, the scene that I liked showed Buddy Rogers and Clara Bow in the position that I'd asked them to be and they both went sound asleep and ended up in each other's arms. They were boy and girl in love with each other and so they were sound asleep when I started to shoot the scene of

them being awakened and I made everyone be quiet and when the old near-sighted janitor came around and flicked them with his duster – thinking to dust them off as he dusted all the wax figures in the morning – they woke up. They looked very sleepy, both of them. It was just right, it was just marvellous because they had been asleep for about an hour.

Q: You gave us the impression though that they had actually fallen asleep while you were shooting it?
A: Yes. They had! They had actually fallen asleep because it would take us quite a while to light sets. I had a very slow cameraman at the time too, who didn't light very fast and we were always working late. Silent pictures … seemed to me we were always working until midnight because there were no guilds or unions at that time to stop us, so we were always working to get out of the set and certainly to get out of a big set like the waxworks.

Q: What do you think Clara Bow's quality was?
A: Clara Bow's quality was like a gamin. She was full of life and energy and moved quickly and darted around. She was attractive to all the boys; she always had men around her. When I took her to be in a picture, I said, 'Now, I don't want a lot of men around here and I don't want any nonsense going on,' and so she used to sit in her dressing room and have the door wide open and say, 'See, there's no one in here.' That's the sort of thing she did. She was charming and I can remember one night we were shooting the last scene of a picture … I think it was *Get Your Man*… It was about 4 a.m. and they both had separate rooms in a hotel and I said, 'Now you come together, meet in the middle and then we fade out,' and of course they and the whole crew burst into laughter saying, 'Now you meet in the middle and fade out'. Clara Bow rushed up and threw her arms around me and said, 'They take a double meaning any time you say anything like that, you know.' Anyway, that's the sort of person she was. She was so good really and I feel everyone

took advantage of her, except I don't think I did. She could cry in a scene and if you felt the scene wasn't going quite right, she could put the tears back in again. She was a marvellous silent actress, full of animation and full of projection of her thinking and emotion through the screen. Then I made her first talking picture which was very difficult for her because to be aware of the pantomime that she was so accustomed to and then have to have words to remember ... she just studied and we had quite a time in the beginning... You've seen *Wild Party*?

Q: Yes. In silent pictures, when you were directing her, did she tend to improvise or did she tend to give you the same performance on each take?
A: I can't remember, I just know she was awfully good and very obedient to do the scene exactly as you asked. I don't ever remember having any controversy of her wanting to do it another way than I'd asked and whichever way she did it, she was so right. She just automatically was a natural because the whole thing was emotional with her and she understood the emotional content of the scene so there was never any quarrel. She did it her way. I never gave people specific line readings and intonation, I just gave them the spirit of the line and what I wanted to get in spirit mostly. I'd help, that way. All the way through my directing, I don't think I remember ever giving anyone a reading except that I had John Boles study with the coach for *Craig's Wife* because I felt that he needed to have some coaching.

Q: Do you think that Clara Bow set fashion or do you think she reflected it?
A: Well, I think she was the outstanding flaming youth, and she *was* flaming, I mean she was so alive it was like a dancing flame and she projected through the screen with such life quality they gave her the name of the It girl. Then she had sex attached to her and all the rest of it but I think that she was the one that really made it popular, the first flaming youth.

INTERVIEW WITH DIRECTOR DOROTHY ARZNER

Q: Can you tell us the saga of *Old Ironsides*?
A: Yes. It's kind of a sad story in some ways because it was … I can't think of the man's first name, Carr was his last name…

Q: Harry.
A: Harry Carr was the one that brought the idea to do *Old Ironsides*. We were doing the American history story. Stephen Decatur (played by Johnny Walker) was the lead who commanded *Ironsides* and you saw the whole layering and that he was just a boy in his father's shop who designed *Ironsides* and then later he commanded it and later as, I think history tells, Lord Nelson said he freed the seas of piracy. But in the meantime *What Price Glory?* (written by Laurence Stallings) was such a success in New York and Stallings evidently got talking to Jesse Lasky and he sold him the idea that we were just making an old-fashioned picture.

He said that Stephen Decatur wasn't the hero, it was the merchant ships that were the heroes, and he went into this symbolism of the merchant ship being the heroine and *Ironsides* being the hero and he sold Lasky a bill of goods. So they changed the whole story and Carr was dismissed and we started making the *Ironsides* that is now showing, which was the story of just a farm boy who was taken onto a merchant ship and fell in love with the daughter of the man that commanded the merchant ship. And then the meeting up with *Ironsides*, the big ship, and the war between the Tripolitans and *Ironsides*. So the whole story to me was no longer American history and of course on *Covered Wagon* everything sort of worked for us and everything went along even though the weather was bad and the hardships were great, everything worked. But on *Ironsides* everything went against us from the first day we looked for locations. We were in a terrible storm and then we were always having days we couldn't shoot.

It would take four or five hours to line up all the ships and then the wind would come along and blow them all haywire. It was a man-killing job to even get the picture and finally we got into the trough of the sea and all the masts crashed over our heads so we had to go against history and show *Ironsides* as though it had had its masts blown off. And then in blowing up the masts to cover that, three men were killed and Jim Cruze was held for murder.

Q: How did that happen?
A: Well, because he ordered the men to go up to dress the mast and the shots went off to blow up the mast too soon. The powder men I guess. I shouldn't say it. It was an accident and I wasn't present. That was the last day's shooting and I had gone. And the first thing Jim Cruze said when he came back to Hollywood was, 'If you'd been there, it wouldn't have happened,' because I was always saving people.

The first time we went out on *Ironsides* we were passing the *Virginia*, the battleship, and we had a broadside loaded, so that the motion picture company could fire a broadside as we passed and salute the *Virginia*. We had all these twelve-year-old boys as powder monkeys and I said to Jim, 'Don't have them so close to those guns, Jim,' and he was busy getting the shot going and it had to go off just at the right time and he practically said, 'Don't bother me, you know,' and I tugged at his coat again and said, 'Please move those little boys back from the guns.' He finally did yell out, 'All you boys get back!' and they did move back and just then they fired the guns and all the breeches blew out, which is the rear end of the cannons that were made at Paramount studios. They all blew out and there were piles of suitcases behind them and there wasn't a little piece of cloth left intact. They would have blown those boys to pieces and from then on almost anything I said to Jim, Jim would say, 'Come on Dot, let's see...' I'd say, 'You can't shoot today, the weather's too awful,' and he'd say, 'Well, come on we're going out to find out,' and I'd have to go out with him in this tug boat and we'd be under the ocean and waves rolling over us. I remember a big wave hit us and I'd say, 'You see, we can't shoot today', and he said, 'I think you're right. Well then, turn around and let's go back.' So we didn't shoot that day.

It was just one hardship after another. We had no motors in the square rig sailing vessel. We brought all the sailors, the old sailors from square-riggers from around the east coast and up in Oregon. Every place we could gather them, you know, and when they were out with us they started deserting every day. Finally, we ended up with the cowboys from *The Covered Wagon* manning the ship; they did it better than the sailors. They just learned by being around. Jim Cruze always had a certain bunch that were loyal to his western pictures. He made a lot of western pictures and so he had them on the picture and the first thing he knew they could haul down the sails. We did keep a few of the sailors. There was one fantastic Scandinavian man who could jump four and five feet up. We had 210-foot masts and he could jump from one to the other and roll up the sail and all the rest of it. It was fantastic what some of these Scandinavians could do on a square-rig sailing vessel. We were terribly impressed with them.

Q: Tell me the story of being rescued by Art Bridges.
A: We were out on the *Esther*, which was the merchant ship, and we hit this storm and the superstructure was being broken off and washing away and the sand ballast … the ship was leaking and we were out on the other side of Catalina Island in this storm, sixty-five mile an hour winds and we were lost at sea. The captain wanted to head out to sea and Jim Cruze ordered him to go back to San Pedro. The old captains believed that in a storm, you go out where it's safe, not near the coast but Jim wasn't for doing that, he wanted to get back to San Pedro. Well, we just didn't get back, we kept being washed toward Point Dume and I think we were there all day and all night and the next day and into the night. Until Art Bridges, who was the tug boat captain who had always been around with us – pushing the boats – he was looking for us and finally about dawn he saw us and picked us up. He threw a rope on us and hauled us and just as we were getting into San Pedro, he ran out of diesel fuel. Then we

were in trouble. So they burned mops. The navy was sitting in San Pedro and they burned mops on the deck and we blew a distress signal but you couldn't hear it in the storm. I remember we were just going nearer and nearer to Point Dume. It was a dangerous spot. They finally took it out of the entrance into San Pedro harbour, but we were going right towards the lighthouse, you could almost reach out, like towards that window, and I remember Jim Cruze saying, 'Now, when we hit you go up the bow and you'll drop off onto the island.' I've forgotten what that island was called. It was all rock. At any rate, just then came the great big old red stacker that the navy had sent to us and they threw a line to us and saved us and I remember Wally Beery saying, 'Well, I was all prepared to tie Dot to a hatch cover,' and Jim Cruze said, 'Don't ever tie her to anything, she's better off by herself than tied.' He had to cover it up; people were always concerned about what was going to happen to me. But we had Duke Kahanamoku on the set (Hawaiian swimming champion, who worked as a stunt man and actor, credited with popularising the ancient Hawaiian sport of surfing). He was always alert to see that I didn't fall into the ocean and drown. I fell in once between the two ships and he just reached over and grabbed me up and set me back on the shore.

Q: How did Cruze get off the murder rap that he was on?
A: I don't really know because I wasn't in on too much that he did. I know that Paramount didn't stand behind him too strong. I think they finally proved it was an accident. The only thing was that he naturally ordered the men up on the yard arm and when the things went off just too soon, they weren't quite in a safe position. They were supposed to be in a safe position for the yard arms to be blown and they hadn't quite got there when the dynamite went off. It was loaded into the mast and they fell about 200 feet to their death. I think there were two or three men killed. I saw Jim Cruze grow grey on that picture; having black hair, he was white almost by the time he'd done it.

Every night I used to say, 'What am I doing giving my life

for a motion picture?' You know I kept arguing that I shouldn't do it, it was foolish and then the next morning there'd be a rap on the door. Because I'd have a nice room close to where Jim Cruze was and he'd come by and rap on the door and say, 'Dot, come on to breakfast,' and out you'd go and start every day. But every night you'd say, 'What am I doing, giving my life for a movie?'

Q: And when the picture was released, was it a hit?
A: Not quite, not as much as they would like to have had. I don't know why but later it became successful. I think it would have been much better if it had been American history. I think it was just a little off-beat with Laurence Stalling's modern view of a story for *Ironsides*.

Q: Didn't this have a special screen process for the print?
A: Yes, when *Ironsides* came in full sail toward us, the screen suddenly enlarged to the great big Magnascope Screen (filling the proscenium) but that had been done in *Wings* and then we came along and used the same thing. It was pretty handsome, that shot was beautiful and there was nothing more thrilling than being on that boat in full sail because it was carrying 210-foot masts on the hull. It should only carry 180 feet and you felt you were just flying. But it was top heavy and it would get this roll and still went pretty fast for this big boat and it was a very thrilling ride. We always thought it was dangerous at every minute.

Q: And then you're about to leave Paramount and you get a break?
A: That was after I finished *Ironsides* and I had written a script for Harry Cohn and then I'd said I wouldn't write another one unless he'd let me direct it because I did write scripts that could be shot. I mean, I put down close ups, medium shots and it told exactly what the camera should cover so it was a shooting script and he wanted me to do another one. I said I would only

do it if I could direct it, so he says, 'There's no reason why you can't direct one, do the next one.'

I went back to Paramount to close out my salary from *Ironsides* and it was an unusual incident because there was no one there except Ben Schulberg. It was late in the afternoon and I'd cleaned up everything and I decided that I should like to say goodbye to Mr Schulberg and the secretary wouldn't let me see him. He was in conference and I said, 'Well, I don't mind waiting,' and she said, 'No, there's no use waiting, he has a dinner engagement and he's going right out after that so no more appointments.' I remember saying, 'You don't mind if I sit here, do you?' and she said, 'Yes I do,' so I remember going out to my car and having my hand on my car door and saying to myself, 'No, I'm going to go back. I've been here for twelve years and I'm leaving and I should say goodbye to somebody important.' So I went back in again and she said, 'Are you back?' I said, 'Yes, I'll just wait and see if I can't catch him as he goes out, I just want to spend one second with him,' and she still said 'No,' and just then Walter Wanger went by the hall and I said, 'Oh you'll do,' because he now was quite a big shot in the eastern studio and he was out visiting and I knew he was an important man in Paramount. He said, 'Well, Dorothy come on in to my office,' and I went in and put my hand out and said, 'I just want to say goodbye to somebody important and you're important enough because I'm leaving,' and with that he picked up the phone and called Ben in this conference, and said, 'Ben, Dorothy's in my office and she says she's leaving,' and with that he was in in about two minutes, and he says, 'What do you mean, you're leaving?' and I said, 'I'm leaving to direct,' and he said, 'Where are you going to direct?' and I said, 'I won't tell you because you'll ruin it. It's a Poverty Row company.' It was Harry Cohn's company and he'd been making pictures for about $12,000 or something like that. And he said, 'Well, what if I said that you could direct here? Come into our scenario department and then we'll think about you directing,' and I said, 'Nope, if I get into the scenario department I'll never get out of it,' and he said, 'Well, what do you want to do then?' and I said, 'I want to be out on a set in two weeks directing an 'A' picture with an important star, otherwise let me go,' and with that he jumped up and went into his office and brought back this French farce which was called *The Best-Dressed Woman in Paris* and said, 'Here, get yourself on the set in two weeks.' Well, I didn't … it took three weeks. I nearly killed myself writing the script and shooting and cutting everything, casting and fashion shows and everything else. I was just unconscious practically, but I got through it.

Q: And the release title was?
A: *Fashions for Women*. Esther Ralston was a little cigarette girl and the famous best-dressed woman in Paris had decided to go off and marry and deserted these two couturiers who were the ones that gave this fashion show every year. So you know, it was a Cinderella story that we always had and it was this little cigarette girl Esther Ralston, who was a beautiful girl. She played Dearest in *Peter Pan*, if you remember.

Q: You had another story about *Old Ironsides?*
A: Well, it was another unusual thing because as I was walking down the pier the last week or two of *Old Ironsides*, I was walking with the property man who had practically saved my life and I said to him, 'I know I'm going to be a director as soon as this picture is finished.' And he knew I was going to become a director, which was rather fantastic. I knew it inside me and I had made the statement as we were walking along over in Catalina on the picr about two weeks before we finished *Ironsides*.

Q: Now, you were going to talk about your anxiety not to be over-exploited.
A: Well, that was in the beginning when I was going to become a director, I asked that I'd not have my name big. I just wanted it small down at the bottom, about the same size as where

it said 'A Paramount Picture'. I didn't like the idea that they were going to make something of me being the only woman director that Paramount had. I had seen them over-exploit people like Lila Lea and actresses who were trying to take the place of Mary Pickford and I felt that if you over-exploit any of these things, an audience backs away from you. I wanted to have my picture stand up along with the men's pictures and be box office successes without any idea that a woman had made it. Just let the picture stand on its own.

Q: How much resentment did you encounter?
A: I don't remember really any resentment except when someone appealed to Darryl Zanuck for me to direct a picture at Fox, he said, 'I don't want a woman director,' so that's the only thing. I don't think Warner Brothers particularly wanted to deal with a woman director either but I did not find resentment that I know of. I would find a little bit of it, of them telling me afterwards that they were worried about coming on the set with me, from either a cameraman or an assistant. I had an assistant once who was worried about coming on the picture with a woman director and then he said afterwards, 'You certainly knew your business,' so I forgot very quickly what my feelings were in the beginning. After all, the director at Paramount was the authority. They may have had feelings and they may have resented me but I never was aware of it.

In fact, I wasn't aware of very much outside of what my own job was. I told you the story of Adolph Zukor coming on the set asking me a question early on, when I was doing Clara Bow pictures. He asked me a question, I thought he was a visitor and I started telling him all about the movies and then as he left, my assistant came up and said, 'Did you know who you were talking to?' And I said, 'I haven't the slightest idea who I was talking to,' and he said, 'It's just Adolph Zukor who pays your salary,' and I didn't know. I never was interested in patronising important people, I only dealt with the person who hired me and when they hired me,

I figured they were the ones, the only one I went to, and Ben Schulberg had made me a director so he was the only one I was really aware of.

Q: How did you cope with the coming of sound?

A: It was difficult but it was just something you took in your stride and you did it. Because we were in booths, we couldn't move and the sound man would say, 'There's hums in the system,' but as I said, making pictures was difficult anyway so one difficulty was not much different than another one, you just took them in your stride and solved them as you went along. I know that's how it happened on the first one, with Clara Bow ... because she was so confined by the microphones that hung there and then you couldn't say anything till you'd got over to the other one they hung over there and they just had these (microphones) hanging in spots where the scenes were supposed to be played. In other words, your sound man was laying out your choreography of the scenes and that bothered me because I used to like people talking and moving and so I remember saying to my property man, 'Do you have a fish pole?' and he said, 'Yes', and I said, 'Well, you bring your fish pole and a ladder tomorrow and hang that thing on it and we will make some moving shots,' and that was the beginning at Paramount of the moving microphones, which we did and it worked. Of course the poor soundman who was an expert from MIT just nearly had a fit. He said, 'It's gonna click,' and I said, 'Well, tape it up so it doesn't click.' This was the whole thing of motion pictures in those days; you solved problems. I know that once Esther Ralston was half-fainting or something, and she had to be dragged off the scene and she was so heavy that nobody could do it gracefully, so we did it with a roller skate, a board on a skate and they picked her up and just dragged her off. She had a lovely dress that covered everything, I mean, we had to devise these things.

Q: When you saw the first sound film in the theatre, what were your feelings?

A: Well, it came about so gradually... I think it was Warner Brothers with their first picture, *City Lights,* was it? The first sound picture that Warners made?

Q: *The Jazz Singer?*

A: Well, *The Jazz Singer* [1927] was the first big one but there was one made ahead of it.

Q: *Lights of New York.* [the first all-talking picture, released in 1928]

A: *Lights of New York* or some such thing and I went east and also heard the sound device and that's when I was assigned to do *Glorifying the American Girl* and I came back to Paramount saying, 'We must have that sound device and colour, sound and colour, to do *Glorifying the American Girl*' and that's when they gave me the absent treatment for a few months because I was a dreaming schoolgirl and wanted to change the business. You see, Paramount didn't want to come into sound because they had too much invested in theatres – they had the majority of theatres and they had so much invested in theatres – it would have cost a fortune for them to change over to sound, which they finally had to do, but they didn't want to. They were the last ones to come into sound of the big studios and so because I said I didn't want to do *Glorifying the American Girl* without sound and colour, especially the Follies show I wanted to do, because we were doing parts of the picture in sound and colour in the beginning, I was taken off the picture and somebody else made it in the east and it was a flop, of course. I was pleased it was a flop. It sort of exonerated me as far as knowing what I was doing. I really had quite a great story for it, *Glorifying the American Girl*.

Q: So you approved of sound as soon as you...?

A: Yes, I was the youngest director... I was so young that I was already into things that were coming, just like youth is today. They know more about what's going to happen than we do, than I do, certainly. I'm still hanging onto the past somewhere … not very much but you know, we aren't pioneers any more, which we were then, we were pioneers and wanting to be and eager for whatever was new, because I know that, even with my first picture, I wanted to do what would be transparencies (back projection) but of course they told me it couldn't be done. And I wanted to have the clothes that would be like yachting clothes and be able to have the background with them at sea and just have the wheel of a yacht and have men and women with yachting clothes. I wanted to do a fashion show that was very modern but that was all way beyond – so I was always known as a dreaming schoolgirl who wanted to do things that were impossible to do. Later it was done, but I was reaching all the time for something unusual. I always had something unusual in my pictures if I could catch it because that was the way that I could know that I could draw attention to my pictures.

Q: Well, looking back at the silent era, do you think anything was lost when sound came in?
A: I felt there was when sound came in, and I don't know now whether it was or not. I don't suppose so … sound is progress but they were wonderful pictures, the silent pictures at the time. I know Jo Sternberg's picture (*The Last Command*) about the film extra who had been a great general, was a wonderful silent picture … there were wonderful silent pictures and Murnau's pictures were great too and I remember just thinking that you couldn't touch those pictures with sound because sound began to confine us so. Of course, now with tape and all the rest of it, it isn't quite as limiting as it was in the beginning of sound. I think we all thought that sound would ruin pictures in the beginning because the cameras were in a booth and we just had all kinds of difficulties handling them but later, great flexibility came about.

Note from the Editors
After further research we believe this is one of Dorothy Arzner's last – if not her very last – interview, thereby challenging Karyn

Kay's assumption – shared on the Agnes Films website (see below link) that her 1974 interview is Arzner's last one. http://agnesfilms.com/interviews/interview-with-dorothy-arzner/

Kevin Brownlow

As a film editor, Brownlow worked on Tony Richardson's *The Charge of the Light Brigade* (1968) with Andrew Mollo, and they directed two feature films *It Happened Here* (1964) and *Winstanley* (1975). In 1980, with David Gill, Brownlow directed for Thames TV a thirteen-part TV series, *Hollywood*, devoted to the American silent film. In l980, his five-hour restoration of Abel Gance's *Napoléon* was presented with a score composed by Carl Davis. Following the demise of Thames TV, Brownlow and Gill formed their own company, Photoplay Productions with Patrick Stanbury. Their restorations included the Valentino classic, *The Four Horsemen of the Apocalypse* (1921) and *The Iron Mask* (1929) with Douglas Fairbanks.

In 1995, they completed the six-part *Cinema Europe* to mark the centenary of cinema. David Gill died in 1997. Brownlow and Stanbury continued the tradition with documentaries like *Cecil B. DeMille – American Epic, I'm King Kong,* the career of Merian C. Cooper and *Garbo* for TCM.

Among Brownlow's books are *The Parade's Gone By...* (Knopf: 1968); *David Lean* (Richard Cohen 1996) and *The War, The West and The Wilderness* (Knopf 1979). He is currently working on a biography of director/producer Sidney Franklin.

Dorothy Arzner

There is renewed interest in Arzner at the moment, with a Hollywood biopic coming out and a recent UCLA retrospective about her work in 2015. Plus *Sight and Sound* (U.K. film magazine) celebrating her considerable talents. Arzner is credited with inventing the boom microphone, pioneering directing feats, and 'star making' many legends including Lucille Ball, Clara Bow and Katharine Hepburn. Arzner directed sixteen feature films in the years between 1927 and 1943.

For more on Arzner – see Francesca Stephens' chapter, 'Directors From the Dawn of Hollywood', about early female film directors. (page 146)

9. WOMEN FILM EDITORS FROM SILENT TO SOUND

Tania Field

Once upon a time there were no film editors … and no cuts, filmmakers just filmed what interested them or amused them. They held a shot until they got bored, or the moment passed, or the film ran out.

The 'fathers' of cinema, Thomas Edison in the United States, and the Lumière Brothers in France, were pessimistic about the future of cinema. There was a world-wide interest in seeing images move, but why would the public audience pay money to see something they could see in the street for free? Auguste Lumière went as far to say: 'Cinema was an invention without a future.'

Edwin S. Porter, an employee of Thomas Edison, proved them wrong; Porter discovered that cutting separate shots together could create a story. His film, *Life of an American Fireman* 1903, started 'cross-cutting' (U.S.) or 'inter-cutting' (U.K.) two shots, separate scenes, not related to each other: the fireman responding together with the fire scene miles away, creating an emotional impact on the audience.

But by 1926, when Hollywood was taking off, the *Los Angeles Times* wrote: 'one of the most important positions in the motion-picture industry is held almost entirely by women, whose job it was to assemble thousands of feet of film so that it tells an interesting story in the most straightforward manner. Assembling reels and cutting negatives was tedious work that often fell to young working-class women. However, out of the ranks of these film joiners and negative cutters emerged a handful of women who would help to develop the editing techniques that would become the hallmark of Hollywood's visual style.'

Women were not just screen actresses in the silent era, in the two decades before the advent of synchronised sound motion pictures, women's participation was both deeper and wider than previously thought. The 'mothers' of cinema were making their huge contribution to the history of cinema.

Flashback eight years, in late 1895, keen to continue his development of films, Thomas Edison employed Alfred Clark as supervising director of his film division. Dickson, of course, is the man generally credited with the actual invention of the Kinetoscope, the device patented and distributed by Thomas Edison as a peep-show viewer for the earliest films produced in the United States. Comparatively little has been written on the contributions of Alfred Clark to early American cinema, but this film, *The Execution of Mary, Queen of Scots*, which he directed in 1895, is a testament to the innovations in storytelling that Clark brought to film.

This very short film is one of the earliest to feature a historical re-creation of a scene, making use of special effects; in this case, stop-motion. Clark may very well have been the first filmmaker to utilise this technique. The effect is actually quite convincing here, as Mary (actually played by a male actor) kneels down, the cut is made as she is replaced with a dummy, whose head is, quite realistically, severed right in front of the viewer's eye. It was said to have convinced many audiences that a woman had sacrificed herself for the making of this film.

The film was produced on 28th August 1895, predating the Lumière screenings at the Grand Café by exactly four months. It's worth noting that, while the Lumière films screened at their 28th December show are often heralded as the 'birth' of the motion picture, Edison, Dickson and Alfred Clark had already achieved a remarkable degree of technical sophistication.

Overlooked in the history of both narrative and special effects, Alfred Clark's *The Execution of Mary, Queen of Scots* stands as an important, early landmark film in its use of both techniques, which sowed the seed for things to come.

Almost simultaneous 'trick' editing was being developed by Georges Méliès, in France, his film *The Vanishing Lady* (1896) provided the first European example. With this basic device Méliès would continue to make a significant number of 'trick' films for the rest of the 1890s and into the next century, and their construction became increasingly intricate. It is important to clarify that whereas these trick films by Clark and Méliès have been seen as simply the product of stop motion, they did involve careful editing. The examination of the actual prints of Méliès' films revealed that in every case the stop motion technique was revised through splicing. There were variations in hand-cranked camera speed when stopping and starting, as well as refinements only possible at this stage, which called for an actual cutting of the film at the beginning and the ending of the uninterrupted action and the subsequent splicing of it together. The splices in Méliès' films were managed in order to maintain the flow and rhythm of the acting which merely stopping the camera could not provide.

During the years after 1908 there was a shift from filmed theatre to cinematic expression. This led the way for a complete change from the broader, theatrical performance to a subtler performance style; from long takes at a fixed distance to the multi-distant shots, and the use of editing. This became the essence of the cinema to come. Continuity editing emerged, in the U.S., as a system for creating coherent narrative space and time, creating action that flows smoothly across shots and scenes without jarring visual inconsistencies, establishing a sense of story for the viewer. Surprisingly quickly, however, filmmakers discovered ways of using editing for authorial comment, for enhancing suspense, for creating parallelism and even disorienting the viewer for various purposes.

This huge shift, when moving pictures became the movies,

developed between 1908 and 1920. Major film firms were created in Europe, Denmark, Sweden, and France, including: Nordisk Film, Svensk Filmindustri and Film d'Art. U.S. independents became Hollywood studios: Loews/ Metro, Fox, Paramount, Universal, Goldwyn, United Artists and Columbia. This prompted the emergence of vigorous film creators, big names of silent cinema including: Gad, Gallone, Feuillade, Gance, Griffith, Sennett, DeMille, Ince, and Chaplin. The films they made got longer, and this encouraged audiences to make film-going a grand social event; this same period gave birth to the modern movie theatre, often converted from conventional vaudeville and drama theatres, later to be joined by purpose-built cinemas, and chains of cinemas across the U.S. and Europe.

The movie culture we recognise today was taking form and growing rapidly with the emergence of distinctive stars, genres and formats. The new juggernaut venture of cinema was gaining speed and momentum worldwide, but, each country seemed to be going its own way. The mode of film production in the U.S. (Hollywood) was based on a slick commercial model, across the Atlantic different methods developed inspired by completely different motives, mainly artistic and as a medium for propaganda.

United States

Central to the process in Hollywood were two related phenomena: the careful, highly detailed planning of production, from conception to screening, through the continuity script, and the implementation of the strict division of jobs. The key player in this revolutionising process was Thomas Harper Ince. By 1915 Ince was one of the best-known producer-directors, and is credited as organising production methods into the discipline still practiced today.

The control over production was accomplished primarily through this continuity script, essentially a complete blueprint for, and record of, a film shoot. The continuity script was often held and managed by women who were known as script girls. The continuity script featured many of the same elements as the earlier scenario script, but in much greater detail. It contained shooting dates, highly detailed description of actions, footage estimations for each shot, complete budgetary data, and information on release prints and distribution. The evolution of the continuity script was simultaneous with changes in film style. Filmmakers began to explore scene dissection, or the division of scenes into multiple shots. This emerging style required careful attention and the proper matching of positions and movements across shots, and the most effective way to do so was by planning every detail in advance.

There was a heavy emphasis on efficiency in the American studios. A producer took over the responsibility, from start to finish, for supervising the whole production. The director had some input in the planning and editing, but was mainly responsible for the shooting phase. The post-shoot phase required 'cutters' or 'editors' to assemble hundreds of numbered shots into a film, often with minimal input from the film director.

Within the Hollywood machine, many jobs were not necessarily gender-typed. In the first decade some departments became exclusively organised along gender lines, with editing or joining being the most visibly gendered work. In 1923 the most comprehensive overview of the industry, *Business Woman* listed over twenty different jobs that women held, in addition to actress, which included typist, stenographer, secretary to the stars and executive secretary, telephone operator, hairdresser, seamstress, costume designer, milliner, reader, script girl, scenarist, cutter, film retoucher, film splicer, laboratory worker, set designer and set dresser, librarian, artist, title writer, publicity writer, plasterer molder, casting director, musician, film editor, department manager, director and producer.

For much of Hollywood filmmaking history, there were virtually no fame-inducing opportunities available to women other than screenwriting and acting, with maybe one major exception. Women have been welcomed, and in many instances, preferred by male directors, as film editors, or 'cutters,' as they were originally known. In the early days, the job was regarded as menial labour, which it was. Cutters worked by hand, running film on reels with hand cranks and manually cutting and gluing together the film. They almost never received screen credit. After the introduction of the Moviola editing machine in 1924, the process became faster and easier, but was still tedious and low paid, and is why most cutters remained young, working-class women.

Around this time the job of cutting films became less about just maintaining proper continuity and more about being creative. In Russia the film director Sergei Eisenstein had introduced the concept of 'montage', how splicing, or juxtaposing, separate images or pieces of film together could advance a storyline and manipulate viewers' emotions. This approach became imitated worldwide, not least by some of the more enterprising female cutters in America, some of whom, like Margaret Booth, began to experiment with leftover footage on the cutting room floor, which proved to be quite inventive.

It is difficult to uncover much information about the very early film editors. Some, like Dorothy Arzner, who cut Rudolph Valentino's *Blood and Sand* (1922), moved up from editing to direct and play a more visible role in Hollywood. But more commonly, the women who cut film in the silent era remained unacknowledged in film credits or the trade press. Their work was considered to be merely technical rather than creative, especially during a period when many directors oversaw the editing of their own films. At least once, however, the case was made for the special aptitude women had for editing, as when Florence Osborne wrote in a 1925 *Motion Picture Magazine* article:

> Among the greatest 'cutters' and film editors are women.
> They are quick and resourceful. They are also ingenious

in their work and usually have a strong sense of what the public wants to see. They can sit in a stuffy cutting-room and see themselves looking at the picture before an audience.

During this Golden Age of Hollywood, Louis B. Mayer, Darryl F. Zanuck, D. W. Griffith and Cecil B. DeMille were powerful enough to determine who would work in the studios. The old cliché that behind every great man is a woman, definitely applied to these very tough-minded, dominating men. They all relied on the judgment of the women around them. Zanuck's wife Virginia guided him throughout his life, just as Ida Koverman, Mayer's secretary/majordomo, directed him. DeMille's female creative team, which included his wife Constance and scenarist Jeanie Macpherson, was humorously regarded as his harem.

Three women editors who started their careers in the silent movies, worked from the 1920s through the 1950s, had constant access to each of these men: Margaret Booth with Mayer at Metro-Goldwyn-Mayer, Barbara McLean with Zanuck at 20th Century-Fox Film Studios, and Anne Bauchens with DeMille at Paramount Pictures. Though Anne Bauchens never held an administrative post at the studio like Margaret Booth and Barbara McLean eventually did, she was the film editor of the chief money-maker on the lot, Cecil B. DeMille. Together, Booth, McLean and Bauchens represented three of only eight female film editors working in Hollywood in the 1930s.

Of the three women, Booth had the most pervasive influence throughout the industry. Long after Mayer left MGM in 1951, she continued as supervising editor until 1968 when she was seventy years old. Then Ray Stark hired her as his supervising editor until 1982. In many respects, the politically astute Booth became the doyenne of the film industry, one of the few crossovers between the old and new Hollywood.

Unlike Margaret Booth, Barbara McLean was too shy to involve herself with industry politics, but firmly held the editorial department in her grasp through sheer personal determination and an enviable professional record. Anne Bauchens never really emerged from the shadows of DeMille's persona to establish herself as a versatile editor. Though it could be argued that the annual DeMille spectacles kept the financially unstable Paramount afloat.

Margaret Booth (1898–2002)

Margaret Booth's career began with D. W. Griffith and ended with Neil Simon, almost sixty-five years later. During that period, she was supervising editor at MGM from 1939 through 1968, which was almost the end of the run for the old studio. When she was in her seventies, producer Ray Stark hired her to be his supervising editor for such productions as the Barbra Streisand vehicles *The Way We Were* (1973) and *Funny Lady* (1975).

Margaret Booth was so respected in the industry that, in 1977, when *Film Comment* asked 100 film editors to name the top ten editors in the history of the medium, she was listed number three in the poll. She was still at the top of her game after half a century, and still had nearly a decade of work left in her. Booth was always an MGM woman, however, as evidenced by her selection of three MGM classics as her favorite editing jobs: *Bombshell* (1933), *Mutiny on the Bounty* (1935) and *Camille* (1937). She was reticent about personal publicity and details about her life are rare. Toward the end of her MGM tenure, she consented to an interview with film historian/filmmaker Kevin Brownlow for his landmark oral history book, *The Parade's Gone By*, when she was in London in 1965.

Margaret Booth began work at D. W. Griffith's Los Angeles studio shortly after graduating from Los Angeles High School in 1915. Her brother, Elmer Booth, had been a Broadway performer who acted in a number of Griffith's films for the Reliance Company. When Elmer died in a car crash in 1915, Griffith gave a moving eulogy at the funeral, as *Moving Picture World* reported. Elmer's sister Margaret was then urged to come to work for the studio. There, the only jobs available to an inexperienced, female high-school graduate were in the 'laboratory', where Margaret soon began work as a film 'joiner' assembling two-hundred-foot rolls of film into thousand-foot reels. 'All of the film,' she explains, 'came in rolls and they had young girls … who assembled the reels and … checked to see that it was all right, that it was assembled right and there were no bad frames.' After working briefly as a film joiner, Margaret was promoted to negative cutter, supporting Griffith's cutters, Jimmie and Rose Smith who edited the positive print materials. Margaret Booth and Irene Morra, who would also become a cutter, then matched the corresponding frames in the negatives. In the years before it became common practice to print key numbers on the edges of film negatives, the job of negative cutter was difficult, time-consuming, and intricate, which perhaps explains why it fell so often to women. Key numbers, or edge numbers, finally made it easier to match each frame of a print to its corresponding frame on the negative. Without key numbers as references, Booth and Morra had to match the negative to the positive print by eye. As she recalled to Kevin Brownlow: 'It was very tedious work. Close-ups of Lillian Gish in *Orphans of the Storm* would go on for miles, and they'd be very similar.'

In 1919, when Griffith closed down his Los Angeles studio and moved his production facilities to New York, Margaret Booth was out of a job. She worked briefly at Paramount, assembling tinted films for the studio before she found better work at Louis B. Mayer's small studio, where she got her foot in the door when she helped one of Mayer's cutters, Billy Shea, who was behind schedule and needed a negative cutter on a Sunday. Margaret was soon hired to cut and assemble negatives at Mayer's studio, where she worked exclusively with director John Stahl. She recalls that Stahl explained his principle of the close-up: 'Always play it in the long shot unless you want to punctuate something.' Booth would repeat this advice in her 1938 essay, 'The Cutter': 'A line spoken by a character in a long shot achieves much greater importance if it is stressed and underlined with a close up.' Margaret would also describe rhythm as essential to editing and was convinced that film directors with talent used a distinctive rhythm in all of their motion pictures, and it was the job of the cutter to find that rhythm and bring it out in the editing, difficult to do at a time when cutting was done by hand. Stahl encouraged her to watch him edit his own dailies. 'That way, he taught me the dramatic values of cutting; in fact, he taught me how to edit.'

Margaret Booth appears to have developed the ambition to become a cutter while working with John Stahl. In her interview with Rudy Behlmer she explains that Stahl would always shoot five takes of a scene, print them all, and screen the dailies with her to tell her what he wanted to use from which take. Booth practised editing with the unused footage from his films, staying at the studio late into the night to experiment with the outtakes. At one point, Stahl was unhappy with the way he had edited a scene, and used Booth's footage instead. Soon, Booth was roughing out scenes for the director. In an interview she explains that beginning with *The Dangerous Age* (1923), she began to receive screen credit for editing his films, though she attributed the actual editing to Stahl; 'I got credit for all the John Stahl pictures… They just put my name there, but I was not a cutter there. John Stahl was really the cutter.'

When Mayer's studio was acquired by Marcus Loew of Loew's, Inc. to form Metro-Goldwyn-Mayer in 1924, Margaret found her niche. She became an editor in 1924 when Stahl was impressed with her editing of outtakes. 'After a while, he started to look at these efforts of mine, and sometimes he'd take a whole sequence that I had cut and put it in the picture,' she recalled. 'Then, gradually, I got around to making his first cut, and that's how I got to be an editor.'

But her loyalty was to MGM, not to Stahl, and she refused to join him when he moved to Tiffany-Stahl and then Universal Pictures. As she told Brownlow, she never wanted to leave MGM and, didn't want to work for just one man; she enjoyed working for everyone. Micromanager Mayer, who was suspicious of stars, directors and screenwriters, made Booth his decision-maker and ally, perhaps because he could truly control film content with an editor. This was a tightrope for her because, as she admitted, she mainly worked for Irving Thalberg, 'the greatest man who was ever in pictures,' but who threatened Mayer's supremacy with Nicholas Schenck, the head of Loew's. Irving Thalberg, wanted her to sit beside him at the screenings of dailies, so they could exchange ideas. And it was out of respect for her talents that he coined the term 'film editor' which carried more gravitas than 'cutter'.

She did not remain loyal to the past, however, and welcomed the new editing techniques of the 1960s. 'When I cut silent films, I used to count to get the rhythm,' she said in *The Parade's Gone By*. 'If I was cutting a march of soldiers, or anything with a beat to it, and I wanted to change the angle, I would count, 'one-two-three-four-five-six.' I made a beat for myself. That's how I did it when I was cutting the film in the hand. When Moviolas came in, you could count that way too; you watched the rhythm through the glass…

According to the editor Ralph E. Winters, who worked under the wing of Margaret Booth, every MGM editor was required to bring his or her work to Booth, as supervising editor. 'She had her own projection room and saw all the rushes and cuts for every MGM film. She was empowered to make changes and present the editing of sequences to various producers and directors as she saw fit.' He went on to write that she demanded only the best from the people she supervised: 'Time and again, editors were sent back to their cutting rooms to adjust their work to her liking. But she was consistent and fair, and appreciated both good work and good effort.'

One of the many things Winters learned from her was to always 'keep the story in mind. She hated editing for the sake of editing, but if you had to make a bad edit to advance the story, that was fine with her. She was not afraid to go to the mat with anyone, and producers and directors alike felt her wrath when she thought that they were going in the wrong direction. She fought hard for what she believed, and she was usually right. But, she always protected her editors.'

Although she was nominated for editing *Mutiny on the Bounty* in 1935, Booth would have to wait until the 50th annual Academy Awards ceremony in 1978 (recognising the films of 1977) to receive her only Oscar, an Honorary Academy Award for her contributions to the art of editing, when she was eighty years old. It was a long overdue recognition from the Academy of Motion Picture Arts and Sciences.

'Women in Film' also awarded Booth its prestigious Crystal Award in 1983, and the American Cinema Editors (ACE) bestowed her with a Career Achievement Award in 1990. At its Board of Directors Installation Dinner in 1998, the Editors Guild presented Booth with a commemorative crystal award in celebration of her one-hundredth birthday and her outstanding career as an editor. She died in 2002 at the age of 104.

In contrast to Margaret Booth, Anne Bauchens would work almost exclusively with Cecil B. DeMille, from *We Can't Have Everything* (1918) through *The Ten Commandments* (1956). While Booth became one of the most powerful editors in Hollywood, named by members of the profession as one of the top ten editors in the history of the medium, Anne's career would remain in the shadow of that of the notoriously extravagant director.

Anne Bauchens (1882–1967)

Anne Bauchens probably owed her longevity in the industry as much to her slavish devotion, as to her editing skills. Long before the term auteur was applied to a film director, Cecil B. DeMille was one. He was even his own film editor in the silent era, Anne Bauchens was his negative cutter and then served as his co-editor, beginning with his film *Carmen* in 1915.

The cinematographer Charles Rosher related to Kevin Brownlow (for the book *The Parade's Gone By*) an incident that demonstrates Anne Bauchens' reverence to the director, which may have originated the famous line, 'Ready when you are, C. B.' As Rosher, a cameraman on *Carmen*, recalled, 'DeMille was tough on lunch breaks. One day, about 3pm, he asked, "Anyone hungry?" "We're not, if you're not, chief," Anne Bauchens, his cutter and script girl, replied. I yelled, "Speak for yourself, Anne!" DeMille called lunch.'

The St. Louis, Missouri-born aspiring actress met DeMille while she was working as a secretary for his brother, William de Mille, in 1912. William, who used the small 'de' in his surname, the true family spelling, as opposed to the pretentious Cecil, also became a director, and Bauchens even edited two of his films: *Craig's Wife* (1928) and *This Mad World* (1931). Bauchens obviously thought the 'Big D' was her destiny.

Leatrice Joy, the star of the first version of *The Ten Commandments* (1923), amongst other DeMille epic films, was friends with Anne Bauchens. 'The editor,' she had said, 'was devoted to DeMille, and he was very comfortable with her.' Since the director-producer really wanted to be his own editor, they were like duo pianists. In fact, DeMille even blocked Paramount's efforts to hire another editor.

But this close working relationship did not bode well for Anne Bauchens artistically. According to her contemporary, Margaret Booth, who pointed out to Brownlow in 1965, 'Anne Bauchens is the oldest editor in the business. She was editing for years before I came into the business. I thought DeMille was a bad editor, and made her look like a bad editor. I think Anne really would have been a good editor, but she had to put up with him.' That 'something' determined her nickname, 'Trojan Annie' because of the prodigious work involved in editing the elaborate DeMille epics.

For forty years, although she was forced by MGM and Paramount to edit other films, Bauchens worked 'cheek by jowl' with DeMille, according to film historian and writer Lisa Mitchell, who was an actress in *The Ten Commandments* (1956). DeMille made Mitchell privy to his methodology during this award-winning, swan-song production for both the director and editor. Mitchell recalled the separation anxiety Anne Bauchens experienced during this production; DeMille was shooting in Egypt and the raw footage was flown to Los Angeles in refrigerated containers for her to edit without him, a physically as well as emotionally difficult experience for the then ageing editor.

Anne Bauchens will be remembered as DeMille's editor, only twenty of the sixty-three films she edited were not directed or produced by him. Bauchens also earned the distinction of being the first woman to win an Academy Award for Editing, for DeMille's *Northwest Mounted Police* (1940). She also received Oscar nominations for three other films by the director: *Cleopatra* (1934), *The Greatest Show on Earth* (1952) and *The Ten Commandments* (1956).

Barbara McLean (1903–1996)

Barbara 'Bobby' McLean began her career as a negative cutter for the director Rex Ingram in the early 1920s. She married soundman Gordon McLean, sometime in the late 1920s or early 1930s, and before that she worked for Ingram's film editor, Grant Whytock, and his wife, Leotta, who was also a negative cutter. Her work on such exotic Ingram films for Metro-Goldwyn-Mayer as *Mare Nostrum* (1924) and *The Garden of Allah* (1927) would prepare her for the sleek adventure sagas directed by Henry King at Fox several years later. When Whytock became Samuel Goldwyn's editor in the late 1920s, Barbara followed him as his assistant and worked on films produced by Goldwyn as well as Mary Pickford, both of whom were partners in the recently formed United Artists.

Darryl F. Zanuck, co-founder and head of Twentieth Century Pictures, was said to have admired a film, possibly Frank Borzage's *Secrets* (1933), on which Barbara McLean assisted. He reportedly referred to her as 'one of the best editors in town' and hired her as an editor for Twentieth Century releases *The Bowery* (1933) and *Gallant Lady* (1934), the latter for which she received her first solo editing credit.

When Zanuck and Joseph Schenck bought the Fox Pictures studio in 1935, and merged his company with it to form 20th Century-Fox, he built a true state-of-the-art, three-story editing building. Only the editors were allowed on the second floor. Screenings were arranged on the first floor and producers, rather than directors, made the editing decisions.

Barbara McLean and her second husband, Robert Webb, whom she married in 1951, were an Oscar couple. Webb directed mainly action pictures for 20th Century-Fox such as *Beneath the 12-Mile Reef* (1954) and Elvis Presley's debut *Love Me Tender* (1956), and won his Academy Award as assistant director of *King's In Old Chicago* (1937), a film edited by McLean but for which she received no nomination. A measure of Zanuck's respect for McLean is the fact that he only assigned her to the prestigious dramatic productions.

The studio chief's favourite director after John Ford was King, and McLean edited the bulk of the prolific director's films at Fox, including *Wilson* (1944), for which she received an Oscar.

Ironically, although McLean was nominated for the Academy Award six additional times, she was not nominated for editing *The Robe* (1953), the inaugural film shot and released in Cinemascope. The challenges involved in determining editing cuts in the widescreen process for the first time certainly seemed to deserve a special award. Her nominations include: *Les Miserables* (1935), *Lloyds of London* (1936), *Alexander's Ragtime Band* (1938), *The Rains Came* (1939) *The Song of Bernadette* (1943) and *All about Eve* (1950).

When she was asked by 'Film Comment' in 1977 to answer three questions, she was succinct, almost too much so, in her answers: What is editing? 'Film editing is telling the story with film.' What is good film editing? 'Good film editing is selecting the best of the film.' What is great film editing? 'Great film editing occurs when you begin with great pictures.'

Dorothy Spencer (1909–2002)

Dorothy Spencer cut Elia Kazan's directorial debut *A Tree*

215

Grows in Brooklyn (1945) and multiple films for directors such as John Ford, including *Stagecoach* (1939) and Alfred Hitchcock, including *Lifeboat* (1944) during a career that spanned from 1926 to 1979. She worked with Anne Bauchens to manage the 70,000 feet of film for the epic production *Cleopatra* (1963), reducing it to 22,000 in the edited version. She was nominated for an Academy Award for Best Editing four times and received an American Cinema Editors Career Achievement Award in 1989. She was also presented with a 'Golden Scissors Award' for her editing of the disaster epic *Earthquake* (1974).

Viola Lawrence (1894–1973)

Viola Lawrence is often credited as Hollywood's first female film cutter. She began working in film at the age of twelve when she held title cards at the Vitagraph studio in Flatbush. Six years later, she edited her first film, a Vitagraph three-reeler, *O'Henry* (1912). In 1917, she moved to Hollywood, where she worked at Universal, First National, and Gloria Swanson Productions before arriving at Columbia Pictures, where in 1925 she became the supervising editor, and where she was still editing until 1960. She was nominated twice for Academy Awards for Best Editing for *Pal Joey* (1957) and for *Pepe* (1960), a big-budget musical comedy which involved reducing 500,000 feet of rushes to 20,000 feet of edited film.

Blanche Sewell (1898–1949)

Blanche Sewell started out as a negative cutter shortly after graduating from Inglewood High School in 1918. She assisted Viola Lawrence on the editing of *Man, Woman, Marriage* (1921) and went on to become an editor at MGM where she cut classic films such as *Grand Hotel* (1932) *Queen Christina* (1933) and *The Wizard of Oz* (1939). She remained an editor there until her death, aged fifty, in 1949.

Jane Loring (1890–1983)

Originally from Denver, Jane Loring edited movie trailers before becoming a film cutter for Paramount-Famous Players

Lasky in 1927. She worked for Paramount until the early 1930s, on films such as *Avalanche* (1928) and *Fast Company* (1929). She later moved to RKO to work as an assistant director. However she often went uncredited as an assistant director/production assistant on films such as *Kismet* (1955) and *An American in Paris* (1951).

Dorothy Arzner (1897–1979)

Dorothy Arzner grew up in Hollywood, California, where her father owned a restaurant next to a theatre that was popular with actors. D. W. Griffith, Mary Pickford, Douglas Fairbanks, Mack Sennett, and many of the local actors and directors frequented the restaurant. She went to the University of Southern California and focused on the idea of becoming a doctor. But with a few summer months in the office of a fine surgeon and meeting with the sick, she decided it wasn't for her.

Her work in the film industry began when she started typing scripts for the Famous Players-Lasky Corporation, which would later become Paramount. After six months, she became a cutter and editor at Realart Studio, a subsidiary of Paramount. As chief editor, she cut and edited fifty-two films before being recalled to Paramount to cut and edit the Valentino vehicle *Blood and Sand* (1922), her first 'big picture' and the first film for which she had undertaken some of the filming. Her experience working on this and *The Covered Wagon* (1923) enabled her to move on to directing. Among the many films in her oeuvre are *Christopher Strong* (1933), *The Bride Wore Red* (1937) and *Dance, Girl, Dance* (1940).

(For more about Dorothy Arzner, see chapters 7 and 8 in this book.)

Women Editors in the European Film Industry

Outside of the United States, the cinema was not on the same commercial scale. In Europe, women were employed as film editors and cutters, as the work was low paid and technical. The backroom posts, including the role of montageur

(U.S.S.R.), monteuse (France) and kleberin (Germany) were less celebrated, and less documented. This chapter explores four of the countries where women were known to have made significant contributions as editors but more research is needed to explore the contribution of women film editors elsewhere.

U.S.S.R.

Without Lenin, we wouldn't enjoy Hollywood half as much. The one idea the October Revolution definitely gave us was the notion that a film is made in the editing suite as much as on the set. The Russians adored editing. This was partly because, in the years after 1917, the Soviet Union was encouraging a growing film industry, mainly to be used as the perfect medium to inspire this largely illiterate nation to join the Revolution. Film was being used as propaganda. Russian filmmakers rejected bourgeois stories, and instead of melodrama they wanted to reflect real life.

Would-be filmmakers didn't have enough cameras or film stock to shoot anything. Instead, they experimented in the cutting room with found footage, from pre-revolutionary Russian melodramas to rare Hollywood imports. A crucial moment was the smuggling into Russia of a print of D. W. Griffith's *Intolerance* (1916), the most brilliantly edited early Hollywood film. Under the influential teacher Lev Kuleshov, a group of film students in Moscow re-ran the film constantly, then re-edited it themselves, discovering the radical effects produced when they changed a sequence.

Kuleshov's workshop took this research further. They used a piece of footage of Ivan Mozzhukhin, a famous Russian actor who had fled the country in 1917, and cut the same shot in three sequences. In one, they juxtaposed his face with a plate of soup; in another with a little girl playing; in another with a dead woman. Audiences praised Mozzhukhin's range – showing hunger when he saw the soup, joy in seeing his daughter play and grief for his mother. The Soviets called their editing technique 'montage'.

Kuleshov's most outstanding student was Vsevolod Pudovkin, who went on to promote the workshop's techniques in influential writings which stated 'The foundation of film art is editing.' In the second half of the 1920s, when the Soviets finally got their hands on film and equipment, and established subsidised studios, Pudovkin made some of the liveliest and most perversely moving films of all time.

Pudovkin was a dedicated propagandist, far less ambiguously so than his rival Eisenstein, who was to subvert Stalin in *Ivan the Terrible* (1944/58), and to a degree that shocked his teacher Kuleshov, who thought artists should be independent. Pudovkin used his brilliance in the service of history as he saw it. History let him down, but his silent films, above all his masterpiece *The Mother* (1926), live on.

The Mother was based on a sentimental novel by Maxim Gorky, which justified the need for a revolution. It's the editing, not the plot, that makes this film compelling. His montage effects are different from those of Eisenstein, who believed editing was a way of achieving discord, making a jagged cinema of conflict. Pudovkin was more lyrical. His cross-cuts, while dramatic, do not break up but enhance the narrative.

In early Russian cinema, rarely, but tellingly, women were editors, such as Elizaveta Svilova, professional collaborator of her husband Dziga Vertov.

Elizaveta Svilova (1900–1975)

Born Yelizaveta Schnitt, she entered films at age fourteen as an editing assistant for Pathé in Moscow, and in 1918 became an editor of features at Goskino. Thrilled by the dynamism of Vertov's early agit-prop documentaries, she became one of his most vigorous supporters. In 1922 she joined Vertov's new Cinema Eye studio and would serve as chief editor, and later assistant director, of all his subsequent films, including the revolutionary newsreel 'Kino Pravda', a new series of newsreel magazines of which there were twenty-three issues between 1922 and 1925. The name 'Kino-Pravda' literally means 'cinema-truth'. The group began its work in a basement in the centre of Moscow. Vertov later described it as damp and dark with an earthen floor and holes one stumbled into at every turn. 'This dampness prevented our reels of lovingly edited film from sticking together properly, rusted our scissors and our splicers.' To get an issue out in time, they often worked into the night. 'Before dawn – damp, cold, teeth chattering – I wrap comrade Svilova in a third jacket.'

Dziga Vertov and Elizaveta Svilova married in 1924. Their work together includes: *Cinema Truth*, twenty-three editions, 1922–1925), *Kino Eye* (1924), *Stride Soviet!* (1926), *A Sixth of the World* (1926), *Man with a Movie Camera* (1929), *Enthusiasm* (1931), *Three Songs of Lenin* (1934), and *Lullaby* (1937).

Their most famous film is *Man with a Movie Camera* gleefully using jump cuts, superimpositions, split screens and every other trick in a filmmaker's arsenal. Vertov, along with Elizaveta Svilova, crafts a dizzying, impressionistic, propulsive portrait of the newly industrialising Soviet Union.

Vertov's stroke of genius was to expose the entire artifice of filmmaking within the movie itself. Vertov shoots footage of his cameramen shooting footage. The lengths to which Vertov goes to capture this 'cinematic communication of real events' is startling; his camera soars over cities and gazes up at streetcars; shows objects from absolutely unexpected angles: a train, for example, rushes up over your head from below; it films machines chugging away and even records a woman giving birth. 'I am eye. I am a mechanical eye,' Vertov once famously wrote. 'I, a machine, am showing you a world, the likes of which only I can see.' One famous montage scene shows his wife, Elizaveta Svilova, editing images from the movie into the film. This sort of cinematic self-reflexivity was decades ahead of its time, influencing such future experimental filmmakers as Jean-Luc Godard who in 1968 formed a radical filmmaking collective called The Dziga Vertov Group.

Svilova's reputation as an editor shielded her from the government attacks that adversely affected her husband's career in the late 1930s, and during World War II she was able to get him employment on combat documentaries.

The montage artist Elizaveta Svilova, outlived her husband. She preserved his archives and creative legacy, and she also made a notable contribution in having the Vertov materials published in the 1960s, thus bringing back from oblivion the name and glory of the 'Cinema Eye' creator.

Italy

Esterina Zuccarone (1904–1998)

Esterina was born in Foggia, a commercial hub between northern and southern Italy. In 1912 her family moved north to find work in Turin and one of her older sisters started working as a seamstress. At the age of twelve, Esterina followed her sister and trained as a seamstress too.

In Turin, the nascent motion picture industry employed many young women who were seamstresses in jobs which involved manual dexterity. By the age of fourteen, Esterina had found a job at La Positiva, with Giovanni Pastrone's Itala Film Company. Despite the long hours and attention to detail required, she was soon promoted to supervise a team of men.

Esterina became so skilled that she received many production awards. She was interested in the technical side of the craft and soon moved to Moviola to work as a film editor. After World War I, the Italian motion picture industry was near collapse and smaller companies merged to become part of UCI (Unione Cinematografica Italiana). Rome became more important as the centre of film production and Turin lost out.

Esterina worked for both La Positiva and FERT (Fiori Enrico Roma Torino) and when sound technology was introduced she quickly became a specialist in sound editing. With the turmoil created by World War II, Esterina began training others, including Franco Cristaldi, who went on to edit and produce *Nuovo Cinema Paradiso* (1988). By the end of the war, the Turin studios were closed but Esterina set up a workers' cooperative to try and carry on filmmaking in the town, succumbing to closure in 1951.

Following a move to work for the car manufacturer FIAT, Esterina became involved with their film unit which produced corporate films and adverts, often commissioning directors and overseeing production. A documentary film was made about her life in 1995 in which she was interviewed: *La storia di Esterina*, which was directed by Milli Toja.

France
Marguerite Beaugé (1892–1977)
Throughout the silent period, French film directors retained responsibility from scenario to editing and this meant that they usually edited their own films. The French system did involve an assistant, the 'monteuse'. This person was invariably a woman, responsible for splicing rushes, assembling the negative, and sometimes for executing the editing under strict instructions from the director. One or two French directors had their regular monteuses such as Jean Renoir whose partner Marguerite Renoir edited around sixty films and Marcel Pagnol who worked with Suzanne de Troeye. Director Abel Gance formed a close working relationship with Marguerite Beaugé and they collaborated for over ten years.

Marguerite would sort and glue together the best takes. This crude film was projected for the director, Gance, who would indicate what cuts to make and what re-takes were needed. The monteuse then cut the negative based on the final positive version.

Their collaboration included: *La Dixième Symphonie*, Abel Gance (1918); *La Roue (La Rose du rail)*, Abel Gance (1923); and *Napoléon*, Abel Gance (1927).

Napoléon was an epic silent French film that tells the story of Napoleon's early years. The film is recognised as a masterwork of fluid camera motion, produced in a time when most camera shots were static. Many innovative techniques were used to make the film, including fast cutting, extensive close-ups, a wide variety of hand-held camera shots, location shooting, point of view shots, multiple-camera setups, multiple exposure, superimposition, underwater camera, kaleidoscopic images, film tinting, split screen and mosaic shots, multi-screen projection, and other visual effects. The revolutionary editing must have been incredibly challenging, and with the running length of a staggering 330 minutes, organising the sheer amount of film footage must have been a Herculean task.

She also edited *Pépé le Moko* (1937), directed by Julien Duvivier and *The Passion of Joan of Arc* (1928) directed by Carl Theodor Dreyer, which she cut twice when the original was destroyed by fire. Later films included: *The Raven* (1948) and *It's Adam's Fault* (1958).

Marguerite's daughter Yvonne Beaugé-Martin went on to become a celebrated film editor too, working on *The Trial* (1962), directed by Orson Welles and *Austerlitz* (1960), directed by Abel Gance.

United Kingdom
Alma Reville (1899–1992)

Overshadowed by her husband, director Alfred Hitchcock, Alma Reville's contribution to his films has long been under-appreciated. She moved from Nottingham to London aged fifteen and her father got a job working at Twickenham Studios in the costume department. Reville began in the film industry as a teenage actress with the London Film Company playing roles such as Lloyd George's daughter in *The Life Story of David Lloyd George* (1918) directed by Maurice Elvey. Soon she was assisting Elvey behind the camera and in 1921 she moved to Players-Lasky Studio in Islington to work as an assistant director, continuity supervisor and film editor.

It was while working at Players-Lasky that she met the young graphic designer, Alfred Hitchcock. She was working as a film editor on the silent movie *Appearances* (1921) while Hitchcock was designing the intertitle cards for the same film. In 1923, Hitchcock employed Reville as his assistant on the film *Woman to Woman* and later on his first feature,

The Pleasure Garden (1925), asking her for advice throughout the shoot. She went on to act as an uncredited producer dealing with finance and logistics while abroad on location and she later took charge of the film's editing too.

Hitchcock married Reville in December 1926 and she acted as creative advisor on many of his films for over fifty years, although she was rarely credited for her contribution. She even persuaded Hitchcock to work with the composer Bernard Herrmann and go with his musical ideas for the shower scene in *Psycho*.

Reville also worked as a screenwriter on many other films including *The Lodger* (1926), *The Secret Agent* (1936) and *The Lady Vanishes* (1938) for which she was paid and properly credited.

The pair moved to the U.S. in 1939 and Reville continued to play a major part in the scripting, casting and editing of her husband's films, discussing each day's filming with her husband when he came home in the evening for dinner or occasionally attending the set.

In 2013, Helen Mirren played Alma Reville in the film *Hitchcock*, which portrayed the close working relationship of the couple and went some way to recognising Reville's important collaboration.

Germany
Leni Riefenstahl (1902–2003)

Riefenstahl is most famously known for her propaganda films made during the Nazi years. She was born in Berlin in 1902 to a prosperous family. Her father had a heating and air-conditioning business and was against his daughter going on stage. She began as a dancer, but suffered a knee injury and was seeking treatment when she noticed a poster advertising *Berg des Schickals* (*Mountain of Destiny*), directed by Arnold Fanck, 1923–4). Mesmerised by Fanck's fifth feature film she successfully pursued Fanck and his star, Luis Trenker, convincing them to make her the star of *The Holy Mountain*. It took three days to write and over a year to film on location in the Alps. She starred in several other silent films with mountain themes too.

Writing, directing and editing her first film, *Das Blaue Licht* (*The Blue Light*, 1932), she also played the outsider peasant character, Junta. Riefenstahl later said, 'It's as if it were a premonition of my own life. Junta was loved and hated. It's been the same for me, I've been loved and hated. Just as Junta lost her ideal … in the same way I lost my ideals at the end of that terrible war. To that extent the film was indeed a premonition of my own destiny.' *Das Blaue Licht* received moderate commercial and critical success, winning the Silver Medal at the Venice Film Festival. The film was one of Hitler's favourites and after he became Chancellor in January 1933, he made Riefenstahl 'Film Expert to the National Socialist Party'.

In 1933, Riefenstahl made a short film about the annual Nuremburg Nazi rally and the next year she made a longer film on the same subject titled *Triumph of the Will*. The film won awards in Germany and Italy as well as more surprisingly, the Grand Prix in Paris in 1937, due to its unusual camera angles and shadowy imagery. Riefenstahl's talent as a filmmaker was evident and the film is often referred to as the best propaganda film ever. Her next project, *Olympische Spiele* (*Olympia*), a two-part film on the Olympic Games of 1936, involved managing over fifty cinematographers and cutting over a million feet of film. Riefenstahl's masterpiece was given its premiere in April 1938, on Hitler's birthday. It demonstrated her cinematic genius, combining techniques such as aerial shots, tracking shots, slow motion and underwater shots, accompanied by an emotional score. She visited the U.S. in 1938 to try and find American distribution for the film but the trip was marred by the Nazis' Kristallnacht atrocities and a saboteur, Ernst Jäger within her own entourage. Invitations from Hollywood were hastily withdrawn.

After the war, she spent three years under allied arrest but was eventually cleared of being a Nazi collaborator. It took fourteen years to complete the filming and editing of her adaptation of the opera titled *Tiefland* (1954) but her attempts to revive her film career were unsuccessful.

In the 1960s she reinvented herself as a photographer, living with and photographing Sudan's Nuba tribe. She joined *Greenpeace* and took up underwater photography and on the occasion of her one-hundredth birthday, she released her first film for half a century, *Impressions under Water* (2002).

Conclusion

Women film editors were central to the development of filmmaking in both Europe and America. Although the theory of the male auteur rose to prominence, film has always been a collaborative medium and as we have shown in this chapter, alongside many of the male directing 'geniuses', there were talented and insightful women filmmakers making significant contributions. Their involvement as cutters, editors, writers, advisors and assistant directors often went uncredited. Even when they were at the top of their field, women such as Margaret Booth and Anne Bauchens rarely received the recognition they were due. While continuing research needs to be done to discover more, the art and craft of filmmaking owes much to those gifted individuals who rose through the ranks to exercise more control over the choice of shots, style, pace and emotional expression within the films they edited. This chapter demonstrates the many ways in which they collaborated creatively on films which are now considered classics and how they enabled cinema to flourish and become the global entertainment industry it is today.

Author Biography: Tania Field

Tania is a co-director of Leysfield House Productions. With film editor Christy Hannah, she has founded the Worcester Film Festival. She is a highly-motivated and committed filmmaker, camera operator and graphic designer with experience across the creative board. Her film production portfolio includes short films and corporate videos for RSPCA, Sustrans, BBC TV, Aurora Metro

Arts and Media and Main Academy.

Tania has also contributed to *Celluloid Ceiling: women film directors breaking through*, edited by Gabrielle Kelly and Cheryl Robson.

References

Grieveson, L. J. and P. Kramer. *The Silent Cinema Reader*. London, Routledge, 2004.

Morris, Nathalie and Clare Watson. 'Women and Silent British Cinema (WSBC)', Women's Film History, U.K. & Ireland Network. https://womenandsilentbritishcinema.wordpress.com

'Women Film Pioneers Project', Columbia University Center for Digital Research and Scholarship. https://wfpp.cdrs.columbia.edu/essay/cutting-women/

www.csw.ucla.edu/publications/newsletters/academic.../TG09_dean.pdf

'Thinking Gender'. Published by the Centre for Women's Studies at UCLA.

Making the Cut: Female editors and representation in the Film and Media Industry, excerpt from plenary session by Julia Wright. http://www.csw.ucla.edu/publications/newsletters/academic-year-2008–09/article-pdfs/TG09_wright.pdf

Jones, Jonathon. 'The Silent Revolutionary', *The Guardian*. August 31st, 2001.

ww.theguardian.com/film/2001/aug/31/artsfeatures1

http://www.theguardian.com/film/2001/aug/31/artsfeatures1

Encyclopædia Britannica. http://www.britannica.com/biography/Dziga-Vertov

Film Reference. http://www.filmreference.com/Films-Jo-Ko/Kino-Pravda.html

Encyclopædia Britannica. http://www.britannica.com/biography/Leni-Riefenstahl

Wikispaces, cinewiki. http://cinewiki.wikispaces.com/Riefenstahl,+Leni

10. WHO WAS THE FIRST FEMALE CINEMATOGRAPHER IN THE WORLD?

Ellen Cheshire

Unlike the gender-neutral term 'director' or 'editor', when one thinks about those behind the camera, it seems to be common parlance to refer to them as 'cameraman'. Yet from the early days of filmmaking women have been behind the camera. Their names may not be as well-known as their male counterparts but they too have made significant contributions to early filmmaking.

In the *Guinness Book of Film Facts & Feats* [Robertson, 1993] Rosina Cianelli is credited as being the first female cinematographer in the world for *Uma transformista original [An Original Transformation]* (1915). Here, she received a co-cinematography credit alongside the film's director, Paolo Benedetti, who was also her husband. *Uma transformista original* is a Méliès-style trick film starring the Lazari Brothers, filmed at Brazil's first film studio the Photo-Cinematographica Brasileira. Benedetti has numerous film credits as director, cinematographer, producer and actor, but other than this one mention, little more seems to be known of Cianelli.

It is unlikely that we'll ever know whether this was Cianelli's only film, despite the vast number of books and academics working on this period of film history. This is perhaps why, as you will see, the *Guinness Book* claim could be challenged by a number of other women. With 75% of silent films now lost and a tendency to discuss filmmaking personnel from a male perspective, we will always wonder how many women's contributions to the early days of film have been lost.

In *Hollywood: A Celebration of the American Silent Film* (1980) Kevin Brownlow's and David Gill's ground-breaking television series for Thames Television they dedicated an episode to the skilled creators behind the camera, 'Trick of the Light'. However, even here the narrator (the velvety-voiced James Mason) reinforces the heteronormative assumption that this was an exclusively masculine sphere: 'The job of the cameraman was to make the star look beautiful, to transform a girl into a goddess'. Surely Ally Acker's *Reel Women: Pioneers of the Cinema 1896 to present* (1991) redresses the balance? Sadly this is not the case. There are sections on women directors, producers, editors, animators and stunt artists – but no cinematographers are featured.

During the early silent period, technology and film production roles were often shared. With film in its infancy, the creative person behind the camera was usually also the director, with the technical work being carried out by a crank-turner or camera operator. But as technology evolved – the introduction of lighting, special effects, faster (more light-sensitive) film stock – filmmaking roles transformed and it became standard for there to be a dedicated person who physically handled the camera and used it creatively. By 1919 this role had become so integral and specialist that the American Society of Cinematographers (ASC) was founded 'to recognise the cinematographer's contribution to the art and science of motion picture making'. The following year it launched *American Cinematographer* magazine, which is still published today.

One of the ASC's founding members was Homer Scott, who was its president from 1925 to 1926. Ten years earlier he was first cameraman for Hollywood star director William Desmond Taylor (probably now best known for his mysterious murder) at the Oliver Morosco Photoplay Co. In 1916, *Photoplay* visited the set of their five-reel feature film *Her Father's Son* (1916), an American Civil War drama. However, it wasn't the film's star Vivian Martin that caught their attention but the film's crank-turner, Margery Ordway. This image of Ordway is probably one of the most widely reproduced images of a woman working a camera from these early days of cinema – indeed it is on the cover of this book. This striking photograph was first published in the October 1916 issue of *Photoplay* under the heading 'This is the new fall style in camera "men",' and is known as much for the image as it is for the extended picture caption beneath 'Meaning, the style you could fall for. Nor is this a masquerade get-up. Margery Ordway, regular, professional, licensed union crank-turner at Camp Morosco, has gone into camera work as nonchalantly as other girls take up stenography, nursing, husband-stalking.' However, other than this one image and caption little else is known of Ordway's Hollywood career. Perhaps she took up 'husband-stalking'!

A few months earlier, in January 1916, readers of *Picture-Play Magazine* would have read of A. J. Dixon's incredulity when he learnt of the existence of Grace Davison, who was employed by the Astor Film Corporation of Rockville Center, Long Island.

'How many of you ever heard of a woman cameraman? That such a person exists will doubtless be a surprise to the majority of people in the film business, as well as those outside it', reads the opening to Dixon's article 'The Only Camera Woman'.

Grace Davison was born into a wealthy Long Island family and was educated at both public and private schools in New York City. Prior to joining Astor, she had some experience of taking photographs using a Graflax camera, but it was whilst acting that she became increasingly interested in 'taking the pictures' and when she wasn't in a scene, she'd watch and question the camera man, Harry A. Fischbeck. As her fascination increased she began taking formal lessons, and then filming a scene here and there for director Al Ray. They became a triumvirate when she began sitting-in and commenting on rushes with Fischbeck and Ray. It soon became clear that she was the studio's 'lady camera man'. By the time word had reached Dixon, Davison had been 'turning the crank' for the past three months. Dixon describes his initial reaction to hearing of Davison's work behind the camera, 'I concluded that something must have happened to the regular camera man, and that they had been forced to substitute this girl at the last moment; and I began to picture static, out-of-focus, under and overexposed negative as the result.'

Intrigued, Dixon set out to meet this leading lady turned camera operator. He was particularly sceptical that she can handle the special-effect trick photography required for the short comedies and films this studio specialised in. Once he met Davison he was clearly smitten, describing first her outfit: 'She wore a plain, checked suit that she called her "camera dress", and a cap to match.' Then her face, 'She has a smile that radiates, and it's a genuine smile, too. There is nothing forced in it. And what big brown eyes!' and finally her character 'Good nature is written all over her face…' Upon seeing some of her films: 'The photography was as clear as a bell, and the detail was very sharp, and some of the effects were really beautiful.' And the trick photography that so concerned him:

> 'The film [*Spring Onions*] had an abundance of trick photography in it, one of the most remarkable being where a man looks at himself in a mirror and suddenly it seems as if his breath covers the glass and he fails to see himself in it any longer. Fischbeck informed me that this was one of the hardest pieces of trick photography imaginable.'

And finally her technique:

> 'I know that the regulation crank on an ordinary scene should be one hundred and twenty times to the minute, so I timed her, and she averaged a hundred and fifteen to a hundred and twenty-three, which is accurate as anyone can do it. If she tilted her camera,

or panned over for something, it never interfered with
her cranking hand, she always kept that grinding at the
regular speed, regardless of what she was doing with
her other hand.'

Clearly Davison's work was far from the 'static, out-of-
focus, under and overexposed' negatives that Dixon had first
envisaged.

Davison would later set up her own production company,
and in 1918 produced her first feature film, *Wives of Men*, in
which she also had a small part. Written and directed by John
M. Stahl, it was filmed by her former cinematography mentor
Harry Fischbeck. Sadly, there is no record of her career after
her leading role in the six-reel society melodrama *The Splendid
Lie* (1922) directed by Charles Horam for J. G. Pictures.

Whereas Grace Davison started her career in front of the
camera and was increasingly to be found behind, Francelia
Billington's career path seems to have gone in the other
direction. In December 1914 Katherine Symon interviewed
Billington about her dual roles in front of and behind the
camera for *Photoplay Magazine*.

At this time Billington was assisting the director W. C.
Cabanne at Reliance-Majestic, which was the home of D. W.
Griffith. Symon reported 'Almost any day at the studios it is
possible to see a brown-haired, gray-eyed, olive-skinned girl of
remarkable grace and extreme prettiness standing back of one
of the big cameras, turning a crank as she keeps close watch
on the scene that a group of players are enacting.' Billington
acknowledged that it 'is still a novelty to see a girl more
interested in a mechanical problem than in make-up,' recalling
that she had always been a 'camera fiend'. Her father had given
her a camera when she was ten years old and she would be
found photographing everything on her family's ranch outside
Dallas. She was educated at a convent in Texas, and it was there
that she first acted in school productions.

In 1912 (aged seventeen) she began working at the Kalem

Company's West Coast Studios. She said, that 'In spite of my interest in photography, I hadn't taken much interest in the movies. I'd hardly ever been to see motion pictures and the idea of posing for them, in fact of going on the stage at all, never entered my thoughts.' It was through a friend, George Melford, that she got her first break in movies, as 'He gave me a lead part to take the place of Alice Joyce who had just left Los Angeles. The work wasn't so hard, but the other girls at the studio were awfully nasty to me and that first day was one of ostracism for little me.' She stayed at Kalem for a year before moving to the Reliance-Majestic. In November 1915 Photoplay reproduced a photograph of Billington behind the camera reporting that she was still working at Reliance-Majestic. From this point it seems that she focused on her acting, moving first to Palo Alto Film Corporation and then to Universal. A career highpoint was appearing in Erich von Stroheim's directorial debut, *Blind Husbands* (1918). Although her performance garnered critical praise, she continued to appear in mediocre dramas and westerns and by the mid-1920s her acting work ended. She contracted tuberculosis and died in 1934, aged thirty-nine – her passing went unnoticed in the film community. But on this evidence it seems likely that Billington's work behind the camera in 1914 pre-dates both Rosina Cianelli and Grace Davison.

Therefore, the February 1920 *Photoplay* headline 'The First Camera-Maid' to accompany a one-page article on Louise Lowell, clearly failed to recognise the previous women they had featured in their pages. However, it does seem that Lowell can claim a first – 'the first newsreel cameraperson under contract to Fox News in 1920' (Slide, 1996: 6). The *Photoplay* article outlines her remarkable life. Born in Samoa, Lowell was educated in India and China where she spent her childhood proving that she could be the 'son' her father had always wanted. From as early as she can remember she had a camera with her, taking photos of her adventures in the Far East and South America, where she secured photographs that were used to accompany the articles her father wrote. She moved to England to study aviation, and soon replaced her still camera with a moving picture camera. The happenchance of being in Canada when the Prince of Wales visited was profound. The images she took with her movie camera so impressed the editor of Fox news weekly that she was signed to a contract as 'the first woman news-reporter in the world – and the first aerial one.' As has been a trend in many of these news articles, there has to be some mention of what the subject looks like, and this is no exception as the feature ends with these lines; 'Despite her adventures Miss Lowell remains essentially feminine. The thing she wants more than anything else in the world is – curly hair.'

Sadly, even the claim that Lowell is the first newsreel photographer can be disputed as in *Moving Picture World* (9th June 1917) there is a story of 'Miss Dorothy Dunn, actress, author and traveller', who 'holds the distinction of being the only woman staff photographer in the motional picture field' when she was signed to work for *Universal Animated Weekly*. Before turning to a career behind the camera, Dunn had appeared on-screen. Having a 'mechanical turn of mind' she was soon drawn to the technical side of filmmaking and spent her leisure time learning the mechanics of the camera and filming. Deciding that there would be more adventures covering the news she joined the corps of Universal Animated Weekly's newsreel photographers where as a 'regular member she covers her assignments on the same basis as her male confrères … [operating] a motion picture camera with skill and takes pictures where she is sent, regardless of the danger involved.'

Dunn may certainly have been the first 'woman staff photographer in the motional picture field' but she wasn't the first to confront danger whilst filming.

In 1915, Katherine Bleecker (who owned her own camera equipment) heard that Alexander Cleland, Secretary of the Joint Committee on Prison Reform (JCPR) was looking for someone to document on film prison conditions in three of New York's biggest penal institutions (Auburn, Sing Sing and

Great Meadow). These would be used in the JCPR's campaign for better prison conditions. It was their hope to '…do away with such unspeakable sections of Hades as Sing Sing, and starting farm colonies to better convicts' mental and physical condition while they are serving their terms.' (Bleecker, 1915) She created a series of documentaries and education films for prisoners. Some of these required the prisoners to recreate incidents, rather than filming 'actuality'. Recalling her first film at Auburn, Bleecker said, 'I hadn't the slightest idea that anyone would come forward for that flogging scene, but a youth of twenty stepped up and said he was willing… [After filming the flogging] I gave the word for the guard to lower [him] and told the youth to appear to fall in a faint as he was released. This he did, and was carried out and I thought he was about as clever an actor as I had seen, and started out after him to thank him and found him in a real faint.' Unsurprisingly, Bleecker found the prisoners less enthusiastic at Sing Sing 'The atmosphere is disheartening in the extreme, I was most dejected all the time I was there. With its 3x3x7-foot cells, [it's] such a depressing pile that no one could possibly get anything but gloomy sensations there.' Her final location was 1,100 acre Great Meadow, there she 'took pictures of prisoners farming, building roads, and working on a conservation plot from which 4,000,000 trees are shipped annually – and of the weekly ball game.' The records of the Community Motion Picture Bureau feature three short educational films released in December 1915: *A Day in Sing Sing*, *A Prison Without Walls*, about Great Meadows Prison; and *Within Prison Walls*, about Thomas Mott Osborne's self-incarceration to observe prison conditions.

Sixteen years later, in September 1931, the *Spokane Daily Chronicle* ran a newswire story of Mrs Katherine Meigs' (née Bleecker) appointment as Social Secretary of the Postal Telegraph Company, with the remit 'to correct America's social errors … [she] will solve etiquette problems, arrange entrainments, send flowers, supply shopping assistance, remind husbands of anniversaries – in short, shoulder all the burdens a social secretary might dispatch for anyone in the country who wants this service.' When asked about her previous work, her experiences at the 'depressing' Sing Sing were still vivid as she recalled seeing, '…all those milling convicts [and] not a guard in sight,' adding 'I'll admit I was frightened, but I finished the job and left.'

This experience may have contributed to her subsequent, considerably safer, employment as manager of Universal Film Company's Broadway Theatre on 41st and Broadway, a post she held for a year before starting a family. When asked how she would combine home life and her office duties at the Postal Telegraph company, she commented 'It seems to me children are really benefited when their mothers have interests outside the home… Being constantly with the mother, the modern boy or girl becomes bored with her.'

If one thinks that women working behind the camera in the United States are under-discussed, those working in the U.K. have even less presence. It is here that we may well find female cinematographers that pre-date the work of any of the women working in America.

Jessica Elvira Borthwick's foray into filmmaking was brief but impactful. Born in 1888, she was the daughter of General George Colville Borthwick, who had been commander-in-chief of the Turkish army in Eastern Roumelia and niece to Sir Algernon Borthwick, First Baron Glenesk, and editor of the *Morning Post* newspaper. In 1913 (aged twenty-two) she set off to film and photograph the second Balkan War. She was not a professional camera operator – having had only three days training before setting off – and was not filming for any organisation. This extremely dangerous expedition was purely for her own personal interest. She eventually stayed a year there, enduring severe conditions including imprisonment, near starvation, bullet injuries and at one point was struck by cholera. She witnessed the true horrors of war, which she described in an extensive interview for *The Bioscope* (7th May 1914): 'During the cholera rage in

Adrianople, everything connected with that terrible disease was painted black. The carts in which the dead bodies were carried away were black, for example, as were the coffins in which cholera victims were buried. While the scourge was at its height, I went down into the gipsy quarter to take a film. The people in this part of the city had never seen a camera before, and when they saw me pointing my black box at various objects they thought I was operating some wonderful new instrument for combating the disease which was destroying them. Quickly surrounding me, they came and knelt upon the ground, kissing my feet and clothing, and begging with dreadful pathos that I should cure them. It was a task as sad as it was difficult to explain that their hopes were mistaken, and that I was impotent to help them.'

The films were never shown commercially. She gave a lecture in February 1914 at the Scala Theatre in London but the promise of further lectures did not follow. There are reports that Borthwick subsequently lived an artistic bohemian life in South Kensington, returning to her first artistic-love of sculpting. In 1932 she worked on a BBC programme of Russian singers broadcast through the Baird process. She never married, and died in 1946.

But is it possible to trace any women working behind the camera back even further than 1913, perhaps back to the very moment pictures began to move?

Laura Eugenia Smith (née Bayley) was born in Ramsgate, Kent in 1864. In the 1880s she and her three sisters, Blanche, Florence and Eva performed as part of J. D. Hunter's Theatre Company at the Brighton Aquarium. In 1888 she met and married George Albert Smith. In the early 1880s Smith began performing in small Brighton venues building up an act as a stage hypnotist. In 1892 he acquired the lease to St Ann's Well Garden in Hove, a short distance from Brighton. He transformed this seaside site into a popular pleasure garden. Smith acted as host and performed Magic Lantern shows. On a visit to London in March 1896 he saw a programme of

Lumière Brothers' films at the Empire Theatre of Varieties, Leicester Square. The early films of British filmmaker Robert Paul played in Brighton during the summer of 1896, and by early 1897 Smith had purchased his first camera. He began making films, initially from his Pleasure Gardens, and later (c.1904/5) he moved to Roman Crescent, Southwick near Shoreham Beach, where he erected a small studio in his garden. According to a feature on Shoreham Beach Studios in *Classic Images* (Pedler, 1990:8) Smith was a major innovator of film techniques, having 'anticipated the Méliès camera tricks', 'used both close-ups and large close-up shots some years before the American D. W. Griffith, who is supposed to have "invented" these particular shots' and as early as 1908 'obtained a patent for a color-film process.' L. E. Smith and her three sisters all acted in G. A. Smith's films, and there is evidence that L. E. Smith was an integral part of filming and making the cameras they sold. G. A. Smith with Charles Urban, managed the Warwick Trading Company, for which they developed a film camera for the amateur market, the Biokam. This camera held 17.5mm film, half the width of the standard 35mm, and their intention was to encourage everyone, particularly women, to shoot and screen their own films. The Biokam was also a printer and projector.

Film Historian Tony Fletcher discovered evidence from G. A. Smith's Cash Book that L. E. Smith was a prolific sales rep for The Biokam, reporting that 'the entries for the Biokam are given under the initials "L. E. S." for Laura Eugenia Smith. The entries range from 29th July 1898, to 21st May 1906, and indicate that over 1,000 Biokam films were marketed by March 1900.' On 14th October 1899, G. A. Smith gave an interview to the *Brighton Herald* about the recently launched Biokam which further confirms this: 'Films are being made for this [Biokam Camera] that will cost only 3s/6d a minute... Mrs Smith came in to borrow the identical camera and to go off and photograph the waves breaking over the Hove sea wall.' Fletcher references an article in *The*

Golden Penny from June 1899 by J. K. Cramer-Roberts, in which the accompanying photograph features … a woman, in the mode of the amateur, taking photographs with the Biokam. G. A. Smith retired from filmmaking during World War I, and the last recorded entry in his cashbooks of L. E. Smith's involvement was in 1908.

Given that Britain's contribution to early silent filmmaking is somewhat neglected on the world-stage it is therefore unsurprising that Laura Smith's contribution has been all but forgotten. Tom Ruffles hoped to redress this in his blogpost 'Laura Smith, Film Pioneer' inspired by hearing Tony Fletcher give an illustrated presentation on *Laura Eugenia Smith and the Biokam Films* at the 11th Silent British Cinema Festival at Nottingham in 2008. He writes 'Bearing in mind the important part she played in the film industry in Britain in its earliest years, Laura has not been well served by film history. [G. A.] Smith is often referred to as part of *The Brighton School* or *The Hove Pioneers*, but Laura has never been considered a member in her own right. She is sometimes referred to merely as "Mrs Smith" or "Smith's wife".' He continues 'As an indication of this neglect, while we know about [G. A.] Smith's death, and obituaries were published detailing his achievements, Laura's was shrouded in mystery. Laura died at home – 7 Melville Road, Hove – with her husband at her side, on 25th October 1938, aged seventy-seven. Smith registered her death the following day and put her occupation down as "Wife of George Albert Smith, a Cinematograph Technical Adviser (retired)".'

To be remembered only as the wife of someone, and not celebrated for either her on or off-screen achievements is a sad end to a woman who can claim to be the 'the first female cinematographer in the world'.

Now, where's the telephone number for the *Guinness Book of Records*?

Author Biography: Ellen Cheshire

Ellen is a lecturer in Media and Culture Studies at University of Chichester. She has had books published on Jane Campion, Ang Lee, Audrey Hepburn, The Coen Brothers, Bio-Pics and contributed to books on James Bond, Charlie Chaplin, U.K. counterculture, war films and fantasy films.

www.ellencheshire.com

References

Acker, A. *Reel Women: Pioneers of the Cinema 1896 to present*. B T Batsford Ltd, 1991.

Bleecker, K. R. 'Prison Moving Pictures Taken by a Girl', *The New York Times*. 21st November, 1915)

Borthwick, J. 'A Girl Cinematographer at the Balkan War: Interview with Miss Jessica Borthwick', *The Bioscope*. 7th May, 1914. 625, 627, 629. Reprinted in *The Red Velvet Seat: Women's Writings on the Cinema – The First Fifty Years*. A. C. Lant and I. Periz, Eds. Verso Books, 2006, 628–630.

Brownlow, K. and D. Gill. 'Tricks of the Light', *Hollywood: A Celebration of the American Silent Film*. Thames Television, 1980.

Cramer-Roberts, J. K. 'Unknown title', *The Golden Penny*. 3rd June, 1899). Quoted in Fletcher, T. 'Profile: Laura Bayley', *Women Film Pioneers Project*. 27th April, 2015. https://wfpp.cdrs.columbia.edu/pioneer/ccp-laura-bayley/

Dixon, A .J. 'The Only Camera Woman', *Picture-Play Magazine*. 1[st,] January, 1916) 59–65 Fletcher, T. 'Profile: Laura Bayley', *Women Film Pioneers Project*. 27th April, 2015 https://wfpp.cdrs.columbia.edu/pioneer/ccp-laura-bayley/

NEA. 'Attractive Young Matron Takes Job of Correcting Social Errors of Whole United States', *Spokane Daily Chronicle*. 19th September, 1931, 25.

'All Ready! Now the Villain Enters! Camera!' *Photoplay*. November, 1915, 91.

'This is the new fall style in camera 'men'', *Photoplay*. October, 1916, 103.

'Enter the camerawoman', *Moving Picture World*. 9th June, 1917, 1609.

'The First Camera-Maid', *Photoplay*. February, 1920, 80.

Pedler, Garth. 'Garth's Vintage Viewing: Shoreham Beach Studios by Neb Wolters adapted for Classic Images by Garth Pedler', *Classic Images*. n. 181. July, 1980, 8–11.

Robertson, Patrick. *The Guinness Book of Movie Facts and Feats: 5th Revised edition*. Guinness World Records Limited, 1993.

Ruffles, Tom. 'Laura Smith, Film Pioneer'. 9th June, 2011. *Tom Ruffles Blog*. 27th April 2015. http://tomruffles.blogspot.co.uk/2011/06/laura-smith-film-pioneer.html

Slide, A. *The Silent Feminists: America's First Women Directors*. Scarecrow Press, 1996.

Smith, G. A. 'Interview' *Brighton Herald*. 14th October, 1899. Quoted in Fletcher, T. 'Profile: Laura Bayley', *Women Film Pioneers Project*. 27th April 2015. https://wfpp.cdrs.columbia.edu/pioneer/ccp-laura-bayley/

Synon, Katherine. 'Francelia Billington Who Can Play Both Ends of a Camera Against the Middle', *Photoplay*. 27th April 2015. http://www.welcometosilentmovies.com/features/fb/fb2.htm

11. WHEN THE WOMAN SHOOTS: Ladies Behind the Silent Horror Film Camera

K. Charlie Oughton

Imagine you're a scriptwriter. You have adapted your story into a full feature. The film is still celebrated over a hundred years later. But, the person the books are written about is your creative partner, who also worked on the film, while you are relegated to a few paltry articles on an obscure academic search engine. Alternatively, imagine you are the director of over 400 of the first films ever made and have work ranging from comedy to horror, yet your name is all but lost to time. The achievements are there, all the more impressive for having been completed in an era without the ease of production enjoyed today, and some have survived a century because people recognised their value. You, however, are ignored because of what amounts to little more than fashion. What's more, your successes are 'given', by popular assent, to someone else.

Then imagine you're an actress. Your eyes widen and jitter at the corners, your lips tremble and your clawed hands move to your face ready for the music's crescendo and your silent scream. Your name is remembered primarily for the erotic appeal your looks held for your audience, then and now, rather than for your talent as a performer. What's more, the names of your female friends on the crew are considered unimportant and are subsequently forgotten.

To recall the words of Laura Mulvey in *Visual Pleasure and Narrative Cinema*, we are used to seeing women (particularly scream queens) as the subject of the male gaze in films while women are cast as an 'erotic object' (1999).[1] Adapting her theory from the teachings of Sigmund Freud, Mulvey states that there are three types of 'look' inherent in the filmmaking process. These looks are: 'that of the camera as it records the pro-filmic event, that of the audience as it watches the final product, and that of the characters at each other within the screen illusion.'[2] As so many of our famous films are presented in such a manner, it is perhaps natural that our hegemonic perspective is that women are seen as the material, rather than the master, of movie creation.

This chapter isn't about the scream queens of yesteryear, despite how the command of the likes of Ingrid Pitt enabled them to alter perceptions of women to be powerful as well as pretty.[3] It's about the women who created powerful images but who have effectively been erased from history because the androcentric times in which they lived favoured men. This chapter will redress the balance not simply in the interests of feminism, but instead in the interests of providing a more accurate account of cinema history that incorporates legendary films such as *The Phantom of the Opera* through to forgotten gems such as Alice Guy-Blaché's adaptation of Poe's *The Pit and the Pendulum*. It will discuss the output of women who worked in roles from choreography to scriptwriting and from directing to editing. Following this, it will then assess the differences between the cultural veneration afforded to scream queens whose looks are manipulated and the women who manipulated those looks to ascertain the true cultural importance of these figures.

Silent Visionary

Alice Guy-Blaché is, of course, the name that cannot be missed in a chapter discussing silent horrors and it is an encouraging sign that her work is gradually gaining more recognition in sources ranging from blogs to academic texts (McMahon, Mattson). Guy-Blaché's first foray into film was by becoming the secretary of the Gaumont Film Company. From here she asked for, and was granted, permission to create her own short film on the condition that her secretarial work did not suffer. From then, she went on to create several hundred films, perhaps most famously 1896's *The Cabbage Patch Fairy*.

While Guy-Blaché's status as a pioneer and indeed prolific filmmaker is evident, what is also interesting is that her direction and subject areas include not only the supposedly 'ladylike', but an early dedication to horror. *The Pit and the Pendulum* (1913) is one such title and the background concept will be known to modern genre enthusiasts for Roger Corman's 1961 film starring Vincent Price. Both are based on the work of Edgar Allan Poe. The original story works as an imagining of torture at the time of the Spanish Inquisition. Focused as a study of fear, it comprises of the narrator's sensory recollections of a time when he was left to die in an encroaching, mechanical torture chamber before being rescued at the last moment before death.

Guy-Blaché's adaptation works by adding an intimate, personal plot to explain the motivation for torture, as Hayes (2001) quotes Bush as stating. In this manner, Guy-Blaché incorporated a romance into the narrative. We are introduced to sweethearts Alonzo and Isabelle, as well as to Isabelle's spurned lover, Pedro. Pedro is responsible for the eventual torture of Alonzo. The addition of these characters to the narrative suggests that petty personal malice, rather than the pure politics of Poe's story, are at the heart of physical abuse.

In the opening sequence, Pedro attacks the object of his affection, Isabelle, who is in turn rescued by Alonzo. Pedro is shown from behind in mid-shot, standing up and jamming his hat on his head before stumbling off to the top right of the screen. By not showing his face and thus focusing on his costume and gait, Guy-Blaché indicates an almost child-like quality to his actions as well as a level of unflattering petulance. It also adds a degree of relative innocence to the piece that is the opposite of what is to come. Pedro seeks revenge on Alonzo for 'stealing' Isabelle by framing him for theft of church property, leading to Alonzo's torture at the hands of the church authorities. He is tied down with the iconic, swinging blade of Poe's original story above him.

Sadly, the final reel of the film has been lost over time, and all that remains is an image of the climactic scene showing Alonzo underneath the blade. What we do know from Guy-Blaché's memoirs is that she was an image innovator and that the sequence incorporated the use of rats nibbling at the ropes that restrain the innocent Alonzo. The rats then swarmed across his body and 'penetrated the legs of his trousers' (Blaché and Blaché, 1996) conveying yet more terror and revulsion to the audience, as stated in *The New York Dramatic Mirror*.[4] Projected on-screen rather than left to the imagination, it's an image that would horrify many today, let alone over a century ago. It would also create sympathy for its hero. Without this emphasis on the plight of the hero and the moral judgement of the villain made by Guy-Blaché's camera angles and direction, narcissism and egotistical power may persuade the audience and the other characters within the piece to confer authority on the evil-doer, and this may go unchecked by the film's finale. It is a lesson from history absent from the Roger Corman version of the tale in which the villainous, maddened Vincent Price is cheered for his scene-chewing evil rather more than continuing the story's moral trajectory in which the hero rules the day. As a result of these additional contrasts that she added to Poe's original story, Guy-Blaché may have made her film all the more shocking.

Ghost in the machine

However, cinematic heroes are at the mercy of fashion in the filmic 'pecking order'. Ask any modern musical-film goer to name an important figure in dance-based movies and it's likely that they may speak of Bob Fosse, choreographer of *Cabaret*, *Sweet Charity* and *All That Jazz*. Why mention a man in a chapter about women filmmakers? There is common consent that this man matters. Audiences agree that Bob Fosse was central to the film's visual imagery because of the way he directed people to dance in scenes set in night clubs. Dance is part of what makes those films important and popular, rather than being secondary or incidental.

In this vein, think of the cultural influence of French author Gaston Leroux's novel *Le Fantome de l'Opera* (*The Phantom of the Opera*, 1910). It has been translated into many languages, adapted for both stage and screen with one of the longest runs in musical theatre history. In the 1925 film adaptation of the novel, the very terror – or 'breach from the norm' – is set by pitting Lon Chaney's grotesque, deformed phantom against the grandiose and graceful background of the opera house itself. As a textual insert at the beginning tells us, 'The Paris Opera House, [rises] nobly over medieval torture chambers, hidden dungeons long forgotten' (*The Phantom of the Opera*, 2:57). This elegance is a key counterpoint to what lies underneath, beauty concealing its true nature.

Albertina Rasch's choreography is key to establishing the notional variance in terms of the control of the human body, despite her lack of recognition in the film's credits.[5] Her work is clear from beginning to end. Rasch trained with the Vienna Opera House and *The Phantom of the Opera* is generally held to be her first foray into film. It shows key elements of the style with which she would go on to choreograph many other features. She became known for infusing the precision of ballet with elements of other dance types and narrative storytelling and this can clearly be seen in *The Phantom of the Opera* (Casey, 2012). I argue that her work focuses on the idea of humanity as controllable and regimented versus the emotional impact of events on individuals' actions, providing parallels with the monstrous maestro Phantom.

The first section of Rasch's work is seen after a series of establishing shots that demonstrate first the opulence of the opera house, then the action of the audience as they move from an organised scrum to sitting patiently behind the orchestra. We are then presented with Rasch's choreography, with the *corps de ballet* filling the stage in rows of eight. Their unison is marked by a crane shot then shown as disrupted and human by the break into steps by differing parts of the company. This change in style is underscored by the musical crescendo and cut to a Dutch camera angle as the dancers move forward and backwards in front of the camera before forming into lines as the music subsides. Following a cut to a discussion of the Phantom, we return to the corps, who now carry bough-like props and some proceed to dance to the floor with them. Shown again via a crane shot, these details prove important for the development of the story itself. The next time the girls are seen, their delicate *port de bras* are transposed into flails of terror as they run beneath the stage and catch a glimpse of the Phantom. Even as they describe what they have seen, there continue to be small movements of choreography, such as spins. As well as adding visual interest to the scene, Rasch's direction also adds to their characters as a group of frightened, but nonetheless excited young women performers who are also very much using the turn of events to gain what additional attention they can amongst their group. They attempt to outdo each other with stories of what they saw and how it affected them (at around 11:54). Within the constraints of a normative representation of these female dancers as submissive girls apparently seeking validation for what they think they saw from the male opera house worker, Rasch had nevertheless provided them with a way of upstaging the man by making them the more interesting characters and reducing the man to mere foil, as well as escalating the conflicting effects of the scene on the audience. As a result of the depiction of these women, the mere thought of the Phantom becomes even more exaggerated in the audience's imagination, allowing him to become one of the most iconic villains of all time.

Metropolis
Of course, women writers such as Mary Shelley have long been directly involved in the creation of horrific ideas and it may be

argued that there is nothing scarier than the possibility of the real. *Metropolis* is such an example. Often credited to its famous director, Fritz Lang, Thea Von Harbou's novel, *Metropolis,* from which the film was adapted, is usually classed as a 'drama-sci-fi' owing to its famous imagery of Maria, the android. This is a slight misnomer, as the main narrative thrust of the story is not concerned with the notion of the scientific elements in terms of feasibility, as opposed to how those elements are put to use to act as a moral fable. This may have been attributed to Lang on the basis of his direction of the piece, the set design and the cinematography. Who could forget the terrifying, gigantic face of the Heart Machine as it is discovered by Freder, apparently about to eat everyone around it alive?

Yet this imagery is taken directly from the source material – von Harbou's own novel – and we are left in no illusion as to the terror the narrative is intended to inspire. Indeed, her original novel refers to the building within Metropolis as 'The New Tower of Babel' (von Harbou). This refers to the Biblical structure destroyed by God in Genesis 11. 4–9. The wording of the Biblical passage is the somewhat euphemistic idea that God 'scattered [the Tower's inhabitants] abroad over all the face of the earth', and yet von Harbou accentuates the destructive nuances of the story with her next words: 'So long would the Machine city of Metropolis roar for food, for food, for food … she wanted living men for food.'[6] And these men come, 'Men, men, men all in the same uniform,' as is then depicted in the film.[7]

Lang shot what he was told to by von Harbou, but her influence extended further than that as she also adapted her work for the screen. This can be seen directly when she references the Babel story in the lines 'To the new Tower of Babel – to my Father' (00:16), rather than simply writing 'To the Tower', and when referring to the workers' abode as 'the depths' (22:40), thus emphasising not only the sense of unreachableness, but also by giving it a lack of a proper noun instilling a sense of foreboding in the viewer. It was a vision of horror precisely because of its depiction of the swapped qualities of man and machine, demonstrating the moral ambiguity of industrialisation.[8]

That the feature ends positively, with new links being forged for the benefit of mankind, does not exclude it from its horrific status. As many a good horror film will show, these links are only as strong as the human hands that bond, and the monster can resume at any time if unchecked.

Mystery Women

While the names Albertina Rasch and Thea von Harbou have largely been lost to time, two other names, Marion Fairfax and Alma Reville have recently been reinvestigated.

'The best and first thing for an aspiring playwright to do is to be born a man,' said Marion Fairfax who became an acclaimed playwright and screenwriter. Her best known work is her screenplay for *The Lost World* (1925), which she adapted from the tale by Arthur Conan Doyle. Marrying the horrors of life-threatening peril with the more family-friendly fare of discovering dinosaurs, *The Lost World* (1925) was selected for preservation in the United States National Film Registry as a mark of its significance as a piece of filmmaking.

Fairfax's personal foray with silent horror did not end there, however, and she also provided the screenplay for the rather more obviously sinister film, *Dinty* (1920). Following the fortunes of the romantic heroine and her plucky young son, the titular *Dinty*, the film follows *The Pit and the Pendulum* in its use of torture as a plot device. To emphasise the derring-do of *Dinty*, the finale sees its protagonist saving an unfortunate from certain death restrained to a table complete with a swinging blade lowering closer and closer overhead. Fairfax even took the horrific to somewhat more surreal ends in the scifi-comedy *Go and Get It* (1920), a murder mystery in which the culprit is none other than a gorilla who carries the transplanted brain of a murderer. The conflation of the bodies of the two species, not to mention the conflict it causes, naturally caused some deadly laughs indeed. Contrarily, Fairfax fought society's fears of women in industry and made a further name for herself in editorial departments and as a producer. She established her own film production company in 1921.

Reville was most famous for being 'master of terror' Alfred Hitchcock's wife. However, she was a screenwriter on over twenty films as well as an editor and filmmaker in her own right, in addition to being a close collaborator with Hitchcock for over fifty years (see more in Chapter 9).

She was featured as a character in *The Girl* (2012) and *Hitchcock* (2012). Both of these features about Hitchcock's life saw two highly respected actors play the role of Reville. While this has positive aspects in terms of the profile and kudos involved by attaching Imelda Staunton and Helen Mirren to the roles, it also suggests a level of covert branding. Both of these performances were nominated for BAFTAs, and the actors are known for playing strong female characters. They have achieved a level of fame in popular culture which they are able to use to endorse a project and attract not only audiences but investment. They are known for their iconic status.

This leads us directly to a discussion of the marketing and branding of the movement for recognition of women's horror films in particular. The sheer fact that Hannah Forman's Women in Horror month exists at all, and has led to festivals such as Jennifer's Bodies, has been seen by some as a gimmick rather than as a spotlight for talent. This is the view that covertly suggests that the reason women filmmakers' names are not known is because, anonymous, their work is simply not good enough to be comparable with that of the men they worked with and who did become famous. The contention is that promoting the naming of women is a desperate attempt at political point-scoring.

When a woman does find some success in the horror film industry (often as a result of her own self-promotion and branding as a means of attracting press attention, as discussed in Oughton 2014) the publicity she receives may overshadow her achievements. This overshadowing can be understood as a combination of Judith Butler's theories regarding gender performativity (in Butler 1993) and of Laura Mulvey's theory of the male gaze (Mulvey, 1971). The women can become aware of the expectation (as discussed by Mulvey) that they will be physically attractive to male consumers simply as that is traditional. At the same time, these women are mindful of what Butler has called gender performativity – the idea that we perform gender representations such as particular representations of femininity rather than them being natural. As a method of being seen to control and celebrate their own femininity, the women may perform an exaggerated version of it, presenting public images of themselves that can act to reinforce the so-called male gaze by encouraging the public to enjoy their appearances at the expense of focus on the quality of their films. Sadly, this shows no sign of changing in the immediate future if anonymised evidence on sites such as shitpeoplesaytowomendirectors.tumbrl.com is to be believed. Many of the notes on that site relate not to casual sexism, but instead to sexism that actually prevents women from having production-based roles in the first place.

Modern horror directors The Soska Sisters have tried to tackle this state of affairs, notably through the short film anthology, *Massive Blood Drive* (Burden et al). Each short was directed by women, with one or two of the contributing crews focusing again on imagery designed clearly to encourage the erotic gaze of the (male) viewer. The Soska Sisters' final sequence, however, showed them manipulating partially undressed men seen cleaning their car, the shots being designed to reveal far more of the men's bodies than that of the Soskas'. However, recent university-based debates suggested that these students saw the sequence as comic rather than sexual despite the shooting style. The signifiers were therefore caused to 'slip' and alter that particular audience's interpretation of the directors' original intention, thus again undermining their authority. The audience reaction was culturally generated as a result of their mainstream social-cultural backgrounds. This background and its traditional representations actively work against the very process of filmmaking and innovation through which female filmmakers may become famous for their work. As a result of this, the women who make superb work or who wish to highlight the history of female filmmaking must combat a social perception that women are not capable, all the while ensuring that their reputations are not simply perceived as 'womanness' rather than being famous for their work.

This chapter aims to raise the profile of female film writers, directors and choreographers who worked in the silent horror genre. At this point in time, the names of Thea von Harbou, Albertina Rasch, Alice Guy-Blaché, Marion Fairfax and Alma Reville are known to few people other than feminists, film buffs and the authors of dusty articles archived in hidden internet portals. The only way that we can begin to change that is to circulate knowledge of what these people did in, and for, silent horror film and discuss how their genius impacted on the films they made. If we do this and work to highlight more evidence of their contribution to the cinematic canon the sheer number of women's names associated with horror cinema will force a change in cultural perception and become the norm. As their numbers grow, we will understand the influence they have had on the development of cultural history itself. This is, after all, one of the key messages of Marshall McLuhan's theories of communication – the medium is the message. By appreciating the diverse experiences and backgrounds people can bring to movies, we can recognise and develop true innovation. Until then, some of the people who tell our stories, and illuminate the female perspective of our world, will remain largely silenced.

Author Biography: K. Charlie Oughton

Charlie lectures in Media Communications at Regent's University London and University of the Arts London. Specialising in film studies, Oughton has contributed to *HARTS and Minds* journal and *Intensities: The Journal of Cult Media* and has presented papers at conferences including Cine-Excess, Inter-disciplinary.net and for IAFOR. With a specific interest in horror film, Oughton's work has appeared in Robert Downey Jr. *From Brat to Icon* (McFarland) and for Aurora Metro's *Celluloid Ceiling: Women Film Directors Breaking Through* as well as taking a wider look at cult cinema in *Counterculture UK*. Oughton is currently preparing research on the films of Lucio Fulci and the role of the non-normative romantic hero in travel narratives. Oughton is also active in the media industry and has contributed filmed and written commentary materials to film releases for companies including Lionsgate, Nucleus Films, Highfliers, Network Distributing and Demonhouse Productions. A journalist, Oughton also contributes to publications including Real Crime, Starburst and Ain't It Cool News as well as having served on the juries for the Méliès d'Argent Film Award and twice for the British Horror Film Festival.

charlie1oughton@gmail.com

References

Aitken, R. *The Holy Bible: New Revised Standard Version*. New York, Arno Press, 1968.

'Alice Guy-Blaché's *The Pit and the Pendulum*', *The New York Dramatic Mirror*. 30th July, 1913.

All That Jazz. Dir. Bob Fosse. Perf. Roy Scheider. Columbia Pictures. 1979. Film.

Blaché, R. & S. Blaché. *The Memoirs of Alice Guy-Blaché*. Scarecrow Press, 1996.

Blake, Michael F. *A Thousand Faces: Lon Chaney's Unique Artistry in Motion Pictures*. Oxford, Vestal Press, 1995.

Burdon, C. et al. *WiH Massive Blood Drive P.S.A.* 7th June, 2015. https://www.youtube.com/watch?v=D2w9BFYM6RI

Butler, J. *Bodies that matter: on the discursive limits of 'sex'*. New York, Routledge, 1993.

Cabaret. Dir. Bob Fosse. Perf. Liza Manelli. Allied Artists, 1972. Film.

Casey, C. G. 2012. The Ballet Corporealities of Anna Pavlova and Albertina Rasch. In. *Dance Chronicle*. Vol. 35, Iss. 1. 2012.

Countess Dracula. Dir. P. Sasdy. P. Perf. Ingrid Pitt. Rank Organisation and Hammer Films, 2006. Film.

Dance. [Online]. *The Reader's Companion to American history*. Boston, MA, Houghton Mifflin. 7th June 2015. http://library3.webster.edu/login?url=http://search.credoreference.com. library3.webster.edu/content/entry/rcah/dance/0

Guy-Blaché, A. *The Pit and the Pendulum*. 1913.

Hayes, K. 'Alice Guy's *The Pit and the Pendulum* (1913)', *The Edgar Allen Poe Review*.

Vol. 2, No. 1. Penn State UP, Spring, 2001, 37–42. Available at: http://www.jstor.org/stable/41507819

Hitchcock. Dir. Sacha Gervasi. Perf. Anthony Hopkins. Fox Searchlight Pictures, 2012. Film.

King, S. *Danse Macabre*. London, Hodder, 1981.

Leroux, Gaston. *Fantome de l'Opera*. Pierre Lafitte, 1910.

Mattson, K. 'See No Evil 2 Directors Jen and Sylvia Soska on Reinventing Horror and the Benefits of a Creative Partnership'. 1st June, 2015. http://blogs.indiewire.com/womenandhollywood/see-no-evil-2-directors-jen-and-sylvia-soska-on-reinventing-horror-and-the-benefits-of-a-creative-partnership-video-20141028

McMahan, Alison. *Alice Guy-Blaché: Lost Visionary of the Cinema*. Bloomsbury, 2014.

Metropolis. Dir. Fritz Lang. Perf. Brigitte Helm. Universum Film, 1927. Film.

Mulvey, L. 'Visual Pleasure and Narrative Cinema', 1975 *Film Theory and Criticism: Introductory Readings*. Eds. Leo Brady and Marshall Cohen. New York: Oxford University Press. 1999, 833–844.

Oughton, K. 'The home, the body and otherness: Canadian representations of identity and feminism in Mary Harron's American Psycho, Sarah Polley's Away From Her and the Soska Sisters' *American Mary*', *Celluloid Ceiling: Women Film Directors Breaking Through*. Gabrielle Kelly and Cheryl Robson, Eds. Twickenham, Supernova Books, 2014.

Poe, E. A. 'The Pit and the Pendulum', *The Gift: A Christmas and New Year's Present for 1843*. 1842.

Sweet Charity. Dir. Bob Fosse. Perf. Shirley MacLaine. Universal Pictures, 1969. Film.

shitpeoplesaytowomendirectors.tumbrl.com. Accessed 3rd June 2015.

The Cabbage Patch Fairy. Dir. Alice Guy-Blaché. Gaumont Company. 1900. Film.

The Girl. Dir. Julian Jarrold. Perf. Sienna Miller. Wall to Wall Media, 2012. Film.

The Lost World. Dir. Harry O. Hoyt. Perf. Bessie Love. First National Pictures, 1925. Film.

The Phantom of the Opera. Dir. Rupert Julian. Perf. Lon Chaney. Universal Pictures, 1925. Film.

The Pit and the Pendulum. Dir. Alice Guy-Blaché. Perf. Darwin Kerr. Solax Film company, 1913. Film. 3rd June, 2015. Available at: http://www.wat.tv/video/pit-and-the-pendulum-1913–19zhr_2h0mp_.html

The Pit and the Pendulum. Dir. Roger Corman. Perf. Vincent Price. Twentieth Century Fox, 2004. Film.

von Harbou, T. *Metropolis*. 3rd June, 2015. https://archive.org/stream/Metropolis_63/metropolis-1#page/n9/mode/2up

Women in Horror Recognition month. 5th June, 2015. Available at: http://womeninhorrormonth.com/

Endnotes

1. Reprinted in *Film Theory and Criticism: Introductory Readings*. Leo Brady and Marshall Cohen, Eds. 838.

2. Brady and Cohen. *Film Theory and Criticism: Introductory Readings*. 843.

3. Such as through her commanding performance as the physically changeable villain in *Countess Dracula*.

4. These details demonstrate Guy-Blaché's ingenuity as a filmmaker. Alison McMahan (2014) has commented that Guy-Blaché introduced props such as the rats to a number of her films.

5. Her involvement in the project is stated in sources such as Michael F. Blake's *A*

Thousand Faces: Lon Chaney's Unique Artistry in Motion Pictures.

6. *Metropolis.* 8.

7. *Metropolis.*

8. As has been discussed by Stephen King (1981, 36).

12. CRITICS, REFORMERS AND EDUCATORS: Film Culture as a Feminine Sphere

Shelley Stamp

In order to chart the full scope of women's engagement with American movie culture in the silent era, it is essential to trace a history that goes beyond the pioneering roles played by female directors and screenwriters in early Hollywood. Working as critics, journalists, activists, reformers and educators, women defined the landscape of American movie culture in its first three decades. As Antonia Lant reminds us, the binary notion of women working on 'both sides of the camera' needs to be significantly complicated and expanded in order to accommodate all of the ways in which women engaged with and produced early film culture (548–49). Indeed, looking at the extraordinary scope of women's participation in discussions and debates about the new medium of motion pictures, it becomes clear that women were not only essential players in these early debates; women *built* American movie culture.

Critics and Tastemakers

By 1915, writing about cinema comprised a key element of the culture surrounding motion pictures. Daily newspapers began regular movie reviewing in the mid-1910s, fostering a critical discourse about performance techniques, preferred plot lines, and cinematic style. Newspaper reviews were published alongside a growing body of film journalism that included profiles of movie stars' homes, wardrobes and family lives, advice for those hoping to work in the industry, and commentary on cinema's cultural value and its industry practices. Movie culture thus extended well beyond theater boundaries to encompass a wide range of discourses on stardom, personality, art, industry, gender, race and ethnicity published in an array of sources including daily newspapers, mass-circulation monthlies, fan magazines, trade papers and other publications. Women were central authors of this discourse, the principal celebrities profiled within it, and often its primary audience as well. Far from being a marginal adjunct to mainstream movie culture, women sat at its heart.

Journalists like Mary Heaton Vorse and Olivia Howard Dunbar provided some of the earliest accounts of American movie audiences. Recounting her experiences visiting New York's nickelodeons, Vorse wrote, 'I had gone, as they had, to see pictures, but in the end I saw only them,' finding herself particularly struck by the diversity of women gathered there – young and old, married and single, wage earners and homemakers, recent immigrants and native-born alike. All had incorporated movie-going into their daily routines, she reported, stopping in on the way home from work or market, greeting friends and neighbors there, bringing infants and children along to the show (Stamp *Movie-Struck* 195). Dunbar too visited the city's nickelodeons and, echoing later feminist assessments of early cinema, expressed considerable frustration that 'endangered girlhood is ... so frequently and persistently presented' on-screen (22).

Writing for high-brow magazines like *The Outlook* and *Harper's Weekly*, Vorse and Dunbar interpreted the new phenomenon of movie-going for an educated elite. Even more significant was the role that daily newspapers played in 'shaping audiences' ephemeral experiences of movie-going in the 1910s, as Richard Abel has documented, by publishing profiles of movie stars and filmmaking studios, film reviews and ads, fictionalized tie-ins for early serials like *The Adventures of Kathlyn* (1913), along with news of industry developments. Much of this material, he notes, appeared in newspapers' women's pages or Sunday supplements geared primarily to female readers – and a significant percentage of the material was written and edited by women as well (*Menus* 6–20).

The *Los Angeles Times* was the first newspaper to take an active interest in the motion picture business, assigning Grace Kingsley to be a movie columnist in 1913 and creating a section called 'The Preview' to feature writing on the industry, its stars and its projects (Goodman 149; Gottlieb and Wolt 148). Recent sources sometimes refer to Kingsley as a 'gossip columnist', but her writing furnished detailed portraits of Hollywood's major players, including many of its women. For instance, Kingsley chronicled Dorothy Arzner's move into directing in 1927 with a piece entitled 'Leave Sex Out, Says Director' (Mayne 194). Kingsley was the first of many newspaperwomen who shaped U.S. movie culture in the mid-1910s, aiding the cinema's transition from a marginalized urban working-class amusement to its new place amongst the nation's most popular pastimes.

Like Kingsley, Chicago-based syndicated columnist Gertrude Price helped promote women's work at all levels of the film industry, and in doing so, fostered a keen female fan base for the movies, as Abel documents. Her column, first published in late 1912, soon became 'one of the most widely read sources of gossip and information on the movies' emerging stars'. By Abel's calculation, some two-thirds of Price's articles were focused on women in the industry – performers, directors and screenwriters alike ('Fan Discourse' 140–53). At the *Chicago Tribune* Kitty Kelly began writing on the movies in early 1914, later joined by Francis Peck, better known by her pseudonym 'Mae Tinee'. Writers at other newspapers across the country soon followed suit, almost all of whom were women: Mary B. Leffler wrote the 'Flashes from Filmdom' column at the *Fort Worth Star-Telegram* and edited its film page; Ruth Vinson wrote the 'Minutes 'Mong the Movies' column at the *Cleveland Plain Dealer*; Dorothy Day penned the 'News of the Movies' column in the *Des Moines Evening Tribune*; Daisy Dean's daily column 'News Notes from Movieland' was syndicated in Midwest newspapers; an unnamed 'Film Girl' chronicled releases at the *Syracuse Herald*; Esther Hoffman was a syndicated movie columnist for the Scripps-McRae circuit; Ona Otto who wrote and edited the 'Photo Plays and Players' page at the *Cleveland Sunday Leader*; and at the *Chicago Herald* Louella O. Parsons wrote a daily 'Seen on the Screen' column and edited the paper's Sunday motion picture page (*Menus* 182–245). Mary Pickford's 'Daily Talks' column began a syndicated run in many national papers in 1915, offering advice to women on careers, beauty routines and health, along with profiles of Pickford's 'friends' in the industry – women like Alice Guy-Blaché, Mabel Normand and Lois Weber. As Abel makes clear, this cadre of early film journalists helped 'train' movie-goers to appreciate well-constructed narratives, subtle performances and expert cinematography, all the while drawing attention to the talented artists and craftspeople employed by the growing industry with their authoritative opinions increasingly cited in ads and publicity. If their critical assessments helped authenticate the new medium, their 'chatty voices' drew movie-goers into 'movie fandom's new 'interpretive communities' (*Menus* 243).

If much of this newspaper discourse favored a white, middle-class perspective on cinema, Spanish-language news-papers, like *La Opínion* based in Los Angeles and *La Prensa* based in San Antonio, fostered a film culture for U.S. Latinos. Both papers published regular cinema pages featuring Spanish translations of Parsons' columns and publicity items on stars including Latina actresses like Dolores del Río and Lupe Vélez. Both reported on films they considered offensive to Mexicans and chronicled the influence of American mores on Mexicano moviegoers, especially the controversy surrounding '*las pelonas*' (the bobbed-hair girls) inspired by Hollywood's flapper culture (Monroy 173–87; Gunckel 325–30; Serna 93, 127–38). African-American newspapers, such as the *Chicago Defender* and the *New York Age*, shaped response to the cinema in black communities by circulating reports of films and industry practices they considered racist, promoting the educational and cultural value of cinema for black audiences, and publicizing African-American filmmakers and stars like Edna Morton, dubbed 'Our Mary Pickford' (Everett 159–77; Stewart, 114–54).

Even as female journalists and readers dominated movie coverage in daily newspapers, helping to define American movie culture, industry trade papers remained a largely male domain – with a few notable exceptions. Mabel Condon, west coast correspondent for the *New York Dramatic Mirror*, was one of several women writing for industry trade papers. At *Moving Picture World* Margaret I. MacDonald drew attention to women working in Hollywood and reminded exhibitors and tradesmen about the importance of their female clientele and Marion Howard penned a regular column combining brief film reviews with news about stars and upcoming productions. Patsy Smith's *Variety* column 'Among the Women' offered a mix of movie reviews, often focused on the exploits of female characters; fashion commentary, containing surprisingly intricate descriptions of items worn by women on-screen; information about actresses Smith had interviewed; and details from film production sets Smith had visited. That such a venerable trade publication might place itself 'among' women suggests not only the prominence of women in the trade who might read such a column; but also the value that exhibitors placed on their female clientele, information about which they could glean from Smith's columns. Theater managers might be interested to learn, for instance, about Smith's pronounced disappointment that Griffith's 1919 release, *The Girl Who Stayed at Home,* did not star either of the Gish sisters and that, despite its promising title, was merely another 'familiar Griffith war story' (90).

Mass-circulation women's magazines also devoted considerable coverage to the movies beginning at least as early as 1912 when *Ladies' World* published the first serialized fiction tie-in with the movie serial *What Happened to Mary?* The trend continued in the late 'teens and early 1920s as publications like *Ladies' Home Journal*, *Good Housekeeping*, and *Woman's Home Companion* – all with circulations over one million – published profiles of women working in Hollywood, product ads featuring Hollywood stars, analyses of the 'movie-struck girl' phenomenon, and tips about how to get screenplays sold, all the while exhorting readers to take an active role in advocating for 'better films' in their communities. Writing in *Half-Century Magazine*, a monthly geared towards upwardly-mobile black women, Jean Voltaire Smith argued against the black church's traditional opposition to popular amusements, instead suggesting that cinema might be a medium that could educate African-Americans, while helping to bridge the gap between the less educated and the elite. 'Would it not be better then, to encourage more of our people to produce pictures – films of the clean, helpful sort, that will uplift; urge them to build class moving pictures theaters, rather than discourage them from attending picture shows?' she wrote (quoted in Everett 157). Women's monthlies thus helped to position women as the primary audience for the movies, as well as an important influence on movie-going tastes and habits in others.

While journalists contributed to an evolving critical commentary on movies and movie culture, a growing fan culture provided movie aficionados with intimate details about their favored players. Romances, marriages, divorces, childhoods and children all became targets of increased curiosity, as did homes, kitchens, closets and dressing tables. Fan culture increasingly tailored its appeal to women, by catering to supposedly 'feminine' preoccupations with romance, beauty, decorating and family life, rather than the technical and scientific details that had colored much of the earliest film publicity (Studlar 263–98; Fuller 115–32). Women authored much of this fan discourse, forming its 'backbone', according to Anthony Slide (6). A quick survey of fan magazine writing in the late 1910s and 1920s reveals that at least half of the featured pieces in each volume were written by women. Adele Whitely Fletcher, Gladys Hall, Fritzi Remont, Pearl Gaddis and Aline Carter, among many others, were all regular contributors to *Motion Picture*. At *Photoplay* the majority of writers were women, the best-known being Ruth Waterbury, Elizabeth Peltret, Mabel Condon, Agnes Smith, and Frances Denton. Well-known journalist Adela Rogers St. Johns also contributed to *Photoplay* in the 1920s, bringing her distinctive, emotional style to tales of life in Hollywood in both factual pieces and fiction, most notably a serialized novella dubbing Hollywood the 'port of missing girls' (Morey 'So real'). In some cases, the prominent role played by female writers translated into positions of editorial leadership. Florence M. Osborne became editor of *Motion Picture* in 1925 and Ruth Biery served as west coast editor for *Photoplay;* editorial assistant Kathryn Dougherty also made important editorial decisions at *Photoplay* and eventually took over editorship in 1932 (Barbas *First Lady* 125; Barbas *Movie Crazy* 71; Lant 563).

Alongside fawning portraits of stars' homes, careers, wardrobes, and families, fan culture also spawned a gossip industry reporting on the sometimes less-than-savory aspects of Hollywood life in items with which neither studio publicists nor the stars themselves were complicit. Gossip, perhaps even more than fan magazine reporting, helped female fans negotiate and assimilate rapidly changing gender norms and shifting sexual mores, a view only confirmed by a review of the era's signal headlines: Mary Pickford's 'quickie' divorce and marriage to Douglas Fairbanks in 1920; the star scandals of 1921 and 1922, all of which involved questions of feminine propriety; Charlie Chaplin's marriage to a pregnant and 16-year-old Lita Grey in 1924, after having divorced his similarly teenaged bride, Mildred Harris; and Rudolph Valentino's 'unconventional' marriage to Natacha Rambova. Chief among early gossip columnists was Louella Parsons, best known for her daily column 'Flickerings from Film Land', syndicated between 1926 and 1965 in hundreds of Hearst newspapers nationwide with a readership estimated at six million. Parsons positioned herself *within* Hollywood, becoming a regular at the

Cocoanut Grove night club and parties held at San Simeon and Pickfair, evolving into a kind of celebrity herself, providing readers with a unique and privileged window on Hollywood culture. Parsons was also instrumental in forming the Hollywood Women's Press Club in 1928, a group that included *Photoplay* editor Ruth Biery, Regina Carewe, a film writer for the Hearst syndicate, along with many of the well-known feature writers for *Motion Picture* and *Motion Picture Classic* (Barbas *Movie Crazy* 91–96; Barbas *First Lady* 124–25).

Female journalists writing in daily newspapers, women's monthlies, and fan magazines crafted portraits of female stars and other women active in early Hollywood that fashioned, in Hilary Hallett's words, 'women-made women'. Creating a 'female-centered leisure space' focused around the motion picture industry, 'women experts explained to female readers how ordinary women became extraordinary new women' (71). As Nan Enstad emphasizes, many of these profiles focused on the *labour* of movie-making, stressing the remarkable work performed by women in 'movieland' (93). Readers might learn, for instance, how serial star Helen Holmes combined moviemaking and motherhood, how filmmaker Lois Weber worked collaboratively with her husband, or how two 'girl picture magnates' emigrated to Los Angeles, pooled their financial and artistic resources, set up house together, and established their own production company (Stamp *Movie-Struck* 148–49; Stamp *Lois Weber* 77–91; Jordan).

While oftentimes dismissed as mere purveyors of gossip, female journalists writing for daily newspapers, popular magazines, industry trade papers, and fan publications were much more than that. They were among the first to write about cinema's social impact, to chronicle the new industry, and to review its products. They played a notable role in helping to define cinema's growing impact on society, particularly for young women caught up in its fan culture and for middle-class women active in the reform movement. In doing so, they helped draw attention to the many women, not just high-profile stars, working in the new industry, and helped to foster a critical distance from Hollywood trends, all the while – yes – providing privileged access to the medium's ethereal celebrities and creating a fan culture with women – stars, writers and readers – at its centre.

Regulation and Reform

If female journalists and women's magazines helped shape an evolving critical and cultural discourse about popular cinema, female reformers and educators took an equally active role in evaluating, monitoring, and attempting to regulate cinema and cinema-going. An industry that had invested so much energy into courting female patronage now found those patrons discerning, critical, and always vocal. As Anne Morey remarks, 'women used film-going to advance their own influence, parlaying their role as consumer into a more obviously political function as the arbiters of their own and others' consumption' ('So real' 333). On the one hand, women's activism drew upon an outmoded view of middle-class white women extending a maternal hand into the public sphere, taking care of 'less fortunate' working-class and immigrant communities; on the other hand, this activism also drew upon newly radicalized women's organizations recently successful in their campaigns for women's suffrage and Prohibition, both ratified in 1920.

Positioned as gatekeepers of culture and morality, women were a visible force in regulating cinema early on. No more so than in Chicago where reformers Jane Addams and Louise De Koven Bowen were at the forefront of efforts to research and write about conditions in the city's nickelodeon theaters. They sought to promote motion pictures as an entertainment medium for the city's working-class youth and to encourage public regulation of such a prominent commercial enterprise. For Addams 'cheap amusements' like the movies could convey essential lessons about society and morality and in 1907, at the height of the nickelodeon craze, she famously installed a five-cent theater at the Hull House Settlement where she lived and worked. Film screenings would become part of an ambitious slate of services offered for the neighborhood's working poor that included public bathhouses, park land, vocational training, union organising, and rooms for single working women. Although the Hull House Theater was ultimately short-lived, it later became a model for alternative exhibition outlets (Lindstrom 90–112; Luckett 169–205; Rabinovitz 105–136).

When narrative features began to dominate the market in the mid-1910s, reformers turned their attention to regulating the content of films, rather than the theater conditions that had been their primary concern initially. The National Board of Censorship was the industry's earliest self-regulatory body and was staffed largely by middle-class white women who volunteered to evaluate films prior to their release. By 1915, 100 out of 115 volunteers were female (Grieveson 101). Less is known about personnel who screened films at many of the state film censorship boards, but it is likely that many were also women active in civic clubs or progressive reform. When Chicago replaced its police censorship board with a ten-person commission of salaried civilians in 1914, for instance, women occupied half of the seats (Hallet 20). Women were so identified with the scrutiny of motion pictures that when New York State established its film censorship commission in 1921, *Variety* remarked on the novelty of a 'womanless censorship board', reporting that 'petticoat candidates' had vied (unsuccessfully) for one of the commission's three seats ('Womanless' 44).

Among the many prominent women's organizations taking an active interest in cinema was the Women's Christian Temperance Union (WCTU) which stepped up its scrutiny of the movies after their successful campaign for Prohibition. WCTU members visited local cinemas to rate the appropriateness of current offerings, sending appreciative letters to companies that produced 'wholesome' pictures and protesting to mayors and police chiefs about pictures they considered 'vulgar'. Particularly concerned about the effects of film-going on the very young, local chapters published statistics on children's movie attendance and sent literature on the hazards of moving picture shows to all new mothers in their area. WCTU groups sponsored screenings of educational films in churches and community halls and influenced local politics, successfully preventing the showing of Sunday movies in several states through special elections (Parker 'Mothering' 75–83; Parker *Purifying America* 213–16). Recognizing cinema's new prominence in the cultural domain, the WCTU would proclaim, 'motion pictures are having a far more injurious effect upon public morals in general than the saloon ever had' (quoted in Parker 'Mothering' 87).

A more moderate strain of activism was centered in the better films movement, a grass roots campaign to promote 'quality' pictures coordinated largely through women's magazines and clubs. In 1916 the Motion Picture Committee of the General Federation of Women's Clubs organized a series of lectures by Mary Gray Peck, head of Federation's Drama Committee, intended to advise clubwomen across the mid-west about how best to agitate for better quality pictures in their own communities ('Lecture Tour'). By the mid-1920s these efforts were highly coordinated. Most affiliates of the General Federation of Women's Clubs had established units devoted to the better films movement. The all-woman International Federation of Catholic Alumnae (IFCA) reviewed up to 11,000 films annually, then distributed lists of recommended titles to Catholic schools across the country. The National Congress of Parents and Teachers, comprised largely of women, circulated a pamphlet on 'Endorsed Films' to parent-teacher organizations nationwide. Popular magazines like *Woman's Home Companion* and *Ladies' World* encouraged readers to exercise their civic 'duty' and advocate for quality pictures in their communities by helping to spread the word about recommended titles and demanding better fare from local exhibitors. Through its Good Citizenship Bureau *Woman's Home Companion* ran a Better Films Service that published lists of recommended films for its readership, coordinated by Bureau director Anna Steese Richardson (Lant 271–73; Stamp *Movie-Struck* 13).

As a result, many clubwomen were instrumental in working with commercial exhibitors to fashion 'wholesome and entertaining programs' suitable for children or families – theaters within theaters, if you will. The Women's Civic Club of Independence, Missouri, partnered with a local exhibitor in 1912 to screen films one afternoon and evening each week aiding its campaign 'for sanitation and beautifying the city', confident that images of urban blight and renewal were best conveyed on motion picture screens ('Women's Club'). Women's clubs were particularly active in the campaign for children's screenings. Elizabeth Richey Dessez explained that 'parents and educators all over the country are awakening to the realization that outside their very doorstep has sprung up, within a decade, a shaper of minds and characters of the young of our generation more potent than any influence the world has ever known, except that of the home' (18). Urging 'women who become godmothers of children's Motion Picture shows' to band together, Dessez advised them to make their demands for appropriate juvenile fare 'insistent, consistent and nation-wide'. Only then, she said, would 'the men who control and direct this commercial art' stand up and listen (20). One such effort was made in Pawtucket, Rhode Island, where clubwomen and members of the local Mothers' Club worked with the owner of the town's 1,000-seat Imperial Theater to create a 'Children's Theater' there on Saturdays. For the price of a nickel, children could watch films like *Snow White* and *The Foundling*, 'supervised by matrons who will see the welfare of the youngsters'. Proceeds from the screenings would be used to benefit children in local communities ('Woman's and Mothers' 78). In New York City Laura Cogswell, known as 'The Motion Picture Mother', formed the Children's Motion Picture League in 1913, taking over a commercial theater in the city's impoverished lower east side to provide free matinee screenings for the neighbourhood's children on Saturday mornings ('Children's M.P. League' 299). Similar efforts were made by women's clubs in Atlanta and New Orleans, where clubwomen contracted with a local film manufacturer to make one-reel shorts featuring children who attended their matinee programs (Beatty 1996; 'A Children's Picture' 584).

Not only did female reformers transform commercial exhibition spaces for educational purposes, they also brought film screenings to disenfranchised populations. Prison film screenings became an integral part of the larger movement of humane prison reform in the 1910s, a movement in which women were especially active, as Alison Griffiths has demonstrated. Ella H. Davison donated a motion picture projector to men imprisoned at New York's infamous Sing Sing, along with three months' worth of movies, attending a screening in the prison's chapel shortly there afterwards (429). When New York City found itself in the grip of a white slavery scandal, Mrs. S. M. Haggen, President of the Immigrant Girls' Home, proposed screening films on the topic to female immigrants new to the city, pointing out that motion pictures were an ideal venue for educating these women, many of whom were not yet fluent in English (Brownlow 73–74). Even though Jane Addams' experiment running a nickelodeon at Hull House had ultimately been short-lived, her vision of integrating cinema into the larger project of progressive reform remained influential.

In other cases an interest in promoting quality cinema led better films activists to become involved in the 'little theater' movement that sought to expand the distribution of European art films in the U.S.. Regge Doran founded one such example, Hollywood's long-standing Filmarte Theater, in 1928. That same year New York's Little Picture House was opened by a group of society women (Horak 22; Guzman). They planned to offer programs of films and educational talks aimed at school children and 'women who go to lectures, who go on shopping expeditions, and many who go nowhere and are bored' (quoted in Lant 582).

Although women's magazines and industry sponsors alike often characterized the better films movement as a group of mothers advocating wholesome entertainment for their families and their communities, many women active in the movement had long track records of public activism and social service. Catheryne Cooke Gilman, who led the better films movement in Minneapolis before assuming a position of national leadership, had been a schoolteacher and a settlement worker at Hull House, and had been active in campaigns for women's suffrage, sex education, and children's welfare. As Cynthia Hanson points out, Gilman's interest in motion pictures manifested a decidedly progressive attitude – a belief that if social problems were documented, publicized and discussed, society would respond because, she believed, all Americans shared a common standard of morality (204–5).

One notable example of such activism was the fight by African-American clubwomen against *The Birth of a Nation* in 1915. Concerned about plans to append screenings of Griffith's film with a short showcasing work at the Hampton Institute, one of the country's oldest black universities, black clubwomen banded together. Margaret James Murray, president of the Northeastern Federation of Colored Women's Clubs and the wife of Booker T. Washington, organized a letter-writing campaign protesting the school's association with the racist epic. Positive imagery of African-Americans produced at the Hampton Institute could never 'offset nefarious pictures' like Griffith's, one clubwoman wrote from Connecticut (Field 175). Murray's campaign was successful and ultimately the Hampton Institute re-considered its plan. Campaigns of this kind had a lasting impact on American movie culture, according to Richard Kozsarski, who argues that the better films movement was 'ambitious, well-organized, and certainly the earliest national effort to promote film as a medium of social and artistic importance' (208).

The movie industry took notice to be sure. We look 'to you to give us suggestions, to co-operate with us, to promote the showing of good pictures ... and to banish evil pictures from the screen' *Moving Picture World* writer W. Stephen Bush told clubwomen in 1916 ('Club Women'). Early the following year, his paper published a thirty-two-page pamphlet with information about educational titles and 'wholesome' comedies and dramas 'suitable for the family group and children's matinees', designed for use by exhibitors and 'others interested in the better film movement' ('Educational' 78). Paramount, building a brand identified with quality cinema (and higher ticket prices), invited female movie-goers to speak directly with exhibitors at their theaters about films they wished to see there, piggybacking directly onto the better films movement for its own branding. 'Get acquainted with the manager of your theater', readers of *Movie Weekly* were advised in one Paramount ad. 'If your ideals of quality in photoplays are as high as Paramount's, he wants to know about it... It's no good simply talking among yourselves when your indignation is aroused by some inferior picture. Talk to the man who can change it.' An accompanying illustration showed two well-appointed white women speaking to a male theater manager, other female patrons visible in the background with their children (32). The message of these efforts: we in the movie industry are on your side; we are eager to hear your opinions; we too are advocates for better motion pictures.

Yet even while seeming to embrace the better films movement, industry leaders were careful to cultivate an anti-censorship ethos amongst activists involved in the campaign. Telling clubwomen that censorship was a 'musty institution' unbefitting a modern progressive society, Bush promoted instead 'constructive co-operation between exhibitors and mothers and such organizations as yours', praising the 'really valuable and constructive work' of clubwomen involved in better films campaigns around the country ('Club Women'). Heeding Bush's call, disparate elements of the movement came together in 1919 to form the National Federation of Better Film Workers. Delegates from all of the prominent women's organizations, including the National Council of Women, the WCTU, Daughters of the American Revolution, and the National Woman's Suffrage Association, met in New

York to devise a platform opposed to official film censorship. Censorship was 'too prone to fall under the influence of politicians' and often only succeeded in drawing attention to 'bad pictures', explained the group's president, Harriet H. Barry, former Chair of the Women's City Club of Los Angeles. A group of committed clubwomen, some ten million strong, on the other hand, could exert considerable influence on exhibitors. 'We're not prudes,' Barry assured industry leaders. 'What we want is pictures with a message' ('Ten Million' 65). Barry had worked successfully with exhibitors in California and was eager to put her methods into practice on a national scale: clubwomen, not politically appointed censors, could best protect the interests of their communities – *and* the movie industry, she insisted.

When Will Hays assumed leadership of the Motion Picture Producers and Distributors Association (MPPDA) in 1922, at the height of the star scandals, he wasted no time in cultivating women's groups that had been critical of Hollywood. Hoping to gain their support in his efforts to ward off federal censorship, then becoming a distinct reality, Hays publicly supported the better films movement and efforts to promote children's matinees, spoke regularly to women's organizations, and cultivated relationships with prominent activists like Catheryne Cooke Gilman. When the MPPDA stepped up industry self-regulation in 1927, forming a Studio Relations Committee to evaluate scripts and completed films, representatives from major women's organizations, including the General Federation of Women's Clubs, the IFCA, and library groups, were invited to preview pre-release prints in a special Hollywood screening room (Morey *Hollywood Outsiders* 110–11; Wheeler 81–83). The following year Hays invited clubwomen to elect a designate to serve on the Studio Relations Committee itself. They chose Alice Ames Winter, past president of the General Federation of Women's Clubs, to be, as one observer described, an ambassador for 'the feelings and wishes of womanhood' (quoted in Wheeler 83).

Hays's efforts to woo female reformers were not always successful, however, as several of his allies became disillusioned with the MPPDA's efforts to police the industry from within. Gilman ultimately distanced herself from Hays, particularly outraged that he did not object when Fatty Arbuckle returned to work after Virginia Rappe's death (Hanson 207). Maude Aldrich, director of the WCTU's motion picture department, refused Hays's offer to serve on the MPPDA's public relations council, choosing instead to continue advocating for federal control of motion pictures. Both women joined the Federal Motion Picture Council, formed in 1925, which sought to create an independent commission, similar to the recently-established Federal Trade Commission, that would supervise the film industry, inspecting and modifying, if necessary, films containing 'sex, white slavery, illicit love, nudity, crime gambling, or excessive drinking' (Wheeler 79). Women remained the public face of the group's campaign: The Council proposed that at least four of the commission's nine seats would be occupied by women, and Gilman was elected president in 1928 after the Council's board of directors decided motion picture reform was 'ultimately a woman's responsibility' (quoted in Wheeler 81).

Education, Activism and Advocacy

While reformers and clubwomen focused attention on regulating the movie industry, others saw cinema's educational potential. Female librarians, classroom teachers and distributors lead the cause of visual instruction, mounting a significant challenge to Hollywood's domination of commercial circuits of exhibition. As both arbiters of culture and targets of reform, women were instrumental in promoting, screening and watching films in non-theatrical settings like schools, libraries, museums, clubs, workplaces and community centers. New publications like *Educational Film Magazine* and *Educational Screen* provided information to educators, social workers and librarians, most of whom were women, while books like *Motion Pictures for Community*

Needs: A Practical Manual of Information and Suggestion for Educational, Religious and Social Work, co-authored by Gladys and Henry Bollman in 1922, furnished practical tips on how to book films from exchanges and how to equip and run a screening facility. Many of the 100 film programs suggested by the Bollmans were specifically targeted for female audiences at YWCAs, girls' reformatories, women's clubs and settlement houses.

Women also helped pioneer the distribution of non-theatrical film. Ruth Gould Dolesé became the first head of the Educational Department of the General Film Company when it was formed in 1911. She compiled its first *Catalogue of Educational Motion Pictures,* with films listed in such categories as Religion, Sociology, Natural Science, Geography and Travel, Fine Arts and History. 'I cover practically the same ground as the schools,' Dolesé proclaimed proudly. A highly visible promoter of cinema's educational potential, Dolesé penned articles promoting educational films and spoke about their value in interviews, stressing how watching films of different cultures and locales could engender feelings of 'sympathy and fellowship with the peoples of the great world', echoing broader ideas of cinema's capacity as a new universal language (Peterson 'Knowledge' 286–87). Following Dolesé's lead, Katherine F. Carter founded the Educational Films Corporation in 1915, furnishing motion picture 'entertainments' for 'clubs, hotels and private residences', and offering to equip 'schools, churches and educational institutions with the necessities of moving picture projection' (MacDonald 803). Before forming her own company, Carter had been in charge of General Film's educational division, a situation not uncommon at other commercial studios and exchanges that ran educational divisions headed by women. Elizabeth Richey Dessez, director of the educational department at Pathé Exchange, for instance, had had a long association with the better films movement prior to her appointment.

The introduction of 16mm technology in 1923 further aided the circulation of films outside commercial exhibition circuits – one estimate calculated that some 15,000 churches, schools and clubs were screening films that year alone. By 1927, that number had nearly doubled (Maltby 190). The new gauge particularly helped to spur a 'visual instruction' movement amongst schoolteachers, and the female teacher as projectionist soon figured in accounts of the modern classroom (Waller 129). Anna Verona Dorris, author of *Visual Instruction in the Public Schools* (1928), the first such comprehensive guide, was particularly concerned to help women feel at home using 16mm technology in their classrooms. 'Anyone who is capable of operating an automobile can learn to operate any type of motion-picture projector,' she wrote (quoted in Waller 146). Ella Flagg Young, superintendent of schools in Chicago, embraced the use of motion pictures throughout that city's curriculum as early as 1916. Visual instruction, she said, would allow school children to 'get much more comprehensive ideas' about subjects like geography (Jackson 252). *Motion Pictures in Education: A Practical Handbook for Users of Visual Aids*, co-authored by Don Carlos Ellis and Laura Thornborough in 1923, offered teachers advice on what films to show in their classrooms, including both 'theatrical films suitable for school use' and 'pedagogical films', advice on how to incorporate films into their curriculum at all levels of schooling, examples of how films had been successfully used in schools across the country, and technical advice about the installation and operation of projection equipment.

Librarians, most of whom were also women, were instrumental in supporting non-theatrical screenings and cultivating an educated film culture amongst their patrons, as Jennifer Horne has documented (149–77). Librarians suggested books that might be read in conjunction with screenings at local movie-houses, hosted matinee screenings alongside children's story hours, and programmed groups of travelogues, newsreels and historical dramas together around particular themes. Libraries also began to acquire films for in-house screenings and circulating film collections, becoming major supporters of educational and documentary filmmaking. Recognizing cinema's potential as an instrument of progressive social change, feminist Charlotte Perkins Gilman imagined the construction of free public film libraries across the nation (143-45).

Cinema's educational potential was not lost on more radical groups as well; many early feminist organizations produced films to garner support for their causes. If one strand of female activism focused on policing cinema during these years, another recognized its extraordinary persuasive authority and the importance of visual rhetoric in feminist campaigns.

America's two leading women's suffrage organizations used motion pictures to promote their cause in the early 1910s, as the fight for voting rights escalated nationwide. The Women's Political Union (WPU) produced a one-reel comedy *Suffrage and the Man* in 1912, making light of a young man who learns to value his fiancée's political activism. That same year, the National American Woman Suffrage Association (NAWSA) produced *Votes for Women*, a two-reel drama that included documentary footage from the 1912 suffrage parade in New York, along with screen appearances by the organization's leader, Dr Anna Howard Shaw, and its vice president, Jane Addams. Edison sound recordings of the women's speeches were apparently included in some versions of the film.

More ambitious multi-reel films followed. The WPU's four-reel drama, *Eighty Million Women Want–?* (1913), featured noted British activist Emmeline Pankhurst addressing viewers in its prologue. WPU leader Harriot Stanton Blatch played herself in the dramatic portion of the film, helping the film's heroine lead the group in a victorious campaign. After witnessing the success of serials with younger female viewers, NAWSA joined with Selig Polyscope in Chicago, producer of *The Adventures of Kathlyn*, to make its feature *Your Girl and Mine* in 1914, hiring Gilson Willets, author of the Kathlyn serial, to draft the suffrage feature. NAWSA president Dr Anna Howard Shaw again made an appearance in the film. Both suffrage organizations employed novel exhibition strategies to promote their films in commercial and non-commercial settings, with suffrage leaders often appearing in person at screenings to introduce films and to field questions afterwards (Shore; Stamp *Movie-Struck Girls* 168–76).

The era's other leading feminist cause, the fight to legalize contraception, or 'voluntary motherhood', was also dramatized in several films. Eager to capitalize on the new medium's potential, activist Margaret Sanger co-wrote the 1917 feature *Birth Control,* a chronicle of her storied career as nurse-turned-birth control advocate, playing herself on-screen. Sanger planned to tour the country with the film promoting her cause, but was cut short by successful efforts to ban showings of *Birth Control* in many communities (Sloan 86–7; Norden 263–79). Like activists in the suffrage cause, Sanger saw movie-goers not as innocents in need of moral protection and 'betterment', but as potential fellow radicals who might be marshaled for action. Movie theaters were imagined as spaces of revolutionary organizing. 'Every woman in the world will demonstrate to see it,' Sanger proclaimed of *Birth Control* (Norden 271). Sanger's fight was also dramatized in *The Hand That Rocks the Cradle*, a 1917 feature written and directed by the era's leading female filmmaker, Lois Weber, who also played the film's central character, Louise Broome, a birth control advocate whom contemporary critics recognized as an obvious stand-in for Sanger (Stamp 'Taking Precautions' 286–87). If Sanger's own film ended with the activist in prison, Weber reimagined the narrative to conclude with her heroine released from prison and contraception legalized in the state of Illinois. 'What do *you* think?' the final title asked viewers, inviting women to talk amongst themselves about family planning and, perhaps, to mobilize others for action outside the theater.

Whether monitoring films at their local cinemas, screening films in classrooms, libraries, and settlement houses, opening alternative theaters and exhibition outlets, or producing advocacy pictures, women stood at the heart of early efforts to reform American politics, classrooms, and workplaces through the use of moving pictures and to reform cinema itself. As critics and journalists women played an equally pivotal role in defining American movie culture. They analyzed the new social phenomenon of movie-going, helped pioneer the art of movie reviewing, and crafted a fan culture by, for and about women. A history of cinema that recognizes this work of advocacy and activism moves women from the margins to the center, assigning this labor its rightful place alongside filmmaking and screenwriting in shaping film culture during the silent era.

This article was excerpted and expanded from the article, 'Women and the Silent Screen', originally published in *The Blackwell History of American Cinema. Vol. 1: Origins to 1928*. Roy Grundmann, Cynthia Lucia and Art Simon Eds. Oxford, Blackwell Publishers, 2012, 181–206.

Author Biography: Shelley Stamp

Shelley is author of *Lois Weber in Early Hollywood* and *Movie-Struck Girls: Women and Motion Picture Culture after the Nickelodeon*. She is founding editor of *Feminist Media Histories: An International Journal* and co-editor with Charlie Keil of *American Cinema's Transitional Era: Audiences, Institutions, Practices*. She is Professor of Film and Digital Media at the University of California, Santa Cruz, where she currently holds the Pavel Machotka Chair in Creative Studies..

References

Abel, Richard. 'Fan Discourse in the Heartland: The Early 1910s'. *Film History: An International Journal*. 18.2. 2006, 140–53.

Menus for Movieland: Newspapers and the Emergence of American Movie Culture, 1913–16. Oakland: University of California Press, 2015.

Advertisement. *Movie Weekly*, 15th April, 1922, 32.

Barbas, Samantha. *The First Lady of Hollywood: A Biography of Louella Parsons*. Berkeley: University of California Press, 2006

Barbas, Samantha. *Movie Crazy: Fans, Stars, and the Cult of Celebrity*. London: Palgrave MacMillan, 2002.

Beatty, A.M. 'Special Films for Children in Atlanta', *Moving Picture World*. 30th December, 1916, 1996.

Brownlow, Kevin. *Behind the Mask of Innocence: Sex, Violence, Prejudice, Crime: Films of Social Conscience in the Silent Era*. Berkeley, University of California Press, 1990.

'The Children's M.P. League', *Moving Picture World*, 19th July, 1913, 299.

'A Children's Picture by the Kiddies Themselves'. *Moving Picture World*, 28th October, 1916, 584.

'Club Women Listen to Film Man', *Moving Picture World*. 28th October, 1916, 552.

Dessez, Elizabeth Richey. 'Better Pictures for Children', *Motion Picture Classic.* September, 1916, 17–20.

Dorris, Anna Verona. *Visual Instruction in the Public Schools.* Boston, Ginn and Co., 1928.

Dunbar, Olivia Howard. 'The Lure of the Films', *Harper's Weekly.* 57. 18th January, 1913, 20, 22.

'Educational and Selected Films', *Moving Picture World.* 7th April, 1917, 78.

Ellis, Don Carlos and Laura Thornborough. *Motion Pictures in Education: A Practical Handbook for Users of Visual Aids.* New York, Thomas Y. Crowell, 1923.

Enstad, Nan. *Ladies of Labor, Girls of Adventure: Working Women, Popular Culture, and Labor Politics at the Turn of the Twentieth Century.* New York, Columbia University Press, 1999.

Everett, Anna. *Returning the Gaze: A Genealogy of Black Film Criticism, 1909–1949.* Durham, NC, Duke University Press, 2001.

Field, Allyson Nadia. *Uplift Cinema: The Emergence of African American Film and the Possibility of Black Modernity.* Durham, NC, Duke University Press, 2015.

Fuller, Kathryn H. *At the Picture Show: Small-town Audiences and the Creation of Movie Fan Culture.* Washington, Smithsonian Institution Press, 1996.

Gilman, Charlotte Perkins. 'Public Library Motion Pictures', *Annals of the American Academy of Political and Social Science.* 128. November, 1926, 143–45.

Goodman, Ezra. *The Fifty-Year Decline and Fall of Hollywood.* New York, Simon and Schuster, 1961.

Gottlieb, Robert and Irene Wolt. *Thinking Big: The Story of the Los Angeles Times, Its Publishers, and their Influence on Southern California.* New York, Putnam, 1977.

Grieveson, Lee. *Policing Cinema: Movies and Censorship in Early-Twentieth-Century America.* Berkeley, University of California Press, 2004.

Griffiths, Alison. 'Bound by Cinematic Chains: Film and Prisons during the Early Era', *A Companion to Early Cinema.* André Gaudreault, Nicolas Dulac, and Santiago Hidalgo, Eds. Malden, MA,Wiley-Blackwell, 2012, 420–40.

Gunckel, Colin. 'The War of the Accents: Spanish Language Hollywood Films in Mexican Los Angeles', *Film History: An International Journal.* 20.3. 2008, 325–43.

Guzman, Tony. 'The Little Theater Movement: The Institutionalization of the European Art Film in America', *Film History: An International Journal.* 17.2/3. 2005, 261–84.

Hallett, Hilary A. *Go West, Young Women! The Rise of Early Hollywood.* Berkeley, University of California Press, 2013.

Hanson, Cynthia A. 'Catheryne Cooke Gilman and the Minneapolis Better Movie Movement', *Minnesota History.* 51.6. 1989, 202–216.

Horak, Jan-Christopher. *Lovers of Cinema: The First American Film Avant-Garde, 1919–1945.* Madison, University of Wisconsin Press, 1998.

Horne, Jennifer. 'A History Long Overdue: The Public Library and Motion Pictures', *Useful Cinema.* Charles R. Acland and Haidee Wasson. Durham, Eds. NC, Duke University Press, 2011, 149–77.

Jackson, Rev. W.H. 'About Pictures in Schools', *Moving Picture World.* 8th January, 1916: 252.

Jordan, Joan. 'The Girl Picture Magnates', *Photoplay.* August, 1922, 22–23, 111.

Lant, Antonia, Ed. *The Red Velvet Seat: Women's Writings on the Cinema: The First Fifty Years.* London, Verso, 2006.

'Lecture Tour Planned', *Moving Picture World.* 21st October, 1916, 406.

Lindstrom, J.A. '"Almost Worse than the Restrictive Measures": Chicago Reformers and the Nickelodeons', *Cinema Journal.* 39.1 1999, 90–112.

Luckett, Moya. *Cinema and Community: Progressivism, Exhibition, and Film Culture in Chicago, 1907–1917.* Detroit, Wayne State University Press, 2014.

MacDonald, Margaret I. 'Educational Films Corporation of America', *Moving Picture World.* 31st July, 1915, 803.

Maltby, Richard. '*The King of Kings* and the Czar of all Rushes: The Propriety of the Christ Story', *Screen.* 31.2. 1990, 188–213.

Mayne, Judith. *Directed by Dorothy Arzner.* Bloomington, Indiana University Press, 1994.

Monroy, Douglas. '"Our children Get So Different Here": Film, Fashion, Popular Culture, and the Process of Cultural Syncretization in Mexican Los Angeles, 1900–1935', *Aztlán: A Journal of Chicano Studies.* 19.1 1988–90, 79–108.

Morey, Anne. *Hollywood Outsiders: The Adaptation of the Film Industry, 1913–34.* Minneapolis, University of Minnesota Press, 2003.

'"So real as to seem like life itself"': The *Photoplay* Fiction of Adela Rogers St. Johns', *A Feminist Reader in Early Cinema.* Jennifer Bean and Diane Negra, Eds. Durham, NC, Duke University Press, 2002, 333–46.

Rabinovitz, Lauren. *For the Love of Pleasure: Women, Movies, and Culture in Turn-of-the-Century Chicago.* New Brunswick, NJ, Rutgers University Press, 1998.

Norden, Martin F. 'Revisionist History, Restricted Cinema: The Strange Case of Margaret Sanger and *Birth Control*', *Cultural Sutures: Medicine and Media.* Lester D. Friedman, Ed. Durham, NC, Duke University Press, 2004, 263–79.

Parker, Alison M. 'Mothering the Movies: Women Reformers and Popular Culture', *Movie Censorship and American Culture.* Francis G. Couvares, Ed. Washington, DC, Smithsonian Institution Press, 1996, 73–96.

Parker, Alison M. *Purifying America: Women's Cultural Reform and Pro-Censorship, 1873–1933.* Urbana-Champaign, University of Illinois Press, 1997.

Peterson, Jennifer. '"The Knowledge Which Comes in Pictures": Educational Films and Early Cinema Audiences', *A Companion to Early Cinema.* André Gaudreault, Nicolas Dulac and Santiago Hidalgo, Eds. Malden, MA, Wiley-Blackwell, 2012, 277–97.

Serna, Laura Isabel. *Making Cinelandia: American Films and Mexican Film Culture Before the Golden Age.* Durham, NC, Duke University Press, 2014.

Shore, Amy. *Suffrage and the Silver Screen.* New York, Peter Lang, 2014.

Slide, Anthony, Ed. *They Also Wrote for the Fan Magazines: Film Articles by Literary Giants from e. e. Cummings to Eleanor Roosevelt, 1920–1939.* Jefferson, NC, McFarland, 1992.

Sloan, Kay. *The Loud Silents: Origins of the Social Problem Film.* Urbana, University of Illinois Press, 1988.

Smith, Patsy. 'Among the Women'. *Variety*, 28th March, 1919, 90.

Stamp, Shelley. *Lois Weber in Early Hollywood.* Oakland, University of California Press, 2015.

Movie-Struck Girls: Women and Motion Picture Culture after the Nickelodeon. Princeton, Princeton University Press, 2000.

'Taking Precautions, or Contraceptive Technology and Cinema's Regulatory Apparatus', *A Feminist Reader in Early Cinema.* Jennifer Bean and Diane Negra, Eds. Durham, NC, Duke University Press, 2002, 270–97.

Stewart, Jacqueline Najuma. *Migrating to the Movies: Cinema and Black Urban Modernity.* Berkeley, University of California Press, 2005.

Studlar, Gaylyn. 'The Perils of Pleasure? Fan Magazine Discourse as Women's Commodified Culture in the 1920s', *Silent Film.* Richard Abel, Ed. Brunswick, NJ, Rutgers University Press, 263–98.

CRITICS, REFORMERS AND EDUCATORS

'Ten Million Women Unite for Fight on Censorship', *Variety*. 2nd May, 1919, 65.

Vorse, Mary Heaton. 'Some Picture Show Audiences', *Outlook*. 24th June, 1911, 442.

Waller, Gregory A. 'Projecting the Promise of 16mm, 1935–45', *Useful Cinema*. Charles R. Acland and Haidee Wasson, Eds. Durham, NC, Duke University Press, 2011, 125–48.

Wheeler, Leigh Ann. *Against Obscenity: Reform and the Politics of Womanhood, 1873–1935*. Baltimore, Johns Hopkins University Press, 2007.

'Woman's and Mothers' Clubs Co-Operate to Found Children's Theater', *Moving Picture World*. 7th April, 1917, 78.

'Womanless Censorship Board for N.Y., Gov. Miller's Plan', *Variety*. 20th May, 1921, 44.

'Women's Club Uses Pictures', *Motography*. January, 1912, 20.

13. U.S. WOMEN DIRECTORS:
The Road Ahead

Maria Giese

In recognizing and celebrating the talent of the many women who have helped create the American entertainment industry from its earliest days, it's important to appreciate the tremendous struggle that has persisted over the last century or more, for women to tell their stories through the media of film and television.

The American Civil Liberties Union recently stated that 'Qualified women directors face a systemic pattern and practice of discrimination and exclusion from directing film and television.'

The institutionalized sexism and racism that exist within the U.S. media are currently the subject of both state and federal investigations. This chapter explores how and why this investigation came about.

The Bombshell

Four months ago, on 12th May 2015, *The New York Times* broke a story and published a letter that will almost certainly change the landscape for women directors forever.[1]

The fifteen-page letter, written by ACLU attorneys Melissa Goodman and Ariela Migdal, strongly urged our Federal agency, the EEOC, and two state agencies to launch an industry-wide investigation into Hollywood's rampant discrimination against women directors.

The ACLU now had indisputable evidence that women directors are almost entirely shut out of U.S. media. Liberal, democratic Hollywood, it turns out, has the worst record of sex discrimination, is among the worst violators of Title VII (U.S. equal employment opportunity law), of all industries in America.

The employment numbers are so strikingly low, that even the most hardened skeptic has to finally stop and take note. No matter how you look at it, America's most culturally influential global export – our media (commercials, TV shows and movies) – the very voice of our civilization – are coming almost 100% from a male perspective.

In legal terms, Goodman and Migdal were unequivocal when they wrote: 'These statistics reveal what the Supreme Court has called "the inexorable zero" – a figure, representing "the glaring absence" of women that is highly indicative of systemic employment discrimination.'[2]

Everyone knew what this meant – industry-wide legal action is realistic and viable.

Manohla Dargis wrote in a recent *New York Times* article that our industry's '…refusal to hire more female directors is immoral, maybe illegal, and has helped create and sustain a representational ghetto for women'.[3]

This groundbreaking news, and the ACLU letter to our state and federal agencies calling for an industry-wide investigation – perhaps the biggest of its kind in U.S. entertainment history – rocked our industry.

It was an extraordinary moment for me, and the culmination of four years of full-time, unpaid work.

The next morning, I woke up to a buzzing phone and a photo of myself on the front page of *The Los Angeles Times* with a headline reading: 'ACLU Calls for Investigation Into Gender Discrimination in Hollywood.'

The opening paragraph read: 'On Valentine's Day two years ago, film director Maria Giese met with U.S. Equal Employment Opportunity Commission staffers in downtown L.A. to talk about an issue she said was stalling her career – gender discrimination.'[4]

I recognized the significance of what had occurred, but

I also understood that the road ahead would be a long one. It had been a long journey already, and a wild, often nerve-wracking rollercoaster ride as I challenged the industry and my own Guild, the Directors Guild of America, in an insurgence that *The New York Times* termed 'a veritable crusade'.[5]

The Making of a Revolutionary

In 2011 I had finally reached the end of my tether. I was broke and depressed and angry. I did not feel I could sink any lower. I did not believe I had anything left to lose. I walked into a Directors Guild of America Women's Steering Committee meeting asking questions and demanding answers.

What I found was a politically dead committee, apathetic and fearful women who could not imagine a future of equality, and a Guild that was hostile to change. The few women on the committee who understood the problem, like my friends Melanie Wagor and Rena Sternfeld, were openly snubbed by the co-chairs. I knew at once that we had a big problem.

Something was rotten in Denmark.

There were no feature directors active on the committee when I arrived, and I was later told that the few who had attended meetings in recent years had given up in despair. For women feature directors like me, the numbers were the worst of all, yet it would be almost two years before we knew exactly how bad. The statistics were simply not broadly available yet.

Today we know: according to the ACLU letter last May, a recent USC study 'found that only 1.9% of directors of the top-grossing one hundred films of 2013 and 2014 were women' – 1.9%. That means 98.1% of America's top studio features are coming from the perspective of men.[6]

Only about 4% of all feature films produced by our six studios are directed by women; that's Disney, Universal, Paramount, Fox, Sony and Warner Bros, and three indie studios: Weinstein Company, Lionsgate, and Relativity.

And women of color? They directed almost 0% of top grossing films over the past twelve years.

Almost 100% of the 4% of women who *are* directing studio features are either movie stars or the wives or daughters of movie moguls. While it is gratifying to see women directors getting any work at all, it is very revealing that in order to get the jobs, these women must be rich or powerful enough in their own right to command executives.

And of course, where does that leave us regular women directors? Where does that leave the next generation of American women filmmakers?

Facing an Uneven Playing Field

Twenty-one years ago, in the spring of 1994, Francis Ford Coppola handed me my Master of Fine Arts degree from UCLA's Graduate School of Film & Television. He shook my hand and he said, *'Good luck.'*

I was graduating at the top of my class, having won many of the premier awards and scholarships available to students at the time. Better than that, I was just months away from being green-lit on the first of my two feature films, the two-million-dollar budgeted British feature film *When Saturday Comes* starring Sean Bean and Oscar nominee Pete Postlethwaite.

What I didn't know was that the following year – 1995 – would mark the peak of female director hires in the United States. For the next twenty years, women directors would face stasis and decline in employment and I would experience that in a very real way.

I was literally stepping out of film school in a class of about fifty-fifty male and female students (thanks to Title 9 which prohibits discrimination based on sex in federally funded education and activities), onto a professional playing field that was almost vertical.

Today, in 2015, nothing has changed. Based on the numbers, women film school students cannot reasonably hope to ever get a feature film directing job after graduation. As I was quoted as saying in the *LA Times* a few months ago: 'It's not that it's an unequal playing field; there is no playing field at all.'

After that first Women's Steering Committee meeting, I started writing articles about the disappearance of women directors from the American film industry, about the almost complete exclusion of women from feature film directing, the static pool of women DGA TV directors that could never rise above 16%, no matter what. I analyzed statistics, studied equal opportunity employment laws, and researched previous class-action suits based on sex discrimination.

Then I asked the editor of *The DGA Quarterly* if he'd publish some of them. He said 'No.'

Something had to be done and when I looked around, there wasn't anyone else to do it except me. I could risk my own career (whatever there was left of it), but I couldn't expect other women to do the same.

So in 2011, I started my own blog 'Women Directors in Hollywood,' to collect and publish the stories of other women like me, and to publish my own articles. It was the beginning of my 'crusade'.

Building a Community

I knew I could not do this for myself. It would only work if I did it for all women, for the next generation of women filmmakers, and for little girls like my daughter, Bea, who represent the future of American women filmmakers.

My blog was disseminated by social media – and it was the advent of social media that made it possible to bring us women directors together into a community that had not existed among the women of my generation.

Social media brought me together with directors like Lexi Alexander, who is not just an Oscar-nominated feature director, but also an Arab-German world kick-boxing champion, and I promise you, is not afraid of a fight.

It also introduced me to other extraordinary women who had already been working for years on Hollywood gender equity: Geena Davis and her Institute on Gender in Media, Jennifer Seibel Newsom's *Miss Representation*, and the relentless Melissa

Silverstein of *Women and Hollywood*.

They were already speaking forcefully about the under-representation of women in the industry and that was great. In my mind, however, the connection had not yet been made between gender disparities on the screen and the lack of women directors behind the camera.

The absence of women directors was the lacuna, I thought – the missing link.

Jane Campion said it best: '[Women] gave birth to the whole world. Without them writing and being directors, the rest of us are not going to know the whole story.'

The essential proliferation of the female *point of view* could change the world.

Seeking Solutions

The Directors Guild of America doesn't like me much.

This is true because I know one thing for sure that they don't want to confess themselves: *Hollywood studio executives and showrunners are not the only ones to blame for the fact that women directors don't get hired.*

The real problem is a blockage in the diversity program at the Directors Guild of America itself. The DGA's conflict of interest issue that Judge Pamela Rymer had pointed out had not just lost women the class action case in 1985, it had also kept them from advancing for the past twenty years.

Look, we all know that women are discriminated against in almost all sectors of our global society. We know there is a gender bias that keeps male – and especially female – executives from hiring more women.

Discrimination against women exists, and it is prevalent in every industry in our country. So why is it that of all the industries in the United States of America, liberal Hollywood has the worst numbers of all?

We know quotas are illegal, and who *doesn't* hate affirmative action? But what's new? Every industry in America is like that. So why is the problem of discrimination against women so much worse in Hollywood than anywhere else? What's different here?

Paris Barclay, our current DGA president and a phenomenally successful TV director, helped establish the DGA Diversity Task Force in 2004. This is our union's primary committee designated to make Guild signatories comply with Title VII and hire more women and minorities.

Even so, after eleven years of heading up the DGA Diversity Task Force, he came across as being confused about the issue of women directors when talking to *The New York Times* last January.

According to Manohla Dargis, in responding to a question about why female director numbers were so low, he said with a laugh, 'The number one director was me, that's true. I'm a black, gay man, so I'm virtually a woman… We really believe in this particular fight that solidarity is the way to go.'

In response to Barclay, Dargis made the astute observation: 'Solidarity is a seductive word, but it can also obscure the differences between sexism and racism.'

Consider this: women make up 51% of our population. Minority men make up 18% of our population. So why are women only directing 16% of TV episodes, while minority men are directing 18%?

And what about ethnic minority women? They make up 19% of the U.S. population, yet direct just 2% of TV shows! Why were the DGA-studio diversity agreements serving minority men, but failing women utterly?

It is folly to expect a union run by its majority white male membership to oversee studio compliance of diversity agreements based on Title VII. It's simply a conflict of interest.

Along the same lines, you cannot expect TV directors, like Paris Barclay, who are actively seeking open assignment TV directing jobs to advocate for other women and minority directors through the DGA Diversity Task Force. It's a conflict of interest.

The temptation to advance one's own career is too strong,

as evidenced by the stasis in female director jobs during the eleven years Barclay headed up the Force.

I wanted to find out the answers to these questions and many more. And I did. But I could not have done it without strong and powerful shoulders to stand on.

The Original Six

In 1979, six courageous DGA women directors became the first women in the history of the U.S. film and television industry to spearhead a class-action lawsuit challenging race and gender discrimination. I named them 'The Original Six.'

These women are: Susan Bay, Nell Cox, Joelle Dobrow, Dolores Ferraro, Victoria Hochberg and Lynne Littman.

They are our own heroes who launched the landmark 1980s class action lawsuit that sent women director employment numbers soaring from 0.5% in 1985 (that's one half of one per cent) to 16% in 1995 in just ten years.

From 1979 to 1985 these women risked their careers to create change for all women in our industry. The work they did altered the landscape for women directors and their teams forever.

There is not a single woman director working in Hollywood today who does not have The Original Six to thank for their jobs.

The work that they did came on the heels of the Civil Rights Movement in the 1960s, and the Women's Liberation Movement in the 1970s. Those were revolutionary times.

Furthermore, their work began a year after the U.S. Equal Employment Opportunity Commission prepared a significant report detailing race and sex discrimination in Hollywood.

That EEOC report stated in no uncertain terms that something needed to be done immediately to mitigate Hollywood's bias against women and minorities in the industry. Unfortunately, that report signaled the beginning and end of concerted U.S. state or federal efforts to help solve the problem.

Listening to The Original Six and learning everything I could about their work motivated me even more to study up. I headed to court in downtown Los Angeles and began researching their DGA-led class-action lawsuit filed against three major studios. I read the final ruling by California's 9th District Circuit Court Judge, Pamela Rymer.

In Rymer's judgment in 1985 in favor of the studios, the case summary outcome reads as follows:

> The named individuals' motion to certify the class was denied. The directors' guild was dismissed as a class representative. The named individuals' law firm was allowed to continue their representation of the named individuals in accordance with the requirements for client consent.

While Rymer believed the lawsuit was important and viable and should be *continued*, she had to disqualify the DGA from leading the class because, in her opinion, the Guild did not share the interests of the women and minorities in the class.

As explained in the case summary outcome, in order to qualify to lead a class in a class-action suit, the court required assurance that 'The representative parties will fairly and adequately protect the interests of the class.' It was in this ability, Rymer ruled, the DGA fell short.

This means that the DGA could not lead the class-action case against the studios because, as a Guild run but its majority white male members, the DGA had an intrinsic system that discriminated against women and minorities as much as the studios did.

Also, of key importance, according to the Court Summary overview, 'The court held that the conflict of interest raised by the directors' guild's role was sufficiently concrete and immediate to preclude its representation of the class comprised of females and minorities.'

The DGA was in no position to be pointing fingers and suing the studios. *It was like the pot calling the kettle black.*

Ultimately, as a result of the suit, the DGA and the studios did get together in subsequent Collective Bargaining negotiations to set up diversity agreements and programs in compliance of Title VII.

These programs included TV directing fellowships, mentoring projects, networking programs, panels on various diversity issues, and events to glorify the successes of women directors.

Unfortunately, as time passed, none of these programs were effective for a number of not-so-surprising reasons. (I have written in depth about this on my web forum, 'Women Directors in Hollywood,' so look there for more on that subject).

The important take-away, though, is that after the initial surge in female director employment numbers, from 1995 onward, the number of working women directors fell into stasis and decline.

Why?

Building a Movement

I said that no one did anything for twenty years, and I guess I'm referring mostly to myself, because perhaps a certain measure of complacency on the part of my generation of American women figured into it.

I believe *in my heart* that that must be true, because twenty years ago when I entered the profession I didn't see any community of women filmmakers to join, and I didn't try to create one.

My generation did not seem to carry forth the torch of women's liberation and equal rights as exemplified by The Original Six. So, four years ago, it seems to me, I woke up…

I remember in 2012, walking into a DGA National Board meeting and introducing myself to then Guild president Michael Apted, and Vice President Steven Soderbergh.

The great British actor Pete Postlethwaite had just died after a long battle with cancer. Apted and I had both worked with him on feature films and TV series, but when I told them about my interest in getting women directors back to work, their eyes glazed over.

'Yeah, women and everyone else,' Soderbergh said.

The prevailing attitude among Hollywood's elite producers,

directors and actors seems to reveal a complete lack of understanding about the plight of women directors.

Think of the debate that ensued when *Jurassic World* helmer Colin Trevorrow responded to a Tweet query from Stephan Jansen asking if he thought he might have got the opportunity to direct the 2015 *Jurassic World* if he had been a woman.

Trevorrow was hired to helm the $150 million feature by Steven Spielberg after having directed just one indie feature, the $750,000 budgeted *Safety Not Guaranteed* in 2012. This is something unheard of among women directors.

In a moment of extraordinary audacity, Trevorrow responded that he didn't think women wanted to direct these big tent-pole films anyway. As he put it: 'Many of the top female directors in our industry are not interested in doing a piece of studio business for its own sake.'[7]

This set off a barrage of feminist articles, the best of which was Film Fatale's ReBecca Theodore-Vachon's powerful piece in *Forbes*. She wrote, '…let's be clear, Trevorrow was given access to resources and support most women directors are denied. That sir, is what we call privilege.'[8]

Worse, the whole debate pointed to endemic discrimination that ran from one generation into the next without self-reflection. As Theodore-Vachon pointed out, 'Spielberg has gone on record saying Trevorrow reminded him of a younger version of himself, and was on-set to mentor to the upstart director.'

If powerful male executives are nurturing and hiring the next generation of studio directors based on the concept that they remind them of themselves, what hope is there for women or ethnic minorities to break through the glass ceiling?

To paraphrase a comment from one woman director: 'If that's the DNA for hiring women directors, what hope is there for us?'

The very fact, however, that mainstream media is throwing light on Tweeted comments like this is a clear indication that we are succeeding in our struggle for equality.

The Big Picture

Last December surrounding Ava DuVernay's *Selma* snub at the Oscars, we had exposure for women directors such as never before. Everyone seemed to know the statistics. Journalists were asking: if Academy membership is 94% Caucasian and 77% male, what chance is there for women to excel?

I wrote an article in *Elle Magazine* right after the Oscars in which I pointed out the unfair bias in terms of how the Academy qualifies 'excellence' in handing out Oscars. With a membership so skewed toward white men, how can diverse perceptions of 'excellence' come to be appreciated?

I asked: 'Why do we allow this fortress of secrecy, this bastion of sexism and racism, to function as the grand architect of our nation's projected ethos when we don't agree with it?'

Why do we? If we are to live in a world that honors freedom and equality, then balanced gender perspective must be reflected in our media content.

It turned out that the only support I could find was from a handful of underemployed women directors who had hit rock bottom, too. That said, the support from those women was immense, and it was from that foundation that a whole community has been built.

Soon, our efforts became a cause – and then, thanks to the ACLU and mainstream media, a *movement*.

The DGA Women Directors Summit

Our first major step was producing 'The DGA Women of Action Summit', held at the DGA headquarters on 2nd March 2013. It was the biggest event ever held for women directors in the nearly eighty-year history of the Guild.

DGA women directors like Melanie Wagor, Diane Bartlow, Rachel Feldman and Rena Sternfeld were stalwart in helping me combat the Directors Guild when they tried again and again to prevent us from producing this groundbreaking event.

Even after we had achieved an almost unanimous vote in the Women's Steering Committee (WSC) in favor of the event in 2012 the event was still held up for nearly a year by the Guild leadership.

It finally took a single letter I wrote to Regina Render, the DGA Head of Diversity since 1996, in which I stated: 'I don't think (the DGA leadership) will want to be held accountable in two years from now when our Guild is found complicit in industry-wide Title VII violations.'

Just two days later, Regina told us that our event would take place, after all.

As reported in IndieWIRE's *Women and Hollywood:*

> This past Saturday, March 2, 2013, became an historic day as the DGA Women's Steering Committee hosted the DGA Women of Action Summit in LA bringing together 150 female American directors for a day-long event designed to create solutions to the problem of the under-representation and under-employment of women directors in Hollywood.[9]

The day-long event included an introduction from Geena Davis, speeches by The Original Six, three panel discussions with many of our industry's top women feminists, producers and directors.

After lunch, there was a brainstorming session that included every woman attendee at the event. The final panel included directors and showrunners in an effort to better understand just what keeps the pool of women DGA TV directors so small and static.

The event was a huge success, and even though the DGA would not allow us to include the press, the entire industry sat up and took note.

The DGA Fights Back

While our Summit produced the beginning of a palpable shift in our perceptions about the power of transformation we could create, it also signaled unwelcome change to the DGA leadership. Immediate repercussions to our success included mandated new by-laws to prevent women from speaking out.

We were warned in the weeks preceding the Summit that the DGA National Board had voted to mandate new by-laws to be imposed on our committee. On the surface, the new by-laws appeared to be an effort to strengthen the committee by bringing it under closer scrutiny and control of the Guild leadership. Under the surface, however, there was a darker intent.

Upon close reading of the by-laws, it became evident that these laws would weaken the WSC by moving it away from its original intent of political action for women in the U.S. entertainment industry. The new by-laws appeared likely to curtail the members' freedom of speech, as they created several obstacles to democratic due process.

The most troubling of the by-laws took co-chair elections out of the room and put them into the hands of the Guild administration. We knew instantly that this by-law, if passed, would allow the Guild leadership to 'deputize' a few women who would be loyal to its edict.

The DGA could supervise the elections, control who would become co-chairs and in so doing, take control of the committee. A second by-law then provided those new co-chairs absolute power by allowing them to 'set the agenda' and appoint all co-chairs and participants on the subcommittees of which there are four: Rules & Elections; Proposals; Communications; and Activities & Events.

If we women refused to vote the by-laws into law in the WSC, we could remain independent of Guild control. If we failed, we risked losing the power of the Committee forever.

We women activists fought very hard against these new by-laws, but the Guild used threats and strong-arm tactics to stop us. In the final by-laws meeting, they would not even allow us to have a woman chair our own meeting. Instead, they installed the second in command DGA Associate National Executive Director/Western Executive Director, Bryan Unger, to chair our final by-laws meeting that took place at the DGA headquarters on Sunset Boulevard on 6th April 2013.

We should have walked out then and there, but sadly their tactics worked: women were afraid, and the Guild had stacked the room. Besides having the meeting run by a top male Guild boss, the forty or so women in attendance were intimidated by male Guild security guards both inside and outside the conference room where the meeting took place, a burly male time-keeper, and a not-so-secret ballot vote in which we were forced to sign our names on the backs of the sealed envelopes.

Even women who had been strongly vocal in their opposition to the new by-laws threw in their towels, intimidated into voting for the by-laws with virtually no compromises to the wording of any of them. Just days later, the National Board quickly ratified the by-laws.

By pushing these by-laws through our committee by force, as was done, the diverse voices among DGA women were effectively silenced, therefore eliminating the very reason for the existence of the women's committee: to have a place where women DGA members could freely speak out and fight for greater employment and equality for women directors and their teams.

Today's WSC co-chair seats are indeed occupied by Guild loyalists who are willing to do the bidding of the leadership. They are being rewarded with more jobs and top positions in Guild governance. And there is not one feature film director among the co-chairs.

Today, if you haven't been able to get a job in seven years, you can't run for elected office, not even on the very committee created thirty-five years ago specifically because women so often can't get work for seven years running. And worse, women cannot even volunteer to participate on the subcommittees.

As a result of the by-laws, subcommittee chairs and participants are by appointment only, ending the possibility of having diverse voices contribute to the only diversity committee women have in the DGA.

The DGA Further Silences Women

Now with loyal new co-chairs in place, the next vexing move the Guild made to silence us and further suppress our activism was to try to stop the follow up event to the Summit, which had already been voted on and approved by the previous co-chairs, Melanie Wagor and Rachel Feldman. The event was to be the 35th Anniversary Celebration to honor The Original Six.

In this case, it was the newly elected WSC co-chair and mentee of Paris Barclay, the TV director Millicent Shelton, who sought to stop it. It was she who sent an email notice out to the WSC Events Committee stating that the Women's Steering Committee had actually not been founded in 1979, but sometime around 1991.

Her message stated: 'According to the DGA the WSC wasn't recognized by the National Board until later despite the initial meeting. That's the record. This was discussed at the Activities & Events committee meeting. Any inconsistency with the DGA website should be brought to the attention of the Guild Communications Department.'

Even though the DGA's own official website DGA.org clearly stated that the WSC was founded in 1979, she claimed that it was incorrect. Therefore, in her view, a 35th Anniversary Celebration would be erroneous.

To combat this fiction, we looked back at the 1990/91 DGA Magazine for evidence. I wrote a letter to the DGA and WSC leadership detailing the history of founding of the committee in 1979, a substantial DGA 10th anniversary celebration of the committee in 1990, and I used the Guild's own official history for evidence.

Once again, two days later at a WSC meeting we were informed that the WSC had indeed been founded in 1979. Rena Sternfeld raised her hand: 'May we have our 35th Anniversary Event then?'

The 35th Anniversary event was approved, but the Guild used the by-laws and the newly elected co-chairs to make sure it diverged from our original concept. And worse, we women who had championed it in the first place were entirely shut out of its execution.

The Original Six were used as a polite introduction to the 'actual' event that morphed into a tribute to three women directors who had never expressed any interest in the cause of advancing women directors, two of whom were longtime DGA leaders.

The event was introduced by Paris Barclay, who had opposed it from the start and ironically, Millicent Shelton introduced The Original Six whose true work and history she had denied just months earlier.

How the DGA Keeps Women Directors Shut Out

It's very important to understand the implication behind Barclay and Shelton's effort to alter the true inception date of the WSC. In so doing, they were not only nullifying the reason for having the event, they were also clipping years off the class action lawsuit from history.

One might ask: why were they so adamant about undermining our efforts to bring attention to the success of legal action for women and minority Guild members when they themselves had benefitted so handsomely from it?

Well, the reason is simple:

The directing profession is incredibly competitive no matter how you look at it, and if we women start getting our fair share of jobs, it's going to cut into the giant piece of the pie that white guys comprise – the guys who make up the vast majority of DGA membership.

In other words, white guys need to keep minority guys off their turf, and minority guys need to keep women off *their* turf. So, the few highly-employed women who have a piece of the action know their pool is limited, so they feel they have to keep new, incoming women shut out.

In the end, guess what? Women as a group suffer. We all suffer.

But what if – and just think about this for a moment – what

if women had their own diversity category that DGA signatories had to hire from in order to comply with America's equal employment opportunity law, Title VII?

And that brings me to the very heart of the battle I'm fighting right now, and it's really important.

This disparity in employment advancements between women and male minorities is due to the fact that women get buried under the too-general category of 'Diversity.' Studios and signatories can fulfill diversity agreement obligations simply by hiring male ethnic minorities, and without hiring any women at all.

In an effort to end this loophole that makes it so easy to keep women shut out of directing work, I proposed that the DGA create a separate DGA-studio diversity mandate for women. I asked that upcoming DGA-studio Collective Bargaining Negotiations include working toward establishing a new system to break women out as a separate category from minority men. In this way, studios would have to hire women directors as well as ethnic minority males.

Significantly, this would also provide a numerical edge to ethnic minority women since they would then qualify for *two* diversity pools: once among women of all ethnicities. And *again* among ethnic minorities of both sexes.

A group of us fought this battle in the Women's Steering Committee last spring. We proposed the motion to break women out, but the co-chairs managed to delay the discussion to the following month.

The final meeting took place on 11th April 2014 at the DGA headquarters on Sunset Boulevard.[10] It was a circus. The Guild leadership had stacked the room. Fur started to fly. Threats were made to have women on our side escorted from the meeting by DGA guards.

The feature director, Lexi Alexander, grew so frustrated she started live-Tweeting the meeting. One observer on Mentorless. com wrote in amazement:

> Lexi Alexander live-tweeted the session, and re-tweeted live reactions. I don't think this has ever been done before… From Alexander's tweets, it seems that the room was mostly composed of women filmmakers, and yet, (the motion) was denied. How did they justify it rationally in their heads, I don't know.

Alexander's final Tweet said simply: 'We lost the vote. I'm done.' She has never attended another WSC meeting.

We lost the battle for independence and democracy in our Women's Steering Committee. And so far, we have lost the battle to break women out. But in the overarching war, we are way, way ahead.

The groundbreaking ACLU letter has tipped the scales, and American media knows it. Our social media and mainstream media is now bursting every day with new articles, documentaries, commentaries and postings about Hollywood's refusal to hire women directors. There is so much daily content, you can't even take them all in. The expression 'Woman Director' has become a household term.

So, onward!

The hardest part has been accomplished. We've got the ACLU on our side, and our nation's most powerful state and federal agencies are committed to helping us create change.

Let's give them all the support we can by keeping our voices strong and our vision steady.

As the ACLU's Melissa Goodman wrote: 'Many brave women in Hollywood are speaking up about their experiences. If you are a woman director who has been discriminated against, excluded from directing jobs in television or get less TV work than your male peers, we'd love to hear from you. Tell us your story' (aclu.org).

We know what we have to do. So, please speak out.

As Victoria Hochberg proclaimed to a standing ovation at the 35th Anniversary Tribute to Women Directors:

'THIS IS OUR TIME!'

Author Biography: Maria Giese

Maria wrote and directed two feature films: *When Saturday Comes*, (starring Sean Bean & Pete Postlethwaite) and *Hunger*, based on the novel by Nobel Prize-winner, Knut Hamsun. She introduced the plight of women directors to the ACLU and co-founded the activist/agitator web forum, 'Women Directors in Hollywood', which helped initiate the current EEOC joint government agency investigation. While writing regularly about women directors (*Ms. Magazine, Elle, Film Inquiry, IndieWIRE*), she has recently been featured in *The New York Times, The Los Angeles Times* and on Bloomberg TV, among others. Giese is currently the subject of several documentaries and is working on a book about her work. Educated at Simon's Rock of Bard College, Wellesley College, and UCLA Graduate School of Film and Television, she is an active member of the Directors Guild of America, and is currently attached to direct several feature films.

www.mariagiese.com

Endnotes

1. http://www.nytimes.com/2015/05/13/movies/aclu-citing-bias-against-women-wants-inquiry-into-hollywoods-hiring-practices.html
2. http://www.nytimes.com/inter active/2015/05/12/movies/document-13filmwomen.html
3. http://www.nytimes.com/2015/01/25/movies/on-many-fronts-women-are-fighting-for-better-opportunity-in-hollywood.html
4. http://www.latimes.com/entertainment/movies/la-et-mn-aclu-gender-discrimination-hollywood-20150513-story.html
5. http://www.nytimes.com/2015/01/25/movies/on-many-fronts-women-are-fighting-for-better-opportunity-in-hollywood.html
6. http://www.latimes.com/entertainment/movies/la-et-mn-women-hollywood-usc-study-20140724-story.html
7. http://www.ew.com/article/2015/08/21/colin-trevorrow-women-directors-jaime-king
8. http://www.forbes.com/sites/rebeccatheodore/2015/08/27/colin-trevorrow-male-privilege-women-directors/
9. http://blogs.indiewire.com/womenandhollywood/guest-post-dga-women-directors-foment-a-rebellion
10. http://blogs.indiewire.com/womenandhollywood/dga-womens-steering-committee-rejects-proposal-to-expand-diversity-options-for-women-20150428

References

1985 U.S. Dist. Lexis 16325,* ; 2 Fed. R. Serv. 3d (Callaghan) 1429
Directors Guild of America, INC., Joelle Dobrow, Luther James, Lorraine Raglin and Cesar Torres, Plaintiffs, v. Warner Brothers, INC., Defendant

SILENT WOMEN

Directors Guild of America, INC., Bill Crain, Dick Look, Sharon Mann, Susan Smitman, and Frank Zimiga, Plaintiffs, v. Columbia Pictures Industries, INC., Defendant
Nos. CV 83–4764-PAR; CV 83–8311-PAR
United States District Court for the Central District of California
1985 U.S. Dist. Lexis 16325; 2 Fed. R. Serv. 3d (Callaghan) 1429
30th August 1985

WHAT THEY SAID

'...I thought I could do better... Gathering up my courage, I timidly proposed to Gaumont that I would write one or two short plays and make them for the amusement of my friends. If the developments which evolved from this proposal could have been foreseen, then I probably never would have obtained his agreement. My youth, my lack of experience, my sex all conspired against me.'
— *Alice Guy-Blaché*

'There is no other occupation in the world that so closely resembled enslavement as the career of a film star.'
— *Louise Brooks*

'I don't want to be a silly temptress. I cannot see any sense in getting dressed up and doing nothing but tempting men in pictures.'
— *Greta Garbo*

'You may have a fresh start any moment you choose, for this thing that we call "failure" is not the falling down, but the staying down.'
— *Mary Pickford*

'My philosophy is that to be a director you cannot be subject to anyone, even the head of the studio. I threatened to quit each time I didn't get my way, but no one ever let me walk out.'
— *Dorothy Arzner*

'I have been in Sorrow's kitchen and licked out all the pots. Then I have stood on the peaky mountain wrapped in rainbows, with a harp and a sword in my hands."
— *Zora Neale Hurston, 'Dust Tracks on a Road' (1942)*

'I had no desire to be a film actress, to always play somebody else, to be always beautiful with somebody constantly straightening out your every eyelash. It was always a big bother to me.'
— *Marlene Dietrich*

'Never get caught acting.'
— *Lillian Gish*

'If there's specific resistance to women making movies, I just choose to ignore that as an obstacle for two reasons: I can't change my gender, and I refuse to stop making movies.'
— *Kathryn Bigelow*

'I believe in censorship. I made a fortune out of it.'
— *Mae West*

'I'd love to see more women working as directors and producers. Today, it's almost impossible to do it unless you are an actress or writer with power... I wouldn't hesitate right this minute to hire a talented woman if the subject matter were right.'
— *Ida Lupino*

'The more I see of men, the more I like dogs.'
— *Clara Bow*

'Ignore the glass ceiling and do your work. If you're focusing on the glass ceiling, focusing on what you don't have, focusing on the limitations, then you will be limited. My way was to work, make my short... make my documentary... make my small films... use my own money... raise money myself... and stay shooting and focused on each project.'
— *Ava DuVernay*

'I would love to see more women directors because they represent half of the population — and gave birth to the whole world. Without them writing and being directors, the rest of us are not going to know the whole story.'
— *Jane Campion*

*

If you want to know more about the many extraordinary women who worked in the emergent film industry go to the Women Film Pioneers Project:
https://wfpp.cdrs.columbia.edu/
Help to discover more about these pioneers so that the history of the motion picture industry can be told in full.

INDEX

A

Academy, Academy Award 14, 22, 32, 97, 133, 136-139, 212, 214-216, 227, 277, 291
Akins, Zoë 158
Alexander, Georg 90, 123-124, 215
Alexander, Lexi 284, 297-298
American Civil Liberties Union (ACLU) 280-282, 291, 298-299
Anderson, Doris 158
Arbuckle, Roscoe, 'Fatty' 137, 271
archives 9, 67, 85, 93-94
Arquette, Patricia 32
Arzner, Dorothy 10, 16, 18, 147, 156-164, 178, 179-200, 206, 217, 257, 278, 302

B

Bankhead, Tallulah 138, 140
Bara, Theda 14
Batley, Ethyle 11
Bauchens, Anne 169, 207, 208, 212-214, 216, 226
Beaugé, Marguerite 222-223
Beaugé-Martin, Yvonne 223
Beranger, Clara 103-106, 108
Bertini, Francesca 113, 117-121, 128, 130, 172
Bigelow, Kathryn 18, 32, 303
Billington, Francelia 232-233, 240
Bleecker, Katherine 234-235, 240
Booth, Margaret 169, 206-213, 226
Borthwick, Jessica E. 236-237, 240
Bow, Clara 14, 133-134, 143, 145, 158-159, 170, 186-188, 196-197, 200, 303
Brooks, Louise 14, 134-135, 145, 170, 302
Bullock, Sandra 144

C

Campion, Jane 18, 240, 285, 303
Caspary, Vera 158
censorship 87-88, 137, 141-143, 264, 269-270, 303
Chaplin, Charlie 14, 21, 30, 70, 72, 131, 134, 136, 157, 204, 240, 261
Cinema Eye, Cine Eye, Kino Eye 172, 220-221
Close, Ivy 85
Coppola, Francis Ford 161, 283
Cruze, James 157, 184-186, 190-193
Cunard, Grace 80, 101-102, 106, 108

D

Dargis, Manohla 281, 286
Dash, Julie 38, 66, 68
Davis, Geena 32, 144, 284, 292
Davison, Grace 230-233
de Acosta, Mercedes 138
DeMille, Cecil B. 103, 169, 182, 200, 204, 207-208, 212-214
de Mille, William 103-104, 181-182, 213
Dietrich, Marlene 135, 138-140, 171, 302
Directors Guild of America (DGA) 66, 96, 152, 158, 212, 282, 284-289, 291-297, 299-300
discrimination 13, 16, 31, 280-281, 283-285, 287, 290, 299
diversity 256, 285-286, 289, 294, 297, 299
Dixie Jubilee Singers 41-42
Doherty, Ethel 158
Dulac, Germaine 29, 87, 88-89, 94, 146, 277-278
Dunbar, Olivia Howard 256, 277
Dunn, Dorothy 234
DuVernay, Ava 291, 303

E

Edison, Thomas; Edison Company 103, 109, 150, 201-202, 274
Egede-Nissen, Aud 90-91, 93, 113, 121-124, 126, 128, 173

F

Fairbanks, Douglas 14, 30, 136, 157, 200, 217, 261
Fairfax, Marion 248-249, 251
Fazan, Adrienne 158
Field, Mary 86, 93
Ford, John 101-102, 108, 159, 215-216

G

Gaines, Jane 29, 36, 67, 71-72, 79, 80, 93-95, 108, 130
Gance, Abel 200, 204, 222-223
Garbo, Greta 14, 89, 138-139, 145, 171, 200, 302
Gaumont, studios, the 15, 69, 73-75, 110-111, 147-149, 152-154,
    243, 253, 302
Gauntier, Gene 15, 69, 98-100, 102, 106, 108, 176
Geena Davis Institute on Gender in Media 32, 144, 284
Gish, Lillian 4, 21, 132-133, 143, 145, 168, 209, 259, 302
Gist, Eloyce King Patrick 35, 38, 40-41, 65, 67
Goldwyn, Sam 22, 27, 214
Griffith, D. W. 30, 75, 132-133, 135-136, 145, 151, 154, 157, 164,
    204, 207-209, 217-218, 232, 238, 259, 268
Guy-Blaché, Alice (Alice Guy) 10, 13, 16-17, 29-30, 69, 72-74, 79,
    93, 98, 110, 113, 125, 129, 146-153, 156-157, 159, 161-162,
    165, 242-244, 251-253, 258, 302

H

Harlem Renaissance 36, 38, 44, 49-50, 55, 68
Hays Production Code 107, 137-138, 142
Hays, William 107, 137-138, 140, 142, 270-271
Hayward, Hilda 84-85, 94
Hayward, Lydia 11-12, 175
Hearst, William Randolph 135, 137, 142, 261-262
Hitchcock, Alfred 12, 16, 139, 141, 175, 216, 223-224, 249, 253
Holmes, Helen 25, 262
Hopson, Violet 85-86, 93
Howard, Marion 259
Hughes, Langston 36, 44, 50, 54, 67
Hurston, Zora Neale 15, 17, 30, 33, 36-38, 40-41, 44-57, 64-68,
    163, 302

Hyland, Peggy 86

I

Ivers, Julia Crawford 75-79, 94

J

Jessye, Eva 41-42, 67

K

King, Henry 214-215
Kuleshov, Lev 218-219

L

Laemmle, Carl 27, 43, 151, 154
Lasky, Players- 76-78, 80, 136, 156-158, 184, 189, 216, 223
Lawrence, Florence 70, 72, 79
Lawrence, Jennifer 144
Lawrence, Viola 158, 216
Leahy, Agnes Brand 158
Lenihan, Winifred 158
Library of Congress 40-41, 51-53, 65
Loew, Marcus 43, 204, 210-211
Loring, Jane 158, 216
Lovely, Louise 82
Lovett, Josephine 177
Lowell, Louise 233-234
Lumière brothers, the 73-74, 109, 122, 124, 147-148, 201-202, 238
Lupino, Ida 10, 177, 303
Lyell, Lottie 81-82, 93

M

MacDonald, Margaret I. 259, 272, 278
Margaret Mead Film Collection 40, 53
Marion, Frances 15, 96-98, 105-106, 108, 136, 168, 186
Marsh, Mary 85
Mathis, June 58, 77-79, 93-94, 96, 98
Mayer, Louis B. 41, 78, 138, 207, 209-211, 214

McCall, Mary C., Jr. 158
McDonagh sisters, the 82-83, 94, 174
McLean, Barbara 207, 214-215
Méliès, Georges 147, 203
Metro-Goldwyn-Mayer (MGM) 41, 132, 138-139, 207-208, 210-
    211, 213-214, 216
Micheaux, Oscar 35, 60-61, 66-67
Mitchell, Dora L. 43
Morgan, Marion 158, 161, 163, 186
Motion Picture Classic magazine 262, 277
Motion Picture magazine 29, 35, 43, 110, 136-137, 140, 150-151,
    153-156, 206, 212, 235, 261-262, 265-266, 270-271, 276-
    278
Motion Picture News magazine 151, 153, 155
Musidora (Jeanne Roques) 113, 124-128, 130, 172

N

Nazimova, Alla 78, 80, 167, 182
Nielsen, Asta 87, 89, 93, 112-121, 124-125, 128-129, 176
Notari, Elvira 73, 87-89, 177

O

Ordway, Margery 4, 230

P

Pagnol, Marcel 222
Paramount Pictures, Paramount Studios 27, 55-56, 76-77, 134-
    137, 139-142, 156-157, 159, 164, 181-184, 186, 190, 192-
    194, 196-198, 204, 207-209, 213, 216-217, 269, 282
Parsons, Louella O. 105, 258, 261-262, 276
Pathé 15, 101, 103, 110, 125, 219, 272
Photoplay magazine 4, 76-77, 136, 200, 229, 230, 232-233, 240,
    261-262, 277-278
Pickford, Mary (Gladys Mary Smith) 14, 18, 21, 30, 70, 72, 80, 98,
    132, 135-136, 143, 164, 166, 196, 214, 217, 258-259, 261,
    302
Price, Gertrude 257
Purcell, Gertrude 158

R

racism 39, 280, 286, 291
Rambova, Natacha 78, 261
Rasch, Albertina 245-246, 248, 251-252
Renoir, Marguerite 222
Reville, Alma 12, 16, 175, 223-224, 248-249, 251
Riefenstahl, Leni 173, 224-225, 227
Robeson, Eslanda Goode 15, 36, 41, 44-48, 57-67, 163
Robeson, Paul 47-48, 57-58, 60, 67, 163
Robeson, Paul, Jr. 41, 47, 57-59, 61-63, 65, 67

S

Sanger, Margaret 275, 278
Schulberg, Ben P. 133, 156, 158, 186, 194, 197
Selznick, David O. 71, 94, 137
Sennett, Mack 157, 204, 217
Sewell, Blanche 216
sexism 92, 106, 250, 280, 286, 291
Shipman, Nell 15, 18-34, 164
Shurey, Dinah 86, 93
silent era 20, 35, 38, 70, 72-73, 75, 85-86, 90, 95-97, 99, 106, 107,
        112, 124, 131-132, 199, 202, 206, 212, 255, 276
Silverstein, Melissa 285
Slesinger, Tess 158
Smith, George Albert 176, 237-240
Smith, Laura E. (Laura Bayley) 174, 237-240
Soska Sisters, the 250, 253
Souders, Tressie 35, 43
sound 14, 41, 83, 87, 91, 97, 99, 106-107, 116, 124, 132, 136, 138,
        143, 149, 159, 161, 186, 197-199, 202, 221, 274
Spencer, Dorothy 169, 215
Spielberg, Steven 290
Streep, Meryl 32, 144
Svilova, Elizaveta 172, 219-221

T

Thomas, Olive 137, 145
Thompson, Lucy Heys 85

U

uncredited 12, 42, 143, 217, 224, 226
United Artists 14, 30, 72, 80, 136, 204, 214
Universal 24, 27, 62, 79-80, 91, 100-101, 151, 154, 204, 210, 216, 233-234, 236, 253, 272, 282

V

Valentino, Rudolph 14, 21, 77-78, 93, 183, 200, 206, 217, 261
Vertov, Dziga 219-221, 227
Vidor, King 41-42, 97
Vitagraph 24-26, 103, 150, 216
von Harbou, Thea 247-248, 251, 253
von Stroheim, Erich 157, 233
Vorse, Mary Heaton 256, 279

W

Weber, Lois 10-11, 16-17, 27, 29, 75-76, 80, 98, 146-147, 151, 153-156, 158-159, 161-162, 167, 258, 262, 275-278
West, Mae 141-143, 170, 303
Williams, Maria P. 15, 35, 43
Women Film Pioneers Project 17, 29-30, 66, 79, 93-94, 107-108, 112, 130, 227, 240, 303
Women in Horror Month 249, 253
Women's Steering Committee (WSC) of the DGA 291, 293-296, 298
Wong, Marion 15, 30-33, 165

Z

Zanuck, Darryl F. 196, 207, 214, 215
Zuccarone, Esterina 221
Zukor, Adolph 27, 196

Praise for *Silent Women: Pioneers of Cinema*

'Inspirational and informative, *Silent Women* will challenge many people's ideas about the beginnings of film history. This fascinating book roams widely across the era and the diverse achievements and voices of women in the film industry. These are the stories of pioneers, trailblazers and collaborators – hugely enjoyable to read and vitally important to publish.'
– *Pamela Hutchinson, Silent London*

'A timely and urgently needed collection of essays by a definitive group of scholars on the subject, *Silent Women: Pioneers of Cinema* utilizes the time-honored feminist concept of the silence and voicelessness at the heart of female oppression as its central motivation. The essays in this collection demonstrate how the film industry kept women from certain opportunities in the early years, but also provided them a particular agency to make their marks outside more traditional boundaries. A must-read!'
– *Lisa Stein Haven, author of Syd Chaplin: A Biography (2010) and editor of Charlie Chaplin's A Comedian Sees the World (2014)*

'This book confirms what an exciting time it is for women's cinema history. Every chapter opens tantalising new windows into the fascinating but forgotten or overlooked lives and careers of women working in the early film industry. Every page begs the question – how on earth did these amazing women vanish from history in the first place? I defy anyone interested in cinema history not to find this valuable compendium a must-read. It's also a 'call to arms' for more research into women's contribution and an affirmation of just how rewarding the detective work can be.'
– *Laraine Porter, Senior Lecturer in Film, De Montfort University and Co-Artistic Director of British Silent Film Festival*

'This book shows how women's voices were heard and helped create the golden age of silent cinema, how those voices were almost eradicated by the male-dominated film industry, and perhaps points the way to an all-inclusive future for global cinema.'
– *Paul Duncan, Film Historian*

'In a climate in which the equality that exists within film has become an increasingly visible focus of debate, *Silent Women: Pioneers of Cinema* offers a timely reminder of the historical contribution women have made to the medium. An authoritative and illuminating work, it also lends a pervasive voice to the argument that discrimination and not talent is the barrier to so few women occupying the most prominent roles within the industry.'
    – Jason Wood, Artistic Director of Film at HOME,
    Author and Visiting Professor at MMU

'A long overdue compendium of insightful essays highlighting the oft-forgotten women and the vital roles they played in both the birth of cinema and it's evolution. I was amazed to discover just how crucially they were involved from not just in front of the camera but in producing, directing, editing and much, much more. An essential read.'
    – Neil McGlone, The Criterion Collection

'...honors the women in cinema who actively paved the way for future women in this industry, and brought attention to the issue of gender bias in media, a problem we are still fighting today.'
    – Madeline Di Nonno, CEO of the Geena Davis Institute
    on Gender in Media

'...an inspiring and refreshing set of well-written essays on a subject often forgotten, discussing the fabulous variety of women in film over the years. A must for any fan of cinema/film, or anyone that has an interest in women's history.'
    – Hayley Foster da Silva, The F Word

'...a lively collection, opening up an increasingly vibrant field which promises to raise a diversity of questions for viewers, makers and teachers of film about women's role world-wide in the emergence of cinema.'
    – Professor Christine Gledhill, University of Sunderland

'This book is inspirational reading for any woman who dreams to express her vision through film in any direction this industry takes us. Only by understanding our past can we embrace our greatest future.'
    Gayle Nachlis, Senior Director of Education
    Women In Film Los Angeles